# AN IMPLEMENTATION GUIDE
# TO REAL-TIME
# PROGRAMMING

Selected titles from the YOURDON PRESS COMPUTING SERIES
Ed Yourdon, *Advisor*

BAUDIN   Manufacturing Systems Analysis with Application to Production Scheduling
BELLIN AND SUCHMAN   Structured Systems Development Manual
BLOCK   The Politics of Projects
BODDIE   Crunch Mode: Building Effective Systems on a Tight Schedule
BOULDIN   Agents of Change: Managing the Introduction of Automated Tools
BRILL   Building Controls into Structured Systems
BRILL   Techniques of EDP Project Management: A Book of Readings
CHANG   Principles of Visual Programming Systems
COAD AND YOURDON   Object-Oriented Requirement Analysis
CONNELL AND SHAFER   Structured Rapid Prototyping: An Evolutionary Approach to Software
        Development
CONSTANTINE AND YOURDON   Structured Design: Fundamentals of a Discipline of Computer Program
        and Systems Design
DeMARCO   Concise Notes on Software Engineering
DeMARCO   Controlling Software Projects: Management, Measurement, and Estimates
DeMARCO   Structured Analysis and System Specification
DeSALVO AND LIEBOWITZ   Managing Artifical Intelligence and Expert Systems
DICKINSON   Developing Structured Systems: A Methodology Using Structured Techniques
FLAVIN   Fundamental Concepts in Information Modeling
FOLLMAN   Business Applications with Microcomputers: A Guidebook for Building Your Own System
FRANTZEN AND McEVOY   A Game Plan for Systems Development: Strategy and Steps for Designing Your
        Own System
INMON   Information Engineering for the Practioner: Putting Theory into Practice
KELLER   Expert Systems Technology: Development and Application
KELLER   The Practice of Structured Analysis: Exploding Myths
KING   Creating Effective Software: Computer Program Design Using the Jackson Method
KING   Current Practices in Software Development: A Guide to Successful Systems
LIEBOWITZ AND DeSALVO   Structuring Expert Systems: Domain, Design, and Development
MacDONALD   Intuition to Implementation: Communicating About Systems Towards a Language of Struc-
        ture in Data Processing System Development
McMENAMIN AND PALMER   Essential System Analysis
ORR   Structured Systems Development
PAGE-JONES   Practical Guide to Structured Systems Design, 2/E
PETERS   Software Design: Methods and Techniques
RIPPS   An Implementation Guide to Real-Time Programming
RODGERS   UNIX Database Management Systems
RUHL   The Programmer's Survival Guide: Career Strategies for Computer Professionals
SCHMITT   The OS/2 Programming Environment
SCHLAER AND MELLOR   Object-Oriented Systems Analysis: Modeling the World in Data
THOMSETT   People and Project Management
TOIGO   Disaster Recovery Planning: Managing Risk and Catastrophe in Information Systems
VESELY   Strategic Data Management: The Key to Corporate Competitiveness
WARD   Systems Development Without Pain: A User's Guide to Modeling Organizational Patterns
WARD AND MELLOR   Structured Development for Real-Time Systems, Volumes I, II, and III
WEAVER   Using the Structured Techniques: A Case Study
WEINBERG   Structured Analysis
YOURDON   Classics in Software Engineering
YOURDON   Managing the Structured Techniques, 4/E
YOURDON   Managing the System Life Cycle, 2/E
YOURDON   Modern Structured Analysis
YOURDON   Structured Walkthroughs, 4/E
YOURDON   Techniques of Program Structure and Design
YOURDON   Writing of the Revolution: Selected Readings on Software Engineering
ZAHN   C Notes: A Guide to the C Programming

# AN IMPLEMENTATION GUIDE TO REAL-TIME PROGRAMMING

David L. Ripps

YOURDON PRESS
Prentice Hall Building
Englewood Cliffs, New Jersey 07632

Library of Congress Cataloging-in-Publication Data

Ripps, David L.
    An implementation guide to real-time programming / David L. Ripps.
      p.  cm.
    Bibliography:  p.
    Includes index.
    ISBN 0-13-451873-X
    1. Real-time programming.  I. Title.
QA76.54.R563  1990
004'.33—dc20                      89-34327
                                     CIP

Editorial/production supervision: Jacqueline A. Jeglinski
Cover design: Wanda Lubelska
Manufacturing buyer: Mary Ann Gloriande
Cover photo: Courtesy of The Science Museum, London

LaserJet is a registered trademark of Hewlett-Packard,
Inc.; MS-DOS is a registered trademark of Microsoft,
Inc.; MTOS-UX is a registered trademark of Industrial
Programming, Inc.; MTOS as a substitute for
MTOS-UX is a trademark of Industrial Programming,
Inc.; OS/370 is a registered trademark of International
Business Machines, Inc.; TeleGen2 is a registered
trademark of TeleSoft, Inc.; UNIX is a registered
trademark of AT&T; VAX is a registered trademark of
Digital Equipment, Inc.; VERSA-dos is a registered
trademark of Motorola, Inc.; VMS is a registered
trademark of Digital Equipment, Inc.; XyWrite III
Plus is a registered trademark of XYQUEST, Inc.;
ITC Garamond is a registered trademark of International
Typeface, Inc.; Bitstream is a registered trademark
of Bitstream, Inc.

The publisher offers discounts on this book when
ordered in bulk quantities. For more information, write:
        Special Sales/College Marketing
        Prentice-Hall, Inc.
        College Technical and Reference Division
        Englewood Cliffs, NJ 07632

Printed in the United States of America

10  9  8  7  6  5  4  3  2  1

## ISBN 0-13-451873-X

Prentice-Hall International (UK) Limited, *London*
Prentice-Hall of Australia Pty. Limited, *Sydney*
Prentice-Hall Canada Inc., *Toronto*
Prentice-Hall Hispanoamericana, S.A., *Mexico*
Prentice-Hall of India Private Limited, *New Delhi*
Prentice-Hall of Japan, Inc., *Tokyo*
Simon & Schuster Asia Pte. Ltd., *Singapore*
Editora Prentice-Hall do Brasil, Ltda., *Rio de Janeiro*

To Sylvia, Elana, and Samara
... for their patient understanding.

# CONTENTS

══════════════════════════════════════════════════════════════

# LIST OF ILLUSTRATIONS

# PREFACE

==============================================================

Interest in real-time programming has grown considerably since the author first began in that field over 20 years ago. A primary reason is the availability of relatively inexpensive, relatively robust hardware. It is now practical to move real-time control functions from mechanical devices to electronic ones. New telephone switches don't have mechanical stepping switches anymore. Furthermore, electronic devices are aiding or replacing humans in an ever-increasing number of areas that demand real-time response. Industrial robots are commonplace.

But hardware is only part of the story; the other part is software. Early real-time applications often ran with *ad hoc* programs developed for a specific purpose and not readily altered, expanded, or maintained. The special problems of real-time devices were not well understood. The required techniques to handle these problems were yet to evolve.

Now, real-time programming has matured considerably. Programs are written with well-established techniques and supported by standard, off-the-shelf software. Not that we have an optimum solution to every problem. Real-time programming isn't *that* mature. But enough progress has been made for there to be a cogent body of knowledge worth learning.

This guide is aimed at sharing some of the experience that has crystallized around one of those pieces of standard, off-the-shelf support software. In this case, the software is a general, real-time operating system. The operating system is a natural focal point since it is the center of a real-time application. In a sense, the operating system defines the vocabulary with which the real-time program is written.

To be concrete, we have chosen a specific operating system (MTOS-UX) and discussed real-time programming in terms of its features and facilities. To do otherwise would be as amorphous as trying to explain how to program without ever showing a line of code. Generalities don't carry much weight. Similarly, illustrative sections of application calls to the operating system are written in C and Ada, the two most important languages for real-time work.

Nevertheless, this is not a just a user's guide for a commercial product or a pair of programming languages. The aim is to demonstrate how to write good, robust real-time programs.

The book is intended as a self-contained tutorial on the real-time aspects of programming. The reader is assumed to have already acquired some familiarity with programming in general. It is the special problems and concerns of real time that are at issue.

The author is indebted to many people for their pointed criticism and helpful suggestions. Bernard Mushinsky and Carol Sigda of Industrial Programming read various drafts of the manual and helped to shape its final form. Joe Gwinn of Raytheon and Roy Stehlik of Westinghouse each made detailed critiques of the text and contributed many very helpful suggestions. Ed Yourdon catalyzed the creation of the book, while Ed Moura and Jackie Jeglinski of Prentice Hall made it all happen. The eagle-eyed copy editor, Sally Ann Bailey, made sure the text was consistent within itself, and with the standards of printed English. Finally, thanks are due to Phyllis Rosenberg and Kathy Pruziner who handled endless secretarial functions so well and so cheerfully.

This book was typeset by the author in the Bitstream ITC Garamond Soft-Font and the Courier internal font of the Hewlett-Packard LaserJet printer. The text was composed and printed with the XyWrite III Plus word processing program.

David L. Ripps

# AN IMPLEMENTATION GUIDE
# TO REAL-TIME
# PROGRAMMING

# Chapter 1
# INTRODUCTION

=================================================================

In this chapter we introduce some basic concepts including real-time programming, multitasking, task attributes, operating systems, and operating system services.

## 1.1 NATURE OF REAL-TIME PROGRAMMING

This book is about real-time programming—about programs that run telephone switches, control robot arms, or pilot airplanes. It is not about programs that generate last month's telephone bill, prepare parts lists for items made by a robot, or do cost accounting for an airline company. But before we plunge into technical issues, let us see exactly why the first is a group of real-time programs, while the second is not.

A fundamental property of a real-time program is that some or all of its input arrives from the outside world *asynchronously* with respect to any work that the program is already doing. The program must be able to interrupt its current activity immediately and then execute some predefined code to capture or respond to that input, which is often a fleeting, transient signal. The capture of new data, in turn, may trigger the running of one or more other urgent programs that were waiting for input. Finally, the computer is able to resume its original activity.

To be concrete, consider a telephone switch that is capable of servicing a rotary dial. Dialing, say, a 5, produces five narrow pulses that must be detected immediately as they fly by. Meanwhile, other parts of the dial processing program must cancel the transaction if the caller hangs up, must time-out the call if there is too long an interval between digits, must start finding a special path if the leading digit is a 1, or an area code, or 800 or 911, and so on. Simultaneously, still other parts of the overall switch program are working on calls that have already been placed: searching for a connection path, generating ring or busy signals, recording billing information, and monitoring hangups, among other activities. This is real-time because the timing of the input is completely imposed on the program by unpredictable outside agents (you and me).

In contrast, generating a telephone bill does not have that kind of frantic timing constraints. When the program needs input, it makes a disk access and then waits for the data. (In a multiuser system the billing program may be swapped out during the wait, but that is irrelevant.) If the program takes a long time to compute a bill, there's no catastrophe; the next customer's data will always be there when the program gets around to reading it.

In these two cases the strong difference between real-time and nonreal-time programs arose from the nature of the program specifications, from what the programs had to do. Sometimes the difference arises just from the relative time scales involved. For example, consider a program to control the speed of a rotating shaft. The shaft has a wheel on which are engraved a series of lines that reflect light onto a detector. Shaft speed is computed by counting the number of blips coming from the detector per unit of time, or equivalently, by measuring the time interval between blips. (Assume that there is a high-resolution clock available to the program.) The program enters the raw speed measurements into an averaging filter, compares the result with the desired speed, and then computes the power to be sent to the drive motor. On the one hand, if the shaft is rotating very quickly or there are many lines on the wheel, the blips arrive faster than the time needed to compute the motor power. The power calculation based on the last period's blip count would have to be interrupted now and then to count the blips for the next period. This is clearly real-time. On the other hand, if the speed is low and there are few lines, the program might easily complete the calculation of the motor power in the interval between blips, and then wait to input the next blip. Now, the program has lost its real-time flavor. Thus, the same program requirements can be either real-time or not depending upon the time scale of the input in relation to all the work that must be done by the system.

As we will see in the next section, real-time programs are organized to survive in the face of disturbances that would upset nonreal-time programs. Thus, if there is doubt as to the real-time nature of an application, it is safer to use the more robust real-time organization.


## 1.2  ORGANIZATION OF A REAL-TIME PROGRAM

The need to interrupt one part of a real-time application spontaneously to perform data capture or other more urgent functions forces a particular organization upon such programs. Real-time applications must be written as a series of separate component programs that can execute concurrently. The components are called *tasks* or *processes*; the organization is called *multitasking* or *multiprocessing*. We will use the terms tasks and multitasking. (The adjective "multiprocessing" is too easily confused with "multiprocessor," which describes a computer system having more than one central processing unit (CPU).)

Each task is a complete program that is capable of independent execution. Each task has a segment of code that it executes. Each task has its own private stack and its own local data areas. These are dedicated memory segments in which the task can keep procedure call parameters, return addresses, temporary data, and similar variables that are not shared with other tasks. Furthermore, each task has its own set of values for the program counter and stack pointer, plus any other general, special, and coprocessor registers that the hardware provides. The hardware register set is known as the execution context, or simply the *context*.[1]

Because each task is itself a viable program, each can be started, suspended, resumed, and terminated separately. When an interrupt requires the current task, **C**, to suspend execution in deference to another task, **I**, **C** stops running, its context is saved, **I**'s context is installed in the hardware, and **I** starts running. Later, **C**'s context is reinstalled in the hardware, and it resumes as though there had been no break in its execution (Figure 1-1).

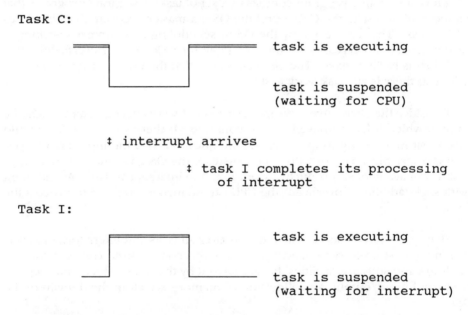

```
Task C:

    ═══════╗         ╔════════════     task is executing
           ║         ║
           ╚═════════╝                 task is suspended
                                       (waiting for CPU)


        ‡ interrupt arrives

                ‡ task I completes its processing
                    of interrupt

Task I:

           ┌─────────┐                 task is executing
           │         │
    ───────┘         └───────────      task is suspended
                                       (waiting for interrupt)
```

FIGURE 1-1: Task Suspension and Resumption in a Multitasking Environment

Often, a real-time application has several different kinds of spontaneous input. Some kinds are more important than others; some engender more impor-

---

[1]Some tasks may share some or all of their code segment with other tasks. Normally, every task will have the same value for certain special registers, such as those that determine the response to external interrupts. Neither type of overlap lessens the completeness of each task as an executable program.

tant responses than others. As a result, task **I** may itself be preempted by yet another task, **I2**.

## 1.3  REAL-TIME OPERATING SYSTEM

The discontinuous execution of a task is invisible to the task. Real-time programs operate under the control of a co-resident piece of code known as the operating system (OS). The OS is the master program; it decides which task executes on a processor and performs the required context switches. It also handles the hardware interrupts that normally announce the availability of fresh input and determines when the response task is to be activated. In short, the OS schedules all processor work.

Thus, a real-time program consists of a set of tasks—separate programs that compete for access to the CPU—and the OS—a master program that schedules CPU access. The work done by the OS in scheduling and context switching is pure overhead; it decreases the time available for task work. Nevertheless, this small loss is easily repaid. The OS makes sure that the CPU is always kept busy as long as there is any task work to do.

Consider the alternatives. Suppose that task **I** were executing and reached a point at which it had to have input to continue. If there were no OS, **I** would have to sit in a polling loop, repeating the question: Has the input arrived yet? This is a terrible waste of CPU time. Instead, the OS gives the CPU to task **C**. Task **C** can accomplish productive work until the interrupt arrives. At that point (with slight additional overhead) the CPU can be turned over to **I** to process the input.

Because of its role as central authority over all tasks and interrupts, the OS is also in the best position to provide centralized services and to control access to hardware and software facilities that are shared by the tasks. Thus, timekeeping, peripheral input/output, and allocation of memory are all in the domain of the OS.

Handling such chores as peripheral I/O within the OS yields considerable space efficiency over duplicating the code in each task that needs the function. Furthermore, the individual tasks rarely have the applicationwide information required to resolve the conflicts that arise when allocating shared resources. Centralization also shortens development time for real-time applications. A debugged general OS can usually be applied immediately to a new project.

In real-time work it is common to have dozens of concurrent tasks. Some have been suspended by the arrival of input that merited immediate attention. Others have been blocked because they requested a service of the OS and that service is not yet complete. (Incomplete services might involve a requested disk access that is still in progress, or some requested memory that cannot yet be allocated.)

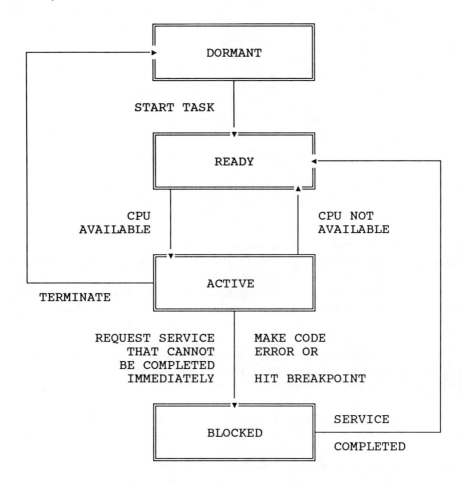

FIGURE 1-2: State Transitions for a Real-Time Task

## 1.4 TASK STATES

To help track the activities of various tasks, OSs commonly maintain the state of each task. One scheme is to classify a task as *Running* if it is currently executing on a processor, as *Ready* if it can execute as soon as a processor becomes available, as *Blocked* if a requested service is not yet complete, or there is some other impediment that prevents its execution, and as *Dormant* if it has terminated after it finished executing or it has not yet been requested to execute.

This is the scheme we will use. The possible transitions between these four states of a task are shown in Figure 1-2.[2]

Different operating systems employ different strategies to choose which task to run next when there is more than one Ready task. The simplest rules are first-come, first-served and equal-execution-time-slice-for-all-tasks. However, at a given moment within a real-time application, each activity has a discernible level of importance or priority with respect to other ongoing activities. Consequently, the tasks that perform the activities carry a corresponding level of priority. A good real-time OS maintains not only the state of each task but the current priority as well. If there is more than one Ready task, the highest priority (most urgent) one gets the processor. Among tasks of equal priority, it can be first-come, first-served.

## 1.5 FURTHER CRITERIA FOR A REAL-TIME PROGRAM

A multitasking organization seems to be the only practical structure for a real-time program. However, programs that have neither spontaneous data nor other aspects of real-time to cope with may also employ multitasking. For example, UNIX, VAX VMS, and OS/370 all use multitasking, even though these operating systems were not designed to support real-time work. Is there anything else, besides the presence of asynchronous input, that characterizes a real-time application?

Two further properties seem to complete the definition of a real-time application: a high degree of interdependence among the component tasks and a need to have very rapid response to interrupts.

In a nonreal-time environment, there is little or no relation among the tasks that are running concurrently; they are a collection of independent programs that happen to have been submitted by the various independent users of the hardware. Thus, the OS need not and does not provide strong facilities to coordinate the tasks. Quite the contrary, for security reasons, the OS tries to make it difficult for one task to interfere with another.

In contrast, in a typical real-time program all of the tasks are highly interrelated: They are all aspects of one overall "embedded" application. Thus, the OS must provide a rich set of facilities for communication, coordination, and synchronization among tasks. Real-time tasks need to be able to send messages to each other, to broadcast that a significant event has occurred, to access shared

---

[2]It is not necessary to make such a strong distinction between Ready, Dormant, and Blocked states. A Ready task can be considered blocked waiting for a CPU to become available. Similarly, a Dormant task is just waiting to be restarted. In this view every task is either Running or is Blocked, waiting for something.

data, to wait for each other to finish some activity, to borrow pooled resources, and much more.

Finally, very rapid response to external stimuli seems to be inherent in the real-time world. The maximum time to recognize that an external interrupt is pending (latency) plus the time needed to suspend the current task and switch to an interrupt handler (context switch time) is commonly on the order of microseconds. UNIX, and similar nonreal-time operating systems, were not designed to react so quickly.

## 1.6 SCOPE OF BOOK

This book discusses several aspects of real-time programming. The overall goal is to teach the reader how to divide an application into separate tasks and then how to make sure that those separate tasks work together as a cohesive, coordinated, and unified program.

Chapter 4 is devoted to the problem of separating an application into tasks. We give some general rules that can help in the rational mapping of functions into a set of tasks. Tasking is often the hardest and the most crucial part of a real-time project. A poor task organization cannot be made to work well, even if the tasks themselves are brilliantly designed and coded. Tasking is especially hard for the beginner since it requires experience with how tasks can and cannot interact efficiently.

The remainder of the book discusses the means by which tasks interact with each other and with the outside world. Topics include how tasks can (1) wait for each other (coordination), (2) send messages to each other (communication), (3) share data without interference (mutual exclusion), (4) apportion memory and other pooled resources (allocation), (5) pause for a given time interval or until a given time of day (synchronization), and (6) exchange information with the external world (peripheral input/output). We describe the treatment of both typical, routine cases and some more challenging special cases. Often, several alternatives are presented since learning is aided by contrast.

## 1.7 INTENDED READERSHIP

The book is intended to be a self-contained introductory text with respect to the real-time aspects of programming. Many of the readers will be technical people who must design, code, or maintain real-time applications. Those who supervise and guide the efforts of real-time programmers are yet another category of readers. A third category is the computer science major who is taking a course in real-time programming.

For many, this book will be their first formal exposure to the special problems, concerns, and techniques of real-time programming. As a result, the text is targeted primarily to programmers with limited or no experience in real-time. The reader is expected to be already familiar with programming in general. Thus, there is no definition of common terms, such as program counter or procedure call. Furthermore, we expect the reader to feel comfortable with short code sequences written in a high-level language. (The examples could have been coded in assembler. However, we choose a high-level language so as not to tie the discussion to any particular instruction set architecture.)

While the primary readership will have little or no prior knowledge of the field, even old hands may benefit from some of the material. Real-time programming is an active field. A great deal of practical experience is being accumulated and is starting to crystallize. A literature of theoretical work is being developed. All this effort is leading to new concepts and techniques, especially in the area of task coordination and communication. For example, the implementation of conditional critical regions via controlled shared variables (Chapter 9) may be new to some seasoned real-time programmers. So may the classification of intertask coordination and communication schemes (Chapter 11).

Finally, many experienced practitioners have worked almost entirely with one OS, or in one application area. These people may be broadened by exposure to another OS and other classes of applications. My advice here is don't be turned off if we took a different approach. Try to understand what we did and why we did it.

## 1.8  REAL-TIME OPERATING SYSTEMS, REVISITED

A premise of this guide is that real-time services are to be supplied by an operating system or kernel.[3] Furthermore, we assume that the OS is separate from the application code and is essentially independent of the application. (More exactly, the real-time OS can be applied to a wide variety of applications.) Alternate approaches are possible.

In the early history of real-time programming, the operating system was not always cleanly separated from the application. A typical real-time program consisted of a series of procedures that performed some function of the application. One procedure might input a certain kind of data by polling at a fixed rate. Another procedure might perform a calculation on the data after polling to

---

[3]An operating system is often depicted as layers or concentric circles around the hardware. The innermost layer (the one closest to the hardware) is called the kernel. Thus, in this scheme, a file system is part of the OS proper. The peripheral I/O services that the file system calls are part of the kernel.

determine that the data were available. Tying all this together was a "main program." It served as a crude OS; it called each functional procedure in a preset order. Generally, the main program would permit each procedure to complete before calling the next one.

This cyclic-scheduler approach to real-time programming has fallen into disfavor. It had many problems. First, the cycle times had to be determined by elaborate experiment and tuning. Every time one of the functions was revised, the dynamics of the program changed and the system had to be retuned. As a result, the programs were a nightmare to maintain and expand.

Equally annoying was that the ad hoc approach to scheduling and service delivery required a new main program for each application. There was too much application-specific code inside of the "operating system." Furthermore, there was little hope of making the execution efficient by performing actions in parallel. Instead of interrupts and preemption there was polling and serial execution. Thus, when a message had to be output to a console, the entire program waited while each character went out.

There is yet another approach to real-time programming that is not so easily dismissed. Time may show it is even the right way to proceed. The idea is to build real-time facilities directly into the task language. Concurrent Pascal, Modula, and Ada incorporate this technique (Be82, Br73, Ho83, LRM83). The approach will be illustrated in Chapter 17 for Ada.

The chief advantages of having real-time features within the tasking language are increased portability and possibly enhanced error checking. In principle, the compiler can do extensive checking for misuse of real-time facilities and potentially dangerous practices.

The chief disadvantage of the linguistic approach is that the real-time primitives may not be adequate or appropriate for your application. Ada provides only one mechanism for coordination and communication among tasks (the rendezvous). But the rendezvous has some very unfortunate semantic properties that were not fully appreciated until after the language had been frozen. [For example, at the First International Workshop on Real-Time Ada issues it was reported that a low-priority task can delay a high-priority task for an unlimited amount of time because the rendezvous has first-come, first-served queuing (Co87).] While these problems are likely to be corrected in the next version of Ada (Ada-9X), this will not occur until well into the 1990s.

Ada restricted the number of real-time features to minimize other problems: compiler size and complexity. The more features you have in a language, the longer the compilation takes. At present, relying upon an independent OS for real-time facilities seems to be a good practical approach to real-time programming.

This book presents each aspect of real-time programming purely from the application (task) side; it does not explain how to write the operating system that supplies the required services. Robust real-time operating systems are commercially available. It is far more economical in money and project time to buy an OS than to plan, write, debug, test, and maintain one of your own. There is no more reason to develop a private OS than to develop a private editor, compiler, assembler, or linker. [If you still doubt that point, see "No Silver Bullet—Essence and Accidents of Software Engineering" by Frederick P. Brooks, Jr. (Br87), in particular, the section headed "Buy vs. Build."]

The real-time OS selected for this book is MTOS-UX, a product of Industrial Programming, Inc. (Jericho, N.Y.). It was chosen for several reasons. The author helped develop it specifically as a realization of the ideas presented here. (More exactly, the ideas and the OS evolved jointly over a 12-year period, with constant feedback from hundreds of users.) MTOS-UX is available for several families of processors, such as the Motorola 680xx and 88x00, Intel 80x86, and National Semiconductor 32x32. It has the richest and most comprehensive set of real-time facilities of any commercially available real-time OS; all others have only a subset of its facilities. Finally, MTOS-UX, together with its immediate predecessors of the MTOS product family, have been used successfully in several hundred very different real-time applications. It is a standard among real-time operating systems.

## 1.9 TOPICS NOT COVERED

Certain topics within the field of real-time programming are not covered within this guide. Not that these areas are unimportant; they were just beyond the limits of the author's direct experience.

The most important area skipped is "hard" real-time (HRT). (This book is about "soft" real-time, SRT.) In HRT, you specify the time at which each task must finish a round of processing and an estimate of the execution time needed. The job of the OS is then to schedule the tasks so as to meet the deadlines, if possible. In SRT, you specify the level of urgency of the tasks and the OS simply assigns the CPU to the most urgent task that is ready to execute. This difference is purely a matter of task scheduling; other aspects of real-time programming remain the same.

A second topic that is barely broached is loosely coupled multiprocessing. In Chapter 15 we discuss real-time applications that have more than one CPU directly executing task code (multiprocessing). However, the main focus is on hardware in which all processors are connected to the same backplane. As a result of this tight coupling, all processors can immediately share as much data as necessary for direct coordination and communication. In an alternate approach, the CPUs are so loosely coupled that the only way to share data is via interprocessor messages. This form of multiprocessing is not explored in depth.

The final topic that is not covered is fault tolerance. We discuss detection of software errors when dealing with debugging in Chapter 16. Nevertheless, we are mute on the whole issue of recovering from significant hardware failures during processing.

## 1.10 LANGUAGE ISSUES

Although we concentrate on the concepts of real-time programming, these can become fuzzy until you see specific examples, coded in real language for a real operating system. The choice of MTOS-UX as the OS was mentioned before. For the language, we chose C, based mainly on its popularity among real-time programmers and its ease of use. Furthermore, if one resists the urge to be overly terse, C can be as clear as any other high-level language. Those who are unfamiliar with C might want to read at least the early chapters of Kernighan and Ritchie (Ke78).

Tasks need not be written in C; all MTOS-UX services can be invoked from assembly language, as well as from FORTRAN, Pascal, or other high-level languages. As we will see in the next chapter, a programmer requests an OS service by calling a procedure, such as *pause* (10 + MS) to pause for 10 ms. All high-level languages that are likely to be used in real-time applications provide some mechanism to call procedures with arguments. In fact, many compilers have the option of generating calls that are compatible with C. Thus, as far as the OS services are concerned, it doesn't matter if the program is expressed in C or in any other language with a compatible interface.

Nevertheless, C, FORTRAN, and Pascal do share a property that sets them aside from a new group of languages typified by Ada. Ada has tasking and other real-time facilities built directly into the language; C, FORTRAN, and Pascal do not. The consequences are so far-reaching that we devote a separate chapter (17) to the use of Ada for real-time applications.

# Chapter 2
## SUMMARY OF OS CONCEPTS
## AND SERVICES

==================================================================

This chapter delves further into the nature of real-time programming and some of the special concerns that are not found in other forms of programming.

### 2.1 MORE ON THE NATURE OF REAL-TIME PROGRAMMING

One of the most difficult aspects of real-time work is getting into the right "mind-set." You must become accustomed to multitasking: to thinking in terms of multiple threads of execution running in parallel. An interrupt can occur between any two instructions within a task. This may require the operating system (OS) to suspend the currently executing task and start another. The suspension and later resumption are handled completely by the OS; they are "invisible" to the task. Nevertheless, this discontinuity can have several important side effects that we will now explore.

In a real-time application, the arrival of an interrupt is normally random with respect to the portion of code that happens to be executing. The interrupt must be serviced. This delays the interrupted code. As a result, the execution time for any portion of task code may be unpredictable. This is true even if the time to perform a given line of (uninterrupted) application code or to supply a given OS service is perfectly predictable. Random variations in performance are inherent in the nature of real-time programs.

Furthermore, under certain conditions, the small variations due to random interrupts can magnify into chaotic behavior. Suppose ordinarily there is barely enough time to perform some sections of a cyclic or repetitive application. Suppose, further, that the program takes a different path when one of these precarious sections is unable to finish in time. On most cycles, there is sufficient time and the program follows its normal path. Occassionally, an unfortunate combination of interrupts causes a time out and then the program diverges onto an alternate path. This variation, in turn, can effect the timing on the next cycle. The result can be a radically different pattern of behavior generated by a very small variation in the arrival time of an interrupt. [For a discussion of chaotic phenomena in real time systems, see "Inner Rhythms" in James Gleick's book on chaos (Gl87).]

A second side effect of a multitasking organization concerns any alterable data that is shared at the task level. Consider a concrete example. Task U is performing some calculations with a set of shared, alterable data. Without any warning, **U** is preempted by task **P**, which happens to be another user of the same data. If **P** were permitted to change the data, the results of the calculations performed by **U** would become unreliable.

The solution to such problems cannot be to disable interrupts. That technique can lead to the loss of any short-lived data whose arrival is signaled by an interrupt.

Nor can the general solution be to raise a task to the highest level of urgency so that no other task can preempt it. In a single-processor system, only one task can protect itself by being most urgent. In a multiprocessor system (i.e., a system with two or more processors executing task code), even the most urgent task may find itself sharing data with a less urgent task that is executing on another processor.

Luckily, there are facilities within a real-time operating system that enable a task to block temporarily other users of the same data (see Section 2.3.3). But this is where mind-set comes into play. The OS cannot automatically set up this type of protection. The designer of the task code must remember to ask for the protection before the first access of the data and must remember to release the protection after the last access.

## 2.2  COORDINATION AND COMMUNICATION

In the first chapter, we defined a task as a complete program that is capable of independent execution. This is true, but needs further refinement. While a task is *physically* complete and executable, it is not *logically* independent of the other tasks.

Each task performs a small part of the overall application, working in parallel with other tasks. At various points, the tasks must coordinate their activities. For example, a task that does an initial analysis of raw data must wait for the task that captures the data to build a complete set of values. The task that performs a deeper analysis, in turn, must wait for the results of the preanalysis. Similarly, when several tasks output reports on a shared terminal, each must wait until it can have exclusive access to the device. Otherwise, the intermixed display might be unintelligible.

Thus, tasks are not independent; they share common goals, common data, and common hardware. As a result, they must rely heavily on the OS to coordinate their individual executions. Planning the way tasks will coordinate and communicate is a major part of the design of a real-time application. These two concepts, coordination and communication, are common threads that are woven throughout the services provided by a real-time operating system.

### 2.2.1 Coordination/Synchronization

Coordination is the blocking of a task until some specified condition is met. With this broad a definition, a task can coordinate with physical events, as well as with itself and other tasks. For example, when a task pauses, it is blocked until the specified time elapses. The task is therefore coordinating with the physical clock.

Often a task coordinates with another task; the condition that task **W** is waiting for is set by another task, **C**. As we will see later, it is even possible for a task to become unblocked by a set of conditions that are supplied jointly by one or more tasks and by a physical device (the clock). Thus, coordination is a very general term for any self-imposed (i.e., requested) suspension of the execution of a task. In every case, it is the OS that performs the requested suspension and eventual resumption of task activity.

In the literature, the term "synchronization" is often applied to what we are calling coordination. Some authors limit synchronization to task-to-task interactions and so would not apply the term to a pause.

### 2.2.2 Self-Coordination

A few services provided by an OS are guaranteed to return immediately with the desired result; they never block the task. Examples are the services that just return information held by the OS, such as the caller's priority or the current time of day.

In contrast, any service that requires the allocation of a resource (such as memory) or that needs a task-level object to be free may be delayed until the resource or object becomes available. Such services involve coordination. In this case, the task is coordinating with itself, or more precisely, with the completion of a service it itself requested.

The simplest way to coordinate is merely to block the task until the service is finished. And in many cases, the simplest is best, especially if the task cannot perform further work until the service is done. Most real-time operating systems provide this coordination mode.

The problem with waiting until a service is completed is that there is no guarantee that the service will ever be completed or that the waiting time will not compromise other more urgent aspects of the task's work. Many critical real-time applications cannot risk any uncontrolled waits. Thus, MTOS-UX permits the basic coordination mode to be augmented by a maximum wait time. If the request cannot be processed within that time, the request is timed out and the task continues. If this occurs, the OS informs the task of the failure. The interval can be zero to provide "fail unless immediately available."

"No coordination" is another mode available for many services. Thus, the OS permits a task to send a message with no coordination if the sender does not care when the message is received.

Finally, there are times when a task needs a service performed, but would like to defer coordination until later. Suppose task **R** wants to have three other tasks started now, but would also like to continue to do other work. Upon the completion of that other work, **R** is willing to wait for the termination of the three tasks it started. Such deferred coordination is permitted under MTOS-UX through the event flag machinery. (To preview a later discussion, each start request would specify a different local event flag, an internal bit that can be set when the service is completed. Later, task **R** would ask the OS to block it until all three bits have been set.)

### 2.2.3  Communication

Communication is the transfer of information between tasks. Input/output (I/O) covers the transfer of information between the external world and a task.

As we will soon see, communication can proceed directly from one task to another. For example, when task **S** starts task **T**, **S** can transmit an argument to **T** (just as the caller can pass an argument to a procedure). Often, however, communication is best mitigated by a separate object, called a message exchange. This is a public queue to which any task can send a message and from which any task can receive a message.

Commonly, communication involves coordination. It is unusual to seek a message and not to wait for it to arrive. However, the sender of a message may not need to wait for it to be received.

### 2.3  OS OBJECTS AND THEIR FUNCTIONS

A real-time operating system is an object-oriented program. The primary objects it deals with are executable objects (tasks), communication/coordination objects (message exchanges, event flag groups, semaphores, and controlled shared variables), and I/O objects (peripheral units). Objects can be created and destroyed. Each object has a set of functions that apply only to that class of objects: You can start a task executing; it is erroneous to request a message exchange to start executing.

One measure of the richness of a real-time operating system is the number of distinct types of objects it provides and the number of manipulations on those objects that it permits. By that measure, the illustrative OS chosen for this guide (MTOS-UX) is a very rich system. In fact, one of the reasons for choosing that particular OS is that it has examples of so many objects and functions.

The objects and service functions supported by MTOS-UX are summarized very briefly in the next eight sections. Each synopsis is greatly expanded in a later chapter.

### 2.3.1  Task Control Services

One task can create another task. The creator specifies the basic attributes of the new object: its entry point, stack size, default priority, and so on. A newly created task is not yet executing; it is Dormant.

Any task (**R**) can request that any task (**T**) start executing. **R** can select the priority with which **T** will begin to run. **R** can pass an argument on to **T**. **R** can indicate what should happen if **T** is already executing, and thus cannot be restarted immediately. The choices are: (1) to queue the restart request or (2) to abort it. Finally, **R** can specify if it will: (1) continue to execute in parallel with **T**, (2) wait until **T** starts because of this request (in case **T** is not immediately available for restart), or (3) wait until **T** both starts and terminates because of the current request. As will be explained in Chapter 4, there are cases in which all three types of coordination are required.

When a task finishes executing, it can simply terminate. This makes the task available for restart by another task. Alternately, a task can terminate now and be automatically restarted at a specified future time. This latter option is needed for cyclic tasks that perform some action periodically.

A task can dynamically change its own priority. It can also change the priority of another task.

In many real-time applications, tasks persist for the entire life of the system. Nevertheless, a task can request to be both terminated and then deleted.

A complete list of task services is given in Figure 2-1; the primary discussion is in Chapter 4.

| | |
|---|---|
| **crtsk** | Create task. |
| **start** | Start given task. |
| **tstart** | Start given task and transfer coordination to new task. |
| **contsk** | Connect given task to interrupt. |
| **setpty** | Set current priority of given task. |
| **exeprc** | Set (or reset) processor on which requesting task can execute. |
| **getkey** | Get key of given task. |
| **gettid** | Get identifier of task with given key. |
| **getdad** | Get address of data segments of requesting task. |
| **exit** | Terminate requesting task (without automatic restart). |
| **trmrst** | Terminate task with automatic restart after given interval of time. |
| **dltsk** | Delete requesting task. |

FIGURE 2-1:  Task Control Services Provided by MTOS-UX

## 2.3.2  Event Flags

Event flags broadcast information that can be employed in intertask coordination.  Any task can create a public event flag group.  Each group contains 16 bits that can be independently set or reset by any task.  The individual bits represent information that is meaningful to the application.  For example, setting bit 2 in group 'PNTS' might mean that the printer has been installed.  (Any such logical significance of the bits is unknown to the OS, which just views the event flag group as 16 alterable bits.)

Any task can wait for an AND or OR combination of the bits within a given group.  If an AND combination is specified, *all* the selected bits must be set before the task continues; if an OR combination is specified, the task continues when *any* of the selected bits is set.

When a bit is set, all tasks whose AND or OR conditions are now satisfied become unblocked simultaneously.  The task that sets a bit need not know the specific identities of the tasks that will use the information.  Correspondingly, the task that uses the information does not have to know which task or tasks supply it.  Thus, event flags are a mechanism to disseminate information to any or all tasks that may wish to know.

Event flag bits remain at the last value supplied by a set or reset service call. The act of continuing a task that was waiting for an event flag to be set does not automatically reset the bit.  In other words, event flag bits are not "consumed" by being used for coordination. Event flag services are listed in Figure 2-2; the primary discussion is in Chapter 7.

| | |
|---|---|
| **crefg** | Create group of (global) event flags. |
| **srsefg** | Immediately set or reset event flags. |
| **srslef** | Immediately set or reset local event flags of given task. |
| **sgiefg** | Set event flags after given interval of time. |
| **waiefg** | Wait until event flags are set. |
| **dlefg** | Delete a group of (global) event flags. |

FIGURE 2-2:  **Event Flag Services Provided by MTOS-UX**

### 2.3.3  Semaphores and Controlled Shared Variables

Tasks often share groups of alterable data, such as a set of variables that is maintained jointly by two tasks, **A** and **B**. While **A** is working on the data, **B** must not be allowed to alter any of the variables, and vice versa.

Semaphores are a traditional means to protect shared, alterable data. A task creates a semaphore for a given set of data. Thereafter, every task that needs access to the data first requests the OS to block it until the semaphore is free. If the semaphore is already free, the task continues; otherwise the task waits. Waiting for the semaphore is equivalent to waiting until no other task has access to the same data. When the task that has the semaphore is finished with the variables, it requests the OS to release the semaphore. If any tasks are waiting at that point, the most urgent one is then permitted to continue. If there are no tasks waiting, the semaphore is kept free until the next request for it.

Controlled shared variables (CSV) are an extension of the simple semaphore concept. With a semaphore, a task can request only unconditional access to a given set of variables. All that the OS requires is that the semaphore be free; the variables themselves do not have to satisfy any particular condition. With CSVs, a task can request that the exclusive access not occur until a specified relation between the variables is true. Thus, a task could stipulate that it needs exclusive access to the windows data for the system console, but only when a window of a given size is available. This extension avoids the inefficient task-level polling of the variables that would otherwise be required.

Semaphore and CSV services are listed in Figure 2-3; the primary discussion is in Chapter 9.

### Semaphores

| | |
|---|---|
| **crsem** | Create (counting) semaphore. |
| **waisem** | Wait for given (counting) semaphore to be free. |
| **rlssem** | Release semaphore. |
| **dlsem** | Delete semaphore. |

### Controlled Shared Variables

| | |
|---|---|
| **crcsv** | Create group of controlled shared variables. |
| **usecsv** | Wait for exclusive control over group of controlled shared variables. |
| **waicsv** | Wait for function of controlled shared variables to be true. |
| **rlscsv** | Release group of controlled shared variables. |
| **dlcsv** | Delete group of controlled shared variables. |

FIGURE 2-3: Mutual Exclusion Services Provided by MTOS-UX

## 2.3.4 Message Exchanges

Message exchanges facilitate communication among tasks. Any task can create a message exchange. Thereafter, any task can send a message to the exchange and any task can receive a message from it. A message is queued at the exchange if no receiver is immediately available to take it. Directing messages to a separate communication object (the exchange) makes it possible for multiple tasks to respond to messages held in a common queue. The design was inspired by the single line at a bank with several tellers.

MTOS-UX provides two different implementations of a message exchange. The first is called a mailbox. For this class of exchanges, there is no limit to the size of a message and no limit to the number of messages that can be queued awaiting a receiver. Both the sender and receiver have full coordination capability, so that the sender can wait for the receiver, and vice versa.

The second implementation is called a message buffer. It restricts messages to the size of an address (since the message is typically a pointer to a block of parameters or text). Each buffer has a finite capacity that is specified when the buffer is created. There are only two levels of urgency, equivalent to first-in, first-out and last-in, first-out queuing. The sender always deposits a message without coordination. If there is no message available, the receiver has only two coordination options: to return immediately without a message or to wait without limit for a message. By building in these fixed options—which are the ones most commonly selected when full coordination is available—the exchange services are extremely fast.

Message exchange services are listed in Figure 2-4; the primary discussion is in Chapter 8.

### Mailboxes

| | |
|---|---|
| **opnmbx** | Open mailbox, creating it if it does not already exist. |
| **sndmbx** | Send message to mailbox. |
| **rcvmbx** | Receive first available message from mailbox. |
| **clsmbx** | Close mailbox. |
| **dlmbx** | Delete mailbox. |

### Message Buffers

| | |
|---|---|
| **crmsb** | Create message buffer. |
| **getmsb** | Get identifier of message buffer. |
| **putmsb** | Post message to the beginning of buffer. |
| **putmse** | Post message to the end of buffer. |
| **getmsn** | Get message from buffer. Return if message is not available. |
| **getmsw** | Get message from buffer. Wait if message is not available. |
| **dlmsb** | Delete message buffer. |

**FIGURE 2-4: Message Exchange Services Provided by MTOS-UX**

## 2.3.5 Input/Output

Input, output, and related functions provide a mechanism for communication between a task and the external world. This communication may be performed at the physical or logical level.

At the physical level, a task selects a particular device—a certain console, printer, disk drive, and so on—and performs a fully specified operation on that device. A typical function is to write a given block of text to a console or to read a given sector from a disk into a given input buffer. Once a task requests such a service, the OS performs all the details of the physical transfer, including handling any interrupts generated by the device.

Input and output can also be performed at the logical level via a file system. In this case, the task specifies a file, a function, and the associated input buffer or output data. The file system (not the task) determines the placement of the data on the disk.

Physical I/O services are listed in Figure 2-5. The primary discussion of physical I/O is in Chapter 13. The file system is described in Chapter 14.

**Peripheral I/O**

| | |
|---|---|
| **crpun** | Create peripheral unit to run under given driver. |
| **getstc** | Get identifier of standard console for requesting task. |
| **setstc** | Install given unit as standard console of requesting task. |
| **getuid** | Get identifier of unit with given key. |
| **pio** | Perform I/O and related functions on given peripheral unit. |

**System**

| | |
|---|---|
| **getidn** | Get system identification data. |

FIGURE 2-5: Input/Output Services Provided by MTOS-UX

### 2.3.6 Signals

A signal is a software interrupt that may be handled at the task level. Since a task can send a signal to another task, or to a group of tasks, signals are a means of intertask coordination or communication. A task may also elect to have a signal sent to itself upon completion of a requested service. Thus, signals are also a means of deferred coordination, an alternate to event flags.

MTOS-UX defines 32 signals of which 17 are available for coordination or communication. The remaining 15 are dedicated to error recovery.

Each task selects its own response to the arrival of a signal. A common response is to execute a given task-level procedure and then return to the point of interruption. Other possibilities are: (1) to ignore the signal, (2) to terminate the receiving task, or (3) to halt the task and invoke the Debugger to restart it. A task can determine its current responses and can alter that response dynamically.

A task can pause until a signal arrives. It can also request the OS to send a signal to itself or to another task after a given interval.

Signal handling capability is an inherent property of a task and need not be created. Signal services are listed in Figure 2-6; the primary discussion is in Chapter 10.

| | |
|---|---|
| **getsig** | Get response to given signal. |
| **setsig** | Set response to one or more signals. |
| **sndsig** | Send signal to one task or group of tasks. |
| **cansig** | Cancel pending signals of requesting task. |
| **sgisig** | Send specified signal after given interval of time. |
| **pausig** | Pause until signal arrives. |

FIGURE 2-6:  Signal Services Provided by MTOS-UX

### 2.3.7  Time and Time of Day

A task can pause for a given interval of time. During that time, the task is blocked from executing. The pause can be canceled by another task that wishes the task to resume immediately. To strengthen the use of pause/cancel-pause as a means of coordination, the original pause can be "forever."

Any task can submit an ASCII clock/calendar string to the OS. Thereafter, the OS will update the string every second. Any task can receive the current value of the string. A task can also pause until a given time of day. This can be a definite time, such as 12 noon, or an indefinite time, such as 30 minutes after the hour.

Various services have time-dependent options. For example, if requested to do so, the OS will set a given event flag after a specified interval or will send a given signal to a particular task after a specified interval. The option of limiting the wait for a service to a maximum interval has already been mentioned. So has the service that automatically restarts a periodic task.

Time and time of day services are listed in Figure 2-7; the primary discussion is in Chapter 6.

### 2.3.8  Shared Memory Management

It is quite common for the sum of the maximum memory requirements of each individual task to far exceed the instantaneous needs of all the tasks taken together. For example, each of 20 tasks might need 10K bytes of work space at

**Time**

| | |
|---|---|
| **pause** | Pause for given time interval. |
| **canpau** | Continue given task if it is paused for time interval. |
| **getime** | Get number of milliseconds since system was started. |

**Time of Day**

| | |
|---|---|
| **gettod** | Get time of day clock/calendar string. |
| **settod** | Set time of day clock/calendar. |
| **syntod** | Wait for given time of day. |

FIGURE 2-7: Time and Time of Day Services Provided by MTOS-UX

sometime during their execution (for a theoretical worst case total of 200K). Yet, because of the way the memory needs are phased among the tasks, only 50K are ever needed at any given time. These observations have led to the concept of memory sharing via pools.

A pool is a contiguous chunk of memory that is turned over to the OS to be allocated to individual tasks upon demand. The memory within each pool is divided into blocks of fixed size. MTOS-UX provides two types of pools. In one, a Fixed Block Pool, each allocation delivers exactly one block. In the other, a Common Memory Pool, a task can receive a contiguous area of any desired size even if it spans several blocks.

With either type of pool, a task that seeks an allocation of memory that is currently not available is given the opportunity to wait until the request can be satisfied. All coordination options are available, including limiting the wait and deferring the coordination.

Memory pool services are listed in Figure 2-8; the primary discussion is in Chapter 12.

## 2.4 INVOKING TASK SERVICES

In a traditional programming environment, OS services are requested via a procedure call. Consider the following C program, which outputs a message to the System Console via a built-in service function

```
inient ()
  {
    ...
    printf ("Application started\n\r");
    ...
  }
```

## Common Memory Pools

| | |
|---|---|
| **crcmp** | Create common memory pool. |
| **getcmp** | Get identifier of common memory pool. |
| **alloc** | Allocate contiguous area from common memory pool. |
| **dalloc** | Deallocate area taken from common memory pool. |
| **dlcmp** | Delete common memory pool. |

## Fixed Block Memory Pools

| | |
|---|---|
| **crfbp** | Create fixed block memory pool. |
| **getfbp** | Get identifier of fixed block memory pool. |
| **alofbp** | Allocate one block from fixed block memory pool. |
| **dalfbp** | Deallocate block taken from fixed block memory pool. |
| **dlfbp** | Delete fixed block memory pool. |

FIGURE 2-8:  Shared Memory Services Provided by MTOS-UX

This program could be run under UNIX, MS-DOS, or VMS.  It also runs under MTOS-UX.  In each case, the task need not be concerned with the details of how a given string is physically output.  Physical I/O is the operating system's job.

MTOS-UX provides an implementation of the C formatted output function (*printf*), the character-oriented I/O functions (*getchar* and *putchar*), and some memory allocation services (such as *malloc* and *free*).  In these cases, the functions are completely specified in Kernighan and Ritchie.

Following this model, all OS services are requested by calling a corresponding service function, with options selected via call arguments.  For example, function *pause* blocks a task for a specified interval.  A 10-ms pause is requested by *pause* (MS + 10), while *pause* (SEC + 9) blocks for nine seconds.  (A header file, MTOSUX.H, supplies the numeric value of literals such as MS and SEC.) The following program demonstrates the natural way in which standard C and proprietary OS functions are intermixed in a typical task

```
#include "MTOSUX.H"                 /* file of basic OS definitions */

inient ()
  {
    register long int  time;

    do
      {
        printf ("\n\rEnter 1-9. A bell will sound after that many seconds: ");
        time = getchar ();              /* get users response */
        putchar (time);                 /* echo back */
        time -= '0';                    /* convert to binary */
      }
    while ((time < 1) || (time > 9));
    pause (SEC+time);                   /* pause for given interval */
    printf ("\07\n\rPause over.\n\r");
  }
```

## 2.5  TYPICAL OS SERVICES: MANIPULATING TASK PRIORITY

We can further illustrate how a task invokes OS services by looking at task priority.

The OS employs the task attribute *current priority* to allocate any shared resource for which demand exceeds supply. The range of the current priority is 0 to 255, with 255 being the most urgent and 0 being the least urgent. The allocation algorithm is simply that the highest-priority task gets the resource. First-come, first-served applies in case of equality. The resources include access to processors, peripheral units, allocated memory, messages, semaphores, and controlled shared variables.

There is no limit to the number of tasks at each level. At one extreme, all tasks may have the same priority; at the other extreme, all have different priorities.

The current priority is dynamic. A task may ask to have its priority changed to a given value, say, 125, via

```
#define mine 0L

setpty (mine, USEVAL, 125L);
```

A value of 0 (*mine*) within the first argument specifies that it is the priority of the caller that is to be changed. (By supplying the identifier of a task in place of the 0, *setpty* can be used to change the priority of another task, but we are getting ahead of the story.)

The priority may also be increased by a given amount (with a clamp at 255)

    setpty (mine, ADDVAL, 10L);

or decreased by a given amount (with a clamp at 0)

    setpty (mine, ADDVAL, -10L);

Almost all service procedures return a value to the requesting task. If one of the parameters is inappropriate, the function returns the value **BADPRM** (which is defined in MTOSUX.H as -1). If the parameters are correct, *setpty* returns the new value of the task priority, as an unsigned short integer. Thus, a task can determine its current priority by adding a 0 to its priority

    mypty = setpty (mine, ADDVAL, 0L);

## 2.6 CHANGING PRIORITY IN ALTERNATE OPERATING SYSTEMS

To be concrete, all the preceding examples were drawn from the same OS. Nevertheless, they illustrate the almost universal techniques for obtaining services from a real-time operating system. Note the similarity with the service to set priority within the proposed Microprocessor Operating System Interface (MOSI) standard [MOSI87, Sections 7.3 and E.7.2 (C binding)]

    void oschpri (process_id, new_priority, &error);

where *process_id* selects the target task (process) and *new_priority* is the new priority value. A value of -1 for the latter indicates the default priority, and a value of 0 provides the largest allowable priority for that task. The meaning of other values is implementation-dependent. The function does not return a value (is "void").

A corresponding function appears in the standard proposed by the IEEE (Realtime Extension for Portable Operating Systems) (POS88, Unapproved Draft 2, Section 4.2.1)

    int rt_setpriority (pid, prio);

Here *pid* selects the target task, with 0 designating the caller, and *prio* is the new priority value. The new priority value is bound to a range associated with the current scheduling policy for the system. Negative values are specifically forbidden. The exact semantics of *rt_setpriority* are implementation-dependent, including questions of appropriate privilege to change the priority of another task. Upon success, the function returns the former priority of the selected task.

There are even more OS "standards" that have been proposed or are still being developed.[1] While our main point is to show how services are obtained from an operating system, the painful lack of agreement on even a simple service becomes apparent. There are so many conflicting universal standards that there is no universal standard. Furthermore, in many cases vital semantic details of the standard service functions are "implementation-dependent." Thus, these standards are not even fulfilling their goal of promoting portability of real-time applications. An application behaves differently with different implementations of even the same standard.

## 2.7 MEASURING IDLE TIME

The next program provides further examples of how OS services are invoked and shows how two tasks may cooperate to attain a single goal. That goal is the measurement of the idle time within an application.

    #include "MTOSUX.H"

    #define MAXTLY 21894;   /* maximum value of tally for no tasks running */

    static long  tally;          /* number of loops performed in sample period */

---

[1] In addition to the efforts mentioned above, the VMEbus International Trade Association (VITA) is standardizing on the Open Real-Time Kernal Interface Definition (ORKID) (Ry89), Motorola is offering to make its Real-Time Executive Interface Definition (RTEID) a universal standard (Mo87), and the Japanese are promoting The Real-Time Operating System Nucleus (TRON) as a world standard (Sa87, Sa89).

```
smpent ()                      /* sampling task: */
    {                          /*   this must be the only task at priority 0 */

        while (1)
            ++tally;           /* increment tally, which is reset by reporting task */
    }



prtent ()                      /* reporting task */
    {                          /*   this must be the only task at priority 255 */

        register long pcidle;   /* percent idle */

        while (1)
            {
              tally = 0;                        /* clear tally, which is incremented
                                                      by sampling task */
                pause (1+SEC);                  /* pause during sampling period */
                pcidle = 100*tally/MAXTLY;       /* compute percent idle */
                printf ("Percent idle = %ld\n\r", pcidle);
            }
    }
```

The OS attempts to keep the processor busy all the time. Some processor time must be spent performing requested services, handling clock and peripheral interrupts, and doing similar housekeeping chores. All remaining time is potentially available for task work. As long as there is any Ready task, the OS will let it execute. The processor falls idle only if all tasks are Blocked or Dormant.

We know that tasks always run in priority order. As a result, we can use a pair of tasks to measure the fraction of the potential task time that is unused during a sample period of, say, 1 second. The sampling task (*smpent*) runs at the lowest priority and must be the only task at priority 0. It is always Ready. Because of its low priority, it runs only when there is no other Ready task. The sampling task just sits in a loop, incrementing a static variable, *tally*.

A second task (*prtent*) calculates and reports the results. This task runs at the highest priority level, 255. First, it clears *tally* to 0, and then pauses for the sampling period of 1 second. At the end of the pause, it computes the percentage idle time as 100 times the actual value of *tally* divided by the maximum possible value, *MAXTLY*. *MAXTLY* is previously determined by noting the value of *tally* when no other tasks are permitted to be Ready during the sampling period.

In this simple example, the percent idle time is reported directly; in practice, the values could be smoothed by numerical averaging before being reported.

## 2.8 SUMMARY

A real-time program consists of a set of parallel threads of execution (tasks) that are subject to random interruptions and preemptions. The consequences of such an organization must be constantly in the mind of the application programmer.

At times, the individual threads of execution must also be connected so they can cooperate to accomplish a common goal using common data, resources, and equipment. The OS provides the required coordination and communication services. The OS also permits the tasks to exercise control over their own execution and that of their fellow tasks.

A task requests an OS service via a set of predefined functions. These are modeled after standard functions, such as C's *printf*. All high-level languages have equivalent function-calling facilities.

The major thrust of this guide is how to write a real-time program. But, before we can write a program, we must know what that program is supposed to do. The next chapter discusses the development of real-time requirements, as a first step toward program development.

## EXERCISES

2.1 Consider the following procedure that outputs a given string to the standard console:

```
putstg (stg)        /* output string to standard console*/
  char* stg;        /* string to be output */
   {
      char  chr;    /* string element */

     while ((chr = *stg++) != 0)
        putchar (chr);      /* output each character until null
                              at end of string */
   }
```

Is this a reliable procedure in a multitasking environment? If not, what problems do you foresee?

**2.2** Suppose that an OS has a service, *getime* (*ms_buf*), that returns the number of milliseconds since system start-up in the 6-byte field *ms_buf*. Show how that function can be used to determine the percent idle time with a single task. At what priority must that task run?

**2.3** Write a task that measures the average time to perform the service *setpty*. What problems would be encountered in measuring the time for *printf, getchar*, and *pause*?

# Chapter 3
## DEVELOPING REAL-TIME REQUIREMENTS

===============================================================

Developing a real-time application—or any other computer program—consists of translating a set of notions of what the system should do into a set of program modules that implement those notions. The translation normally proceeds in stages. In the early stages, vague notions of system behavior evolve into a formal statement of the specific system requirements. These requirements are often formulated as abstract models of the desired system behavior.

Ideally, the requirements model should express pure behavior. It should neither reflect the way the model is to be implemented nor bias the implementation in any way. Nevertheless, it would be senseless to include any requirements that cannot be met with any available means of implementation.

The requirements model can have a variety of formats, each aimed at clarifying some aspect of the system behavior. For example, some emphasize the flow and transformation of data, while others highlight the internal transitions caused by the arrival of inputs. Often several different formats jointly constitute the overall requirements model. As a minimum, the requirements model must show:

1. The inputs to the system, differentiating continuously available inputs from transient ones.
2. The various items of data that must be stored.
3. The internal states that the system can attain.
4. The actions that must be taken when the system is in a given state and a certain input arrives. Actions include changes in stored data, generation of outputs, and change of internal state.

The goal of the requirements model is to formulate system behavior as clearly, completely, and correctly as possible. "Clearly" means that there is no doubt as to what the system will do when it is presented with a given time profile of inputs. "Completely" means that all possible combinations of inputs have been considered. "Correctly" means that those who understand the purpose for which the application is being built agree that the actions are appropriate.

With such goals, the language used to express the inputs, stored data, internal states, and outputs is normally drawn from the problem arena and makes

sense to people conversant with that field.  Thus, the requirements for a telephone switch use the vocabulary of telephony.  For problems arising from ordinary life, ordinary English is the language of choice.

### 3.1  DEVELOPING A VERBAL REQUIREMENTS MODEL

We can illustrate the stepwise evolution of a requirements model by consid-
ering how to control access to a single-lane bridge that is shared by both lanes of
a dual-lane road.[1]  Lights RB and LB control access to the bridge from the left-
bound and right-bound directions, respectively.  Traffic flow is light so that most
of the time the bridge is in its initial (empty) state.  In that state both lights are
red.

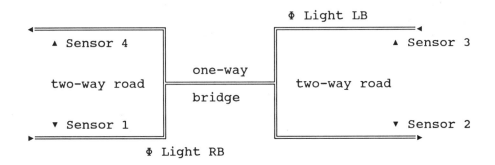

We will start by writing the rules governing the system in purely verbal form:

**1.1**   If the bridge is not in use and a right-bound car approaches (as detected
by sensor 1), then set the number of right-bound cars between sensors
to 1, mark the bridge in use by right-bound traffic, and turn light RB
green.

**1.2**   If the bridge is in use by right-bound traffic and a right-bound car approaches, then increase the number of right-bound cars between
sensors by 1.

**1.3**   If the bridge is in use by right-bound traffic and a left-bound car approaches then increase the number of left-bound cars between sensors
by 1, but take no further action.  (Light LB remains red.)

**1.4**   If the bridge is in use by right-bound traffic and a right-bound car leaves
the bridge (as detected by sensor 2) and the number of right-bound cars

[1]This example was adopted from Section 7.9 (Vol. 1) of *Structured Development for Real-Time
Systems* by Paul Ward and Stephen Mellor (Wa85).

between sensors is not 1, then decrement the number of right-bound cars between sensors by 1.

**1.5** If the bridge is in use by right-bound traffic and a right-bound car leaves the bridge and the number of right-bound cars between sensors is 1, then turn light RB red, set the number of right-bound cars between sensors to 0, and mark the bridge not in use. If at that point the number of left-bound cars between sensors is not 0, then mark the bridge in use by left-bound traffic and turn light LB green, as in Rule 1.6.

**1.6** If the bridge is not in use and a left-bound car approaches (as detected by sensor 3), then set the number of left-bound cars between sensors to 1, mark the bridge in use by left-bound traffic, and turn light LB green.

**1.7** If the bridge is in use by left-bound traffic and a left-bound car approaches, then increase the number of left-bound cars between sensors by 1.

**1.8** If the bridge is in use by left-bound traffic and a right-bound car approaches, then increase the number of right-bound cars between sensors by 1, but take no further action. (Light RB remains red.)

**1.9** If the bridge is in use by left-bound traffic and a left-bound car leaves the bridge (as detected by sensor 4) and the number of left-bound cars between sensors is not 1, then decrement the number of left-bound cars between sensors by 1.

**1.10** If the bridge is in use by left-bound traffic and a left-bound car leaves the bridge and the number of left-bound cars between sensors is 1, then turn light LB red, set the number of left-bound cars between sensors to 0, and mark the bridge not in use. If at that point the number of left-bound cars between sensors is not 0, then mark the bridge in use by right-bound traffic and turn light RB green, as in Rule 1.1.

One way to test a behavioral model for a real-time application is to ask: Does the model provide the proper response when two or more asynchronous inputs are presented simultaneously? In this case, suppose the bridge is not in use and both a right-bound and a left-bound car approach at exactly the same time. We see that both Rules 1.1 and 1.6 are to be applied and that their actions conflict. (Each calls for marking the status of the bridge in a different way. Worse, each sends a car onto the bridge in opposing directions.) Thus, our first attempt at a behavioral model fails because of the essential real-time nature of the problem. We can readily correct the model by requiring exclusive access to the bridge before the status or any other data is altered:

**2.1** If the bridge is idle or in use for left-bound traffic and a right-bound car approaches (as detected by sensor 1), then set the number of right-bound cars between sensors to 1 and request exclusive access to the bridge. When exclusive access is granted, mark the bridge in use by right-bound traffic and turn light RB green.

**2.2** If the bridge is in use by right-bound traffic or right-bound traffic is waiting for exclusive access to the bridge and a right-bound car approaches, then increase the number of right-bound cars between sensors by 1.

**2.3** If the bridge is in use by right-bound traffic and a right-bound car leaves the bridge (as detected by sensor 2) and the number of right-bound cars between sensors is not 1, then decrement the number of right-bound cars between sensors by 1.

**2.4** If the bridge is in use by right-bound traffic and a right-bound car leaves the bridge and the number of right-bound cars between sensors is 1, then turn light RB red, set the number of right-bound cars between sensors to 0, mark the bridge not in use by right-bound traffic, and release exclusive access to the bridge.

**2.5** If the bridge is idle or in use for right-bound traffic and a left-bound car approaches (as detected by sensor 3), then set the number of left-bound cars between sensors to 1 and request exclusive access to the bridge. When exclusive access is granted, mark the bridge in use by left-bound traffic and turn light LB green.

**2.6** If the bridge is in use by left-bound traffic or left-bound traffic is waiting for exclusive access to the bridge and a left-bound car approaches, then increase the number of left-bound cars between sensors by 1.

**2.7** If the bridge is in use by left-bound traffic and a left-bound car leaves the bridge (as detected by sensor 4) and the number of left-bound cars between sensors is not 1, then decrement the number of left-bound cars between sensors by 1.

**2.8** If the bridge is in use by left-bound traffic and a left-bound car leaves the bridge and the number of left-bound cars between sensors is 1, then turn light LB red, set the number of left-bound cars between sensors to 0, mark the bridge not in use by left-bound traffic, and release exclusive access to the bridge.

Note that it is no longer necessary to repeat the actions of Rule 2.5 within Rule 2.4 as we did in version 1 (i.e., "If at that point, the number of left-bound cars between sensors is not 0, then . . ., as in Rule 1.6."). Those actions will automatically occur when exclusive access to the bridge is released and the other side is waiting for similar access.

We can make the model more precise by separating that information which is to be stored as data from that which simply encodes an internal state. In particular, bridge status ("not in use for right-bound traffic," "not in use for left-bound traffic," etc.) just designates the internal state; it is not a stored variable. Thus, we can replace "If the bridge is in use by right-bound traffic" by "If in right-bound state Traffic_Idle" and "mark the bridge in use by right-bound traffic" by "enter right-bound state Traffic_Active."

In contrast, the number of left-bound cars between sensors must be stored and becomes the integer variable LB_Cars. Similarly, "gain access to bridge" becomes "request semaphore variable Access_to_Bridge." (Semaphores are described in detail in Chapter 9. For now, it suffices to say that they are variables that may be Free or may be assigned to one requester or another. However, a given semaphore is never assigned to more than one requester at a time. Thus, they are used to achieve mutual exclusion.)

To complete our demonstration of the evolution of a verbal requirements model, we will recast the verbal rules into a third and final version:

**3.1**   If in right-bound state Traffic_Idle and a right-bound car approaches the bridge (as detected by sensor 1), then set RB_Cars to 1, request Access_to_Bridge, and enter right-bound state Wait_for_Exclusive_Access_to_Bridge. When exclusive access is granted, enter right-bound state Traffic_Active and turn light RB green.

**3.2**   If in right-bound state Traffic_Active or Wait_for_Exclusive_Access_to_Bridge and a right-bound car approaches the bridge, then increase RB_Cars by 1.

**3.3**   If in right-bound state Traffic_Active and a right-bound car leaves the bridge (as detected by sensor 2) and RB_Cars is not 1, then decrement RB_Cars by 1.

**3.4**   If in right-bound state Traffic_Active and a right-bound car leaves the bridge and RB_Cars is 1, then turn light RB red, set RB_Cars to 0, release Access_to_Bridge, and enter right-bound state Traffic_Idle.

**3.5**   If in left-bound state Traffic_Idle and a left-bound car approaches the bridge (as detected by sensor 3), then set LB_Cars to 1, request Access_to_Bridge, and enter left-bound state Wait_for_Exclusive_Access_to_Bridge. When exclusive access is granted, enter left-bound state Traffic_Active and turn light LB green.

**3.6**   If in left-bound state Traffic_Active or Wait_for_Exclusive_Access_to_Bridge and a left-bound car approaches the bridge, then increase LB_Cars by 1.

**3.7**   If in left-bound state Traffic_Active and a left-bound car leaves the bridge (as detected by sensor 4) and LB_Cars is not 1, then decrement LB_Cars by 1.

**3.8**   If in left-bound state Traffic_Active and a left-bound car leaves the bridge and LB_Cars is 1, then turn light LB red, set LB_Cars to 0, release Access_to_Bridge, and enter left-bound state Traffic_Idle.

## 3.2  GRAPHICAL REQUIREMENTS MODEL

As the foregoing sample suggests, the verbal expression of a behavioral model can be laborious to prepare and difficult to comprehend. Verbal rules also put a subtle bias into the implementation. For example, if the bridge is idle in both directions and cars approach from both sides simultaneously, the ordering of the statements suggests that we apply Rule 3.1 before Rule 3.5.

These deficiencies have led to the development of various graphical methods to show the behavior of real-time systems. In their three-volume set *Structured Development for Real-Time Systems*, Ward and Mellor (Wa85) describe a series of techniques that can be applied manually to prepare a comprehensive set of graphical requirements models. [Several companies currently offer alternative methods that employ a graphic workstation in place of paper and pencil. For a general review of computer-aided software engineering tools for real-time systems, see H. Falk (Fa88).]

A full description of the graphical techniques is beyond the scope of this book. Nevertheless, we can give the flavor of the methods by recasting the verbal description into the "transformation schema" of Ward and Mellor (Figure 3-1). The supporting state transition diagrams are in Figures 3-2 and 3-3.

In essence, each graphical method consists of a library of pictorial symbols that represent certain basic elements of the model. For the transformation schema (Figure 3-1), dashed, rounded enclosures represent a transformation on transient binary information (events). Dashed lines entering the enclosure are input events; dashed lines leaving the enclosure are output events. Rectangular areas show stored data; dashed lines delimit the area when binary data is stored; solid lines delimit the area when the data is not binary.

For the state transition diagram that shows the details of the transformations (Figures 3-2 and 3-3), rectangular enclosures represent states. An arrow between states is a transition engendered by the event listed above the horizontal line next to the arrow. Actions taken during the transition are shown below the horizontal line.

The graphical methods permit the behavior model to be developed by elaborating successively greater levels of detail. We get a hint of this by hiding the details of the control transformation within the separate state transition diagram. In more complex (and more typical) real-time applications, several layers of transformations would be needed to show the entire behavioral model.

## 3.3  IMPLEMENTING REQUIREMENTS MODEL

We will not dwell further on the requirements model.  The only purpose in discussing this model is that it is the starting point for our work: the development of implementation procedures.

The premise of the requirements model is that it be independent of the means of implementation.  (When the single-lane "bridge" is a temporary road blockage, the requirements are often implemented by people, unaided by computers.)  When the system is to be realized through a computer, the requirements model must pass through the next stage of transformation, to become an implementation model.  Methods of implementing a real-time application, once the specifications are in hand, is the main thrust of this book.

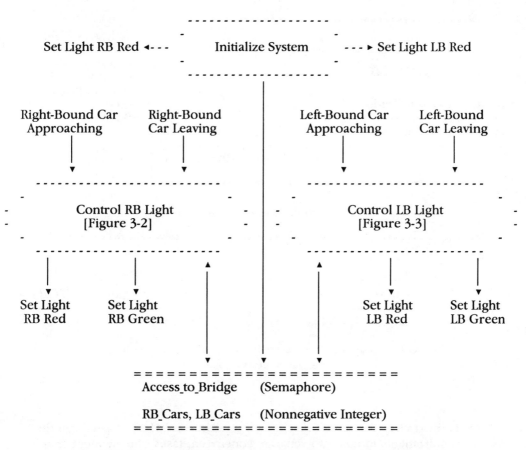

**FIGURE 3-1:  Graphical Representation of Behavioral Requirements:**
**Control Transformations**

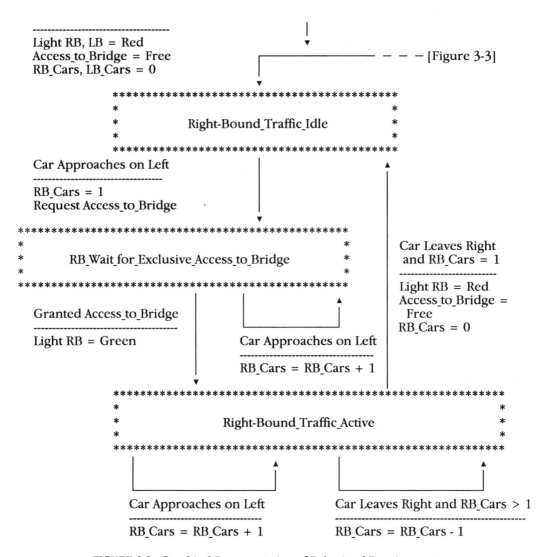

FIGURE 3-2: Graphical Representation of Behavioral Requirements:
State Transition Diagrams

 

 

In the next chapter we will discuss the first hurdle: How to partition the overall requirements model into separate concurrent tasks. Subsequent chapters will deal with techniques for coordinating these tasks, for communicating between them, and for providing other centralized services.

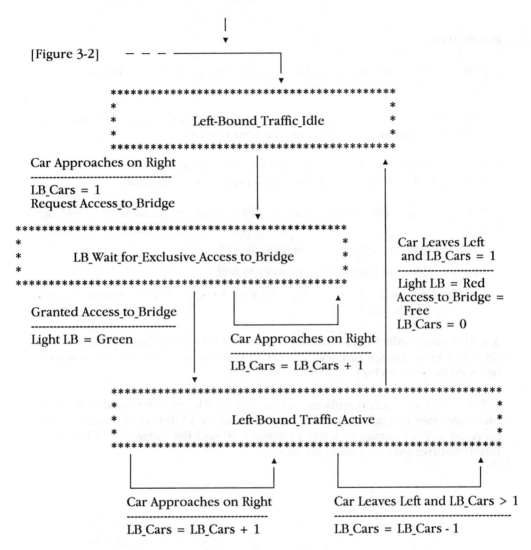

**FIGURE 3-3: Graphical Representation of Behavioral Requirements:**
**State Transition Diagrams**

## 3.4 SUMMARY

The problem of designing a real-time application consists of first preparing a requirements model and then transforming it into an implementation model. An example of a verbal requirements model is given for the simple problem of controlling access to a one-lane bridge. An alternate and preferable graphical model is also shown.

**EXERCISES**

**3.1** Modify the verbal and graphical requirements models to include the follow-ing additional idea:

> If a car is waiting on one side, do not let more than six additional cars pass from the other side before giving the waiting side a turn.

**3.2** Is the requirements model complete? What input/state combinations are not covered? What might be a reasonable response to such inputs?

**3.3** Is the requirements model robust? With the given model what would hap-pen if:

**a.** one of the car-approaching sensors were to fail?

**b.** one of the car-leaving sensors were to fail?

**c.** a car approaches the bridge and then makes a U-turn instead of going over the bridge?

**3.4** Does the model imply anything about how the sensor data will be obtained? (Is it necessary for the physical sensors to generate a change-of-state interrupt, or could the sensors be polled?)

**3.5** Could the requirements model be replaced by one that used a single all-inclusive state instead of the dual right-bound and left-bound states? Would there be any advantage to such a change? Would the answer be different for interrupt-driven versus polled sensors?

# Chapter 4
## TASKING

In constructing a requirements model, we strive to be independent of the specific methods that might be employed to achieve the requirements. Once we come to design an implementation model, however, we want to reveal the methods so that they can be analyzed and ultimately coded. The remainder of this book is concerned with implementation. This chapter is devoted to the central issue of the implementation model: tasking.

Tasking is the distribution of the functional requirements (as contained in the requirements model) among concurrently executing programs (the tasks). The problem of tasking in real-time work is akin to structural organization (distribution of functions to subprograms) in traditional programming. Many of the same concerns and principles apply in both cases. Nevertheless, real-time tasks run concurrently and can be started, suspended, and terminated individually. This imposes even stronger design restraints than would be necessary for a singly threaded traditional program.

In real-time work, the problem of tasking is more than just the assignment of the application's functions to various concurrent tasks. You also have to select the method by which the task will be activated and receive its inputs, as well as the function the task will perform once it is active.

### 4.1 TASKING HEURISTICS

Despite the importance of proper tasking, there are only a few general rules that can be set down to guide the newcomer. Eight rules are given in Figure 4-1. [This is an expanded version of a six-rule set published earlier (Ri79).] The rules are almost too obvious to be called basic principles. But any more specific rules would have to be hopelessly complex, if they could be expressed at all.

#### 4.1.1 Use Tasking to Aid Development and Maintenance

The first rule warns the designer not to complicate a task by including several separate and functionally independent components. The memory overhead for each task is the size of an internal task control block (about 300 to 400 bytes for MTOS-UX) plus the size of the task stack. While this is significantly more than that for just another subprogram, the designer should not be afraid to create a separate task if it clarifies the overall logic of the application.

**A.** Obey the rules of structured design to help make the application easy to design, implement, test, and maintain:

   **1.** Each main (functionally distinct) activity should be assigned to at least one separate task.

   **2.** Closely related functions should be kept in the same task. "Closely related" means that they perform operations that must be logically consistent; that is, a change in one is likely to engender a change in the other. However, in cases where it is desired to perform the same function but other considerations dictate separate tasks, the desired consistency can be achieved by using common subprograms or even common task code.

   **3.** It is preferable that functions that deal with the same inputs, data, or outputs be kept in the same task.

**B.** Try to keep the processor (or processors) always busy with productive work:

   **4.** Try to isolate as a separate task any subfunctions that frequently encounter significant delays such as wait for peripheral I/O to be completed, pause to allow mechanical or electrical events to occur, and wait for information produced within another functional component.

**C.** Functions that have different attributes must be assigned to different tasks:

   **5.** Functions that are initiated or coordinated by different means must be assigned to separate tasks.

   **6.** It is preferable that functions that are initiated or coordinated by the same means must be assigned to the same task.

   **7.** Functions that have significantly different levels of urgency must be assigned to separate tasks.

   **8.** Functions that proceed at different time scales must be assigned to separate tasks.

**FIGURE 4-1: Rules for Real-Time Tasking**

Separating main functions into different tasks is especially important because changes in specifications inevitably become necessary. Ideally, the alterations generated by a single change in the functional specifications should not extend beyond a single task.

By the same reasoning, it is preferable that closely related functions and functions that deal with the same inputs, data, or outputs be kept in the same task.  Closely related functions are those that have operations that must be logically consistent; that is, a change in one is likely to lead to a change in the other.

Unfortunately, in embedded, real-time applications, all functions are somewhat intertwined since they share interrelated goals and common data.  Judgment with respect to the particular application dictates what are distinct main functions (that should be in separate tasks) and what are closely related aspects of the same function (that should be in a single task).

We will not dwell on this category of rules since they are amply covered in numerous books on principles of good structured programming [(De78), (Pa72), (Pa88), and (Yo79)].

### 4.1.2  Take Advantage of Concurrency

The next rule is unique to real-time work.  Most often a task will specify that the operating system is to block the task until a requested service is completed. (If a task needs input from a peripheral it usually cannot proceed until the input is available.)  Thus, if we have Task **TkAB** designed as shown in Figure 4-2, the processor cannot even begin to get input **B** until it has finished with **A**.  There is no problem if another task can keep the processor busy until **A** comes in.  But if there is no such task work to do, the processor must be idle.  In that case, if the processing of **B** does not depend upon **A**, a more productive organization would be that depicted in Figure 4-3.  Now we are utilizing the benefits of task concurrency.

### 4.1.3  Respect Differences in Functional Attributes

The final category of rules provides the strongest constraints on tasking within a real-time application.

Every major function has three attributes that determine how it is to be implemented in terms of tasks.  These are its method of activation, its level of urgency, and its time scale.  The rules state that functions that do not have the same attributes should not be housed in the same task.

As a simple example, suppose that there were just one task for all emergency processing in a certain application.  Suppose further that this task had already been started by a safety violation when a power failure occurs.  Since the task is busy, it cannot be restarted immediately to respond to the power failure, even though power failure has the highest level of urgency.  Unless you complicate the processing of safety violations by frequent checks for power failure, the system may shut down before the power failure interrupt is ever serviced.

TASK 'TkAB'():

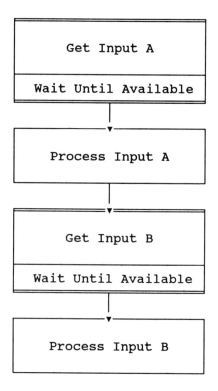

FIGURE 4-2: Serial Processing of Real-Time Inputs

TASK 'TskA'():                    TASK 'TskB'():

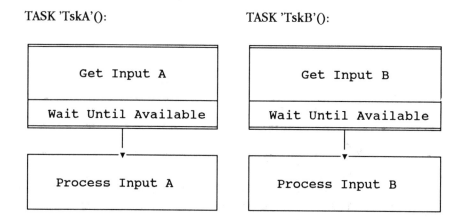

FIGURE 4-3: Parallel Processing of Real-Time Inputs

To appreciate these rules better you must understand the four basic ways in which a task can become active. The first could be called *periodic self-activation*. A task **PdSA** is started initially. (The details of the initial start are not relevant.) **PdSA** performs its part of the application. When that function is complete it issues an OS service call to terminate it with restart after a given interval (say, 15 ms) based on its last start time. Thus, **PdSA** takes the form:

TASK 'PdSA'():

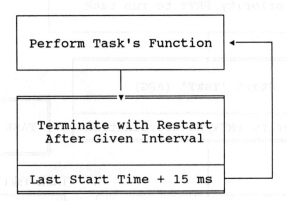

MTOS-UX computes the time at which the task should be restarted as the sum of the last start time plus the given interval. If it is already at or past the restart time, the task begins immediately. Otherwise, the task is suspended until the computed time arrives. In either case, the task restarts back at its entry point, ready to begin a new cycle.

**PdSA** is a periodically active task, with 15 ms as its period. (We may assume that **PdSA** runs at sufficiently high priority to complete its execution within the given interval.) It is self-activated; its own request to terminate carries with it the order for its next restart. Because it starts itself, it does not receive any information when it begins. As we will see shortly, a task that is started at the request of another task may receive parameters, in a way analogous to a simple subprogram call.

An input scanning task (**INPS**) is usually periodic. Typically, it runs with a short interval (5 to 20 ms) and very high priority (200 to 250). It scans external inputs that are mapped into memory bits or are read from hardware ports. When it finds a change, **INPS** reports the change to other tasks by means to be described shortly. This arrangement allows **INPS** to complete the scan cycle quickly, leaving it to the other tasks to process the changes more slowly and with lower priority.

TASK 'INPS'():

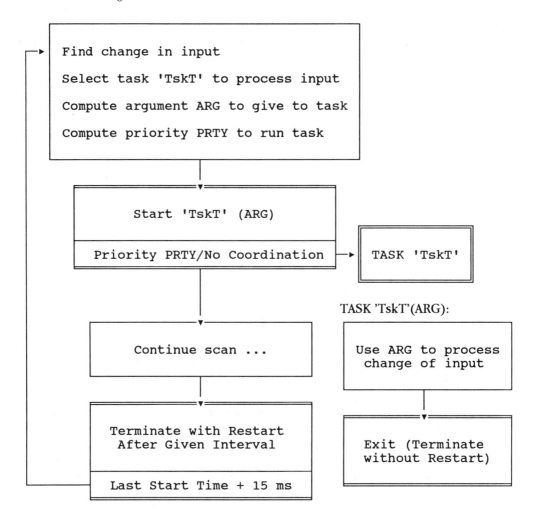

FIGURE 4-4: Typical Input Scanning Task

Another use for periodic tasks is for summary reporting. Now, a typical period is 1 hour to 1 day, and the priority is often rather low. (Commonly, all we need is sufficient priority to complete the processing before the time for the next cycle.) Such a task would produce a summary report and output it to a printer or to another computer. Input for such tasks is usually already in memory or is obtained from records left on a disk.

The scanning and reporting functions would have to be in separate tasks: by Rule 7 because they have different priorities and by Rule 8 because they have different time scales. If there were two different summaries produced, one output every 30 minutes and the other every hour, the designer would have a choice. On the one hand, two tasks may be the simpler and clearer arrangement (Rule 1). Furthermore, if there is appreciable peripheral input or output, Rule 4 would also favor two tasks so that one could proceed while the other waits for I/O. On the other hand, if both reports use similar data or similar algorithms, Rule 2 implies that both be produced in one 30-minute task, with a counter to skip alternate periods for the hour report.

In describing the scanning task, we mentioned that it passes change-of-input information on to other tasks. One possibility is for **INPS** to have the OS start that other task. The MTOS-UX *start* service is the second method of task activation. It permits the requesting task to select a particular task to start (the "target," **TskT**), to pass parameters to **TskT**, to set the priority at which **TskT** begins to run, and to queue the start request automatically if **TskT** happens to be still running, among other options.

It is quite common for fast, high-priority input-capture or preprocessing tasks to start other tasks that complete the processing at lower priority. Task **INPS** would normally select the target and its priority based on the type of input (Figure 4-4). For the *start* request to be honored immediately, the target task must be currently Dormant. Otherwise, the request is queued internally to be completed when the target terminates without timed restart; that is, via *exit*.

With *start*, activation involves the full restart of the target from its entry point. There is an alternate class of activations that do considerably less. To employ this class, **TskT** must be organized as a cyclic task, but not a periodic one (Figure 4-5). In this form, **TskT** never terminates. Instead, after (a possibly empty) initialization section, it enters an endless loop. It waits for input, using any of several mechanisms such as wait for any length message at a mailbox, wait for a 4-byte or 6-byte message at a message buffer, or wait for 1 to 16 bits of coordination data at an event flag group. (Which mechanism to use is the subject of several subsequent chapters. At this point, our interest is only in the tasking, which transcends the details of the wait facility. To be concrete, we will employ a message buffer.)

If **TskT** reaches the wait before the message, the OS blocks it until the message arrives. If the message gets there first, it is queued awaiting the task. If need be, the message queue can be very long. The corresponding form for **INPS** is given in Figure 4-6. In the alternate formulation, activation means start the next cycle rather than start the whole task. That is a minor detail.

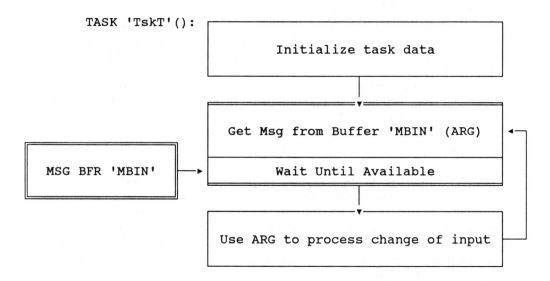

TASK 'TskT'():

Initialize task data

Get Msg from Buffer 'MBIN' (ARG)

MSG BFR 'MBIN'

Wait Until Available

Use ARG to process change of input

FIGURE 4-5:  Cyclic Task Activated by Messages

Of the two task couplings, message activation is faster than full start.  Thus, for a scan-type task, the message is preferable.

There are also many cases in which *start* is the method of choice.  Scan is special; it starts other tasks, but does not wait to coordinate with them.  Suppose, however, that an application function is being processed by a certain task (**TskO**).  At some point, the work is to be continued by one or more other tasks, say, for reasons of structural clarity (Rule 1) or improved CPU utilization (Rule 4).  Often, **TskO** must know when these concurrent sections are completed.  As we will see in Chapter 5, *start* has the option of coordinating with the termination of the target task.  Furthermore, it is easy to have **TskO** start several tasks, continue on, and later request that it be blocked until all those tasks have finished.  It is not so easy to arrange this with messages alone.  Thus, when coordination with the end of a subfunction is needed, *start* can have advantages over other tasking arrangements.

We have still not exhausted the methods of activating a task available under MTOS-UX.  This operating system contains a set of internal programs that perform peripheral I/O.  They are known as drivers.  They service task-level requests for peripheral I/O.  Drivers can also handle unsolicited input, such as text that is typed at a console without a corresponding read request having been given.

TASK 'INPS'():

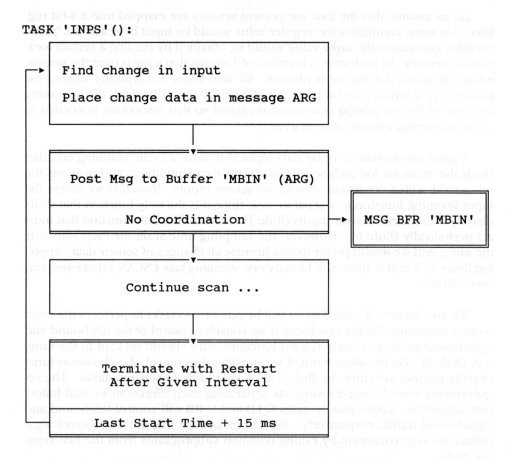

**FIGURE 4-6: Message-Based Formulation of Input Task**

A common response to unrequested input is to activate a task to process it. Debuggers and command line interpreters are often started in this way. Normally, the driver selects which task to start (if any) based on the first character of the unrequested text.

## 4.2 SIMPLE EXAMPLE: TASKING FOR SHARED BRIDGE CONTROL APPLICATION

We can illustrate the rudiments of task design by working out the tasking for the shared bridge control system of the previous chapter.

Let us assume that the four car-present sensors are mapped into a 4-bit register. On some computers the register value would be input by reading a "port";
on other computers the same value would be obtained by reading a certain location in memory. In each case, a bit value of 1 means that a car is over the sensor,
while a 0 means that no car is present. We also know that typically when a car
passes over a sensor, the bit is on for 100 to 300 ms. However, the beginning
and end of the on period is somewhat ragged so that smoothing is needed to
prevent counting a noise spike as a car.

A good way to handle noisy data input is to have a cyclic scanning task that
reads the status bit for each sensor, performs data smoothing, and presents the
other tasks with a consistent view of the sensor inputs. Note that we assign the
input scanning function to a separate task since it is the only function that deals
directly with the raw sensor inputs (Rule 3). It is also the only function that must
act periodically (Rule 6). However, the sampling time scale for each sensor is
the same, and we would prefer to synchronize all changes of sensor data. Apply-
ing Rules 2, 3, and 6, there will be only one scanning task ('SCAN') that runs, say,
every 20 ms.

We now have to decide if there will be one or two tasks to perform the main
control functions. On the one hand, if we consider control of the left-bound and
right-bound traffic as closely related functions, they should be kept in the same
task (Rule 2). On the other hand, if we consider the control of each side as functionally distinct activities, by Rule 1 they should be in separate tasks. The requirements model strongly suggests separating each direction; we will follow
that suggestion. Consequently, tasks **C_LB** and **C_RB** will control left-bound and
right-bound traffic, respectively. We can make sure that the two control algorithms are kept consistent by calling common subprograms from the two separate tasks.

The two control tasks will compete for the right to send cars over the bridge.
The competition will involve gaining exclusive access to the bridge, as
represented by the semaphore **ACCS**. While either task is waiting for the
semaphore, it cannot be restarted to maintain its corresponding Cars tally. However, we can easily assign maintenance of the Cars tallies to task **SCAN**.

The value of the Cars tallies will change asynchronously with respect to any
actions that tasks **C_LB** and **C_RB** may be taking. Hence, the control tasks must
be careful in how they use the information within the tally for its direction.
Fortunately, what a control task is really interested in is not the value of the tally
per se, but in the binary information: Is the tally zero or nonzero? For example,
**C_RB** must become active when LB_Cars becomes nonzero (that is, when the first
left-bound car approaches the bridge). Later, **C_LB** needs to wait until LB_Cars
becomes zero again (signifying that the last left-bound car has cleared the

bridge). As a result, we can hide the actual tallies within task **SCAN** and employ only the binary zero/nonzero information for coordination.

MTOS provides an easy mechanism to have a task wait until a binary bit is set: the event flag group. We can create an event flag group (**STAT**) within which we assign two bits for each direction. **SCAN** sets one bit when the corresponding tally is zero and the other when the tally is nonzero. (The event flag wait function only waits until flags are set; there is no wait until reset. This restriction is easily overcome with dual bits.)

The overall tasking and coordination mechanisms for the shared bridge control application may be pictured as:

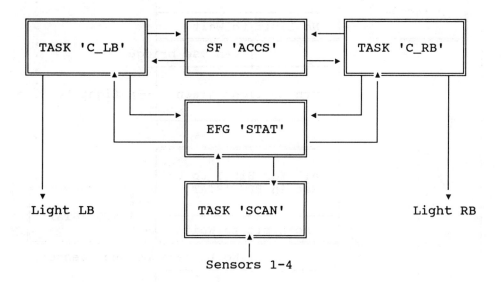

A more detailed implementation model for the LB control task is shown in Figure 4-7. (The corresponding RB task would use bits 2 and 3 of **STAT**.) The implementation model for the **SCAN** task is outlined in Figure 4-8. To complete the tasking, there would normally be an initialization task (**INIT**) whose only function is to create all the support objects for the application (**ACCS**, **STAT**, **C_LB**, and **C_RB**), start the other tasks, and then terminate itself (Figure 4-9).

## 4.3 OTHER EXAMPLES

The literature has not been generous in supplying examples of the steps that lead to a design model for real-time applications. An exception is a detailed description of the design of a robot controller presented by H. Gomma (Go84). In

TASK C_LB():

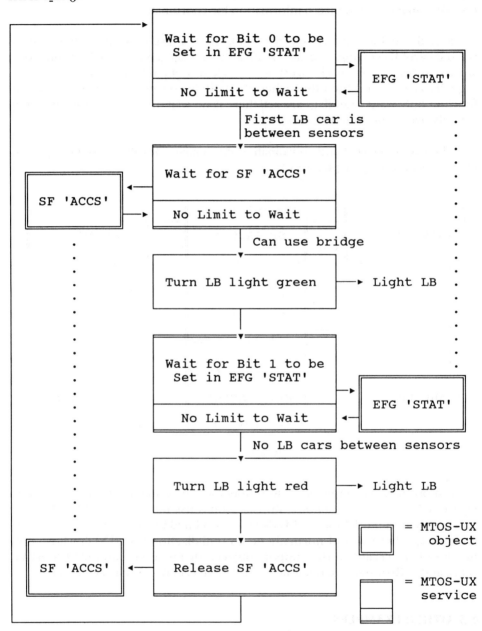

**FIGURE 4-7: Graphical Representation of Implementation Model: Control Task**

this example Gomma employs his "Design Approach for Real Time Systems" (DARTS).

DARTS starts with a requirements model formulated as a data flow diagram. The diagram shows data stores (repositories) connected through transformations that carry out the functions of the system.

TASK SCAN():

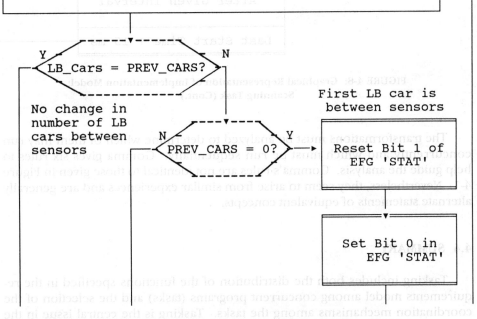

```
(1) Save LB_Cars as PREV_CARS

(2) Read hardware status bit for Sensor 1 and smooth
with previous values for Sensor 1 to give CUR_VAL;
If CUR_VAL is ON and PREV_VAL_1 was OFF then
   add 1 to LB_Cars;
Save CUR_VAL as new PREV_VAL_1;

(3) Read hardware status bit for Sensor 2 and smooth
with previous values for Sensor 2 to give CUR_VAL;
If CUR_VAL is ON and PREV_VAL_2 was OFF then
   subtract 1 from LB_Cars;
Save CUR_VAL as new PREV_VAL_2;
```

Y / LB_Cars = PREV_CARS? \ N

No change in number of LB cars between sensors

First LB car is between sensors

N / PREV_CARS = 0? \ Y → Reset Bit 1 of EFG 'STAT'

Set Bit 0 in EFG 'STAT'

**FIGURE 4-8: Graphical Representation of Implementation Model: Scanning Task**

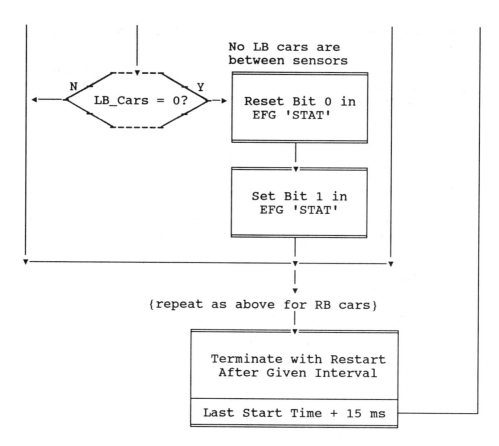

**FIGURE 4-8: Graphical Representation of Implementation Model:**
**Scanning Task (Cont.)**

The transformations must be analyzed to determine which of them may run concurrently and which must be run sequentially. Gomma gives six rules to help guide the analysis. Gomma's rules are not identical to those given in Figure 4-1. Nevertheless, they seem to arise from similar experiences and are generally alternate statements of equivalent concepts.

## 4.4 SUMMARY

Tasking includes both the distribution of the functions specified in the requirements model among concurrent programs (tasks) and the selection of the coordination mechanisms among the tasks. Tasking is the central issue in the design of a real-time application.

Eight heuristic rules that can guide the functional distribution are:

TASK INIT():

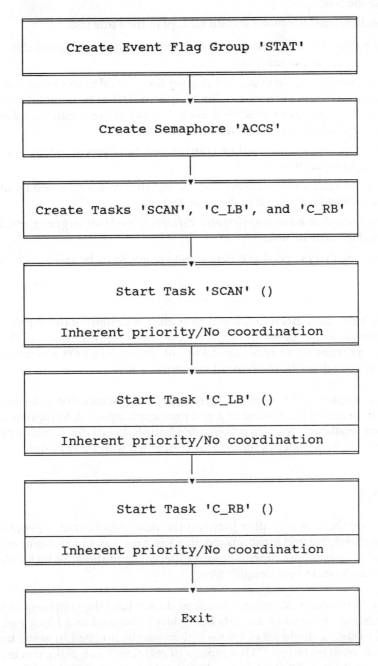

FIGURE 4-9:  Graphical Representation of Implementation Model:
Initialization Task

**1.** Each main (functionally distinct) activity should be assigned to at least one separate task.

**2.** Closely related functions should be kept in the same task.

**3.** It is preferable that functions that deal with the same inputs, data, or outputs be kept in the same task.

**4.** Try to isolate as a separate task any subfunctions that frequently encounter significant delays such as wait for peripheral I/O to be completed, pause to allow mechanical or electrical events to occur, and wait for information produced within another functional component.

**5.** Functions that are initiated or coordinated by different means must be assigned to separate tasks.

**6.** It is preferable that functions that are initiated or coordinated by the same means must be assigned to the same task.

**7.** Functions that have significantly different levels of urgency must be assigned to separate tasks.

**8.** Functions that proceed at different time scales must be assigned to separate tasks.

These rules have been employed to outline a design model for the shared bridge example of the previous chapter. A pictorial representation of the resulting design permits us to hide the details of the required OS services until we have a chance to describe them in subsequent chapters.

In this chapter we have introduced some of the factors that a designer must consider in planning the tasking of a real-time application. A full appreciation of the options available requires much more knowledge of the facilities provided by the OS. The remainder of the book is concerned with these issues.

**EXERCISES**

**4.1** Suppose there is a conflict between the rules of structured programming (say, keep closely related functions together) and the rules of real-time programming (such as never mix functions with different attributes). Which rules have greater precedence in task design? Why?

**4.2** Many embedded real-time applications do not have the simplicity of transaction processing. Instead of the data being nicely encased in a block that moves from task to task, a single set of values is dynamically updated by some tasks and dynamically used by others. What aspects of real-time work make this especially difficult to deal with? What type of real-time support facilities might be needed to protect alterable, shared data?

**4.3** What problems does multitasking introduce in the use of common I/O devices, such as a printer or console? How might the OS overcome these problems?

# Chapter 5
## BASIC TASK SERVICES

================================================================

This chapter is devoted to the basic task services: create a new task, start an existing task, terminate the requesting task, change the priority of a given task, and delete the requesting task.


### 5.1 A TASK OBJECT

As we have already seen, a task is the basic unit of execution for a real-time application. However, a task is not an inherent part of the C language; tasks must be created and maintained by the OS.

A task is a complex object consisting of four basic components:

1. A segment of executable code, normally in the form of a procedure having a single parameter. (We will consider the nature of the parameter later in this chapter.) Starting a task is equivalent to calling the procedure with a given value of its parameter. In most real-time applications, the executable code already resides in memory before the task is created. The code has been either "burned" into read-only memory or downloaded into read-write memory. Nevertheless, the code may also exist as a file on disk. In that case, the code is loaded into memory during task creation.

2. A set of fixed attributes, such as stack length and default priority. These attributes are specified when the task is created. The entry point (the starting address within the code segment) is among the fixed attributes.

3. A set of dynamic properties, including register values, current priority and status (Active, Blocked, etc.). These properties are maintained by the OS, but are influenced by service requests (such as the one to set priority).

4. A few portions of support memory, primarily for the program stack and Task Control Block (an area to house the dynamic properties). The OS allocates these resources when it creates a task and does not release them until it deletes the task. Thus, a task retains its support memory even while it is Dormant.

Other task-level objects, such as message exchanges and pools, are only somewhat simpler; they lack the code segment but have the remaining three components.

## 5.2 CREATING A TASK

A task may be created automatically as part of system start-up, or it may be created upon the request of a "parent" task while the application is running. In either case, the OS is presented with the fixed attributes enclosed in a structure called the Task Control Data (TCD). The OS computes the amount of support memory required and allocates it from appropriate pools. Finally, part of the memory is initialized to preserve the fixed attributes and to establish the starting values of some of the dynamic properties. A newly created task is Dormant.

The ability to create tasks and other task-level objects permits an application to be completely self-installing, that is, to be configured at run time from within the application itself. In particular, upon start-up MTOS-UX always creates and then starts a task whose entry point is labeled *inient*. This is a user-written application Initialization task. At first, it runs as the only Active task in the system. It normally creates memory pools, message exchanges, and other task-level objects; builds the initial application data base; creates and starts the other application tasks; and then exits. For example, suppose that an application is composed of three permanent tasks. The task creation part of the Initialization task might be:

```
#define SCAN      0x5343414E      /* ASCII constants: 'SCAN' etc */
#define C_LB      0x435F4C42
#define C_RB      0x435F5242

long int  scnent(),clbent(),crbent();    /* task entry points */

long int  scntid,clbtid,crbtid;          /* task identifiers */

struct tcd  scntcd = {SCAN,ABS,-1,C,250,0,scnent,1024,0,0,0,0,0,0};
struct tcd  clbtcd = {C_LB,ABS,-1,C,200,0,clbent,1024,0,0,0,0,0,0};
struct tcd  crbtcd = {C_RB,ABS,-1,C,200,0,crbent,1024,0,0,0,0,0,0};

inient()
  {
    scntid = crtsk (&scntcd);            /* create tasks */
    clbtid = crtsk (&clbtcd);
    crbtid = crtsk (&crbtcd);
    ...
  }
```

The *tcd* structure contains all of the fixed attributes of the task being created. The first element is the key. Every task-level object has two names, one external and one internal. The external name is called the key. It is convenient to compose the key from four printable ASCII characters, such as 'SCAN'. (This permits the System Debugger to display messages that refer to objects with greatest clarity.) Nevertheless, a key can be any 4-byte binary value. Within each class of objects, all keys must be unique. The key of the Initialization task is 'INIT'.

Following the key within the *tcd* is a parameter that specifies where the task code is to be found. The literal **ABS** signifies that the code is already stored in memory in ABSolute form. The alternative to **ABS** is **REL**, which causes the System Loader to be invoked to load the code from a RELocatable UNIX or MTOS-UX file.

The −1 parameter designates a global task, that is, a task that can execute on any CPU in a configuration with more than one processor. If a task is not global, then it is bound to a particular processor. This is indicated by supplying a processor number (0 to 15) in place of the −1. (Multiprocessor configurations are discussed in detail in Chapter 15.)

The next *tcd* parameter, **C**, specifies the primary language of the task. The 250 (200, 200) gives the inherent or default priority, the 0 specifies that no co-processors are in use, the external function name (xxxent) is the entry point, and the 1024 is the stack length, in bytes. The remaining zeros apply to special options that need not concern us for now.

## 5.3  TASK IDENTIFIER

All create services return a long word identifier when they are successful in creating the requested object. For *crtsk*, the identifier is the internal name of the task; it is used in subsequent services to specify the task. The identifier points directly to the support memory for the task. Thus, use of the identifier avoids the time-consuming search that would be required if the key were the specifier.

For failure, a specific error value is returned to indicate which of the *tcd* parameters was found to be incorrect. Each error code is a small negative number whose hexadecimal representation as a long integer always starts with 0xFFFFFF. The high-order six digits of a proper identifier are never of this form. Thus, an easy way to catch all failures is:

```
if ((scntid & 0xFFFFFF00) == 0xFFFFFF00)
    {
    ...   /* code to handle failures */;
    }
```

There are several ways in which a task identifier can become known to a task other than the one that issued the *crtsk*. The identifier can be stored in a global variable or it can be sent to another task through a message exchange. Alternately, any task can issue:

    scntid = gettid (SCAN);

to determine the identifier of the input task. If there is no task corresponding to the given key, the result is **BADPRM** (= −1).

A task is set Dormant as soon as it is created. A separate request is needed to start it running.

### 5.4 STARTING A TASK

In many ways a task is like a procedure that can be called (started) upon the request of another task. The analogy is helpful in understanding the nature of the task start, particularly the communication (argument passing) aspects. But the analogy is not perfect, because a task is much more than a procedure.

One of the differences is that a task is an independent program capable of concurrent execution. Depending upon the options selected in the request, a *start* can begin a thread of execution that runs concurrently with the task that issued the request. Starting a task thus has special concerns that have no counterpart with procedure calls: coordination, priority selection, and request queuing.

A *start* request carries five arguments, the first of which specifies which task is to be started. We call this the "target" task. The remaining parameters jointly provide the options for priority selection, coordination, communication, and queuing. The purpose and effect of each option is best explained through examples.

To begin, consider how the Initialization task starts the Scanning task of the previous chapter. **SCAN** is typical of a cyclic task that once started perpetuates itself in an endless loop. In such cases, a sensible priority option is **INHPTY**, a value that tells the OS to start the target task at its INHerent PrioriTY. This ensures consistency within the application. The designer of the Scanning task is expected to supply as the inherent priority a proper value at which this cyclic task is to execute. The designer of the Initialization task is merely deferring to the designer of the Scanning task. Furthermore, there is no reason for the Initialization task to take note of exactly when **SCAN** executes or to coordinate with it in any way. Thus, ConTinUe with NO Coordination (**CTUNOC**) is stipulated within the start request:

```
long int  dummy;

start (scntid,INHPTY,0L,&dummy,CTUNOC);
```

Even though we specify "no coordination," the variable *dummy* still receives an indication of the result of the service: 0 for success, a small negative value for failure. Thus, **CTUNOC** really means that the task will not wait for service to be completed and that it does not need any stronger indication of completion than the eventual storage of *dummy*. Since the OS may store a value within *dummy* after the procedure that contains the *start* request has exited, *dummy* must be an external, not a local variable. This is illustrated in the paragraphs that follow.

Priority selection and coordination are only two of the components that enter into a task start. As with a procedure call, a task start can also pass information on to the target when it starts. Even the Initialization task, **INIT**, may benefit from this option, as we will now see.

Recall that **SCAN** communicates with **C_LB** and **C_RB** via a global event flag group. It is convenient to have **INIT** create this group (using a service described in Chapter 7). Similarly, **C_LB** and **C_RB** share a semaphore that **INIT** can also create. In each case, the create service returns an identifier analogous to that for a task. **INIT** can store these identifiers in a structure and then transmit the address of the structure to the target task as it starts running. The Initialization task thus takes the form:

```
long int  dummy;              /* make results buffer external to inient */

inient()
  {
    long int  ids[2];         /* id for status EFG and access SF */

    ids[0] = crefg (---);     /* create EFG */
    ids[1] = crsem (---);     /*  and  SF */

    start (scntid,INHPTY,ids[0],&dummy,CTUNOC); /* start SCAN */
    start (clbtid,INHPTY,ids,&dummy,CTUNOC);    /* start C_LB */
    start (crbtid,INHPTY,ids,&dummy,CTUNOC);    /* start C_RB */
      ...
  }
```

The third parameter of *start* now contains some information that the requesting task (**INIT**) wishes to send to the target tasks (**SCAN**, **C_LB**, and **C_RB**)
as a so-called "run-time argument." To complete this facility, the target task is
composed as a procedure having a single argument. When the target task is
started, the OS automatically transfers the value of the run-time argument to the
task. Thus, **C_LB** can retrieve the identifiers as:

```
clbent (ids)
    long int  ids[2];                /* id of status EFG and access SF */
    {
        ...
        waisem (ids[1],WAIFIN);      /* wait for access SF (without
                                        time limit) */
        ...
    }
```

MTOS-UX makes no assumptions as to the content or meaning of the run-
time argument; it may be a simple integer as well as the address of an array or
structure. Because the argument can be a pointer to a structure, there is practi-
cally no limit to the amount of information that can be transmitted to a task when
it starts. This is particularly convenient when the task performs some work for
the calling task. In such cases, the structure would be likely to contain the parameters of the required work.

A structure pointed to by the run-time argument can also contain variables in
which a worker task can return information back to the calling task:

```
struct wrk_prm
    {
        long int  in_arg_1;          /* input argument 1 */
        long int  in_arg_2;          /* input argument 2 */
        long int  out_arg_1;         /* output argument 1 */
        long int  out_arg_2;         /* output argument 2 */
    };
```

The calling task enters the values of the input arguments and then starts the
worker. The worker computes the value of the output arguments and stores
them in the structure before it returns. After the worker returns, the calling task
can pick up the output arguments for use in its further processing.

For this mechanism to be effective, however, the calling task has to coordinate with the worker task. In this case, the caller would specify **WAIFIN** +
**CTERM**, instead of **CTUNOC** within the *start*:

```
    struct wrk_prm  arg;          /* parameter block for worker */
    long int  result;            /* result of start request */

    arg.in_arg_1 = 1;            /* set input data for worker */
    arg.in_arg_2 = 2;            /* in parameter block */

    start (wrktid,INHPTY,&arg,&result,WAIFIN+CTERM);   /* start worker */
    ...


  wrkent (prm)
    struct wrk_prm  *prm;       /* addr of parameter block */
    {
        ...
      prm->out_arg_1 = 10;  /* store return data in parameter */
      prm->out_arg_2 = 20;  /* block */
    }
```

With coordination mode **WAIFIN+CTERM** the OS will block the calling task until the target terminates after having been started as a result of this call. Thus, with this coordination mode the earlier analogy between starting a task and calling a procedure is very strong; in each case the caller does not resume execution until the target terminates.


## 5.5  GRAPHICAL REPRESENTATION OF TASK START

In Chapter 3 we saw that a graphical representation could clarify a verbal requirements model. Implementation details can also be aided by a graphical treatment. The basic ideas remain the same. Each building block (such as an OS service or a created OS object) is represented by an icon. These are connected as in a traditional flow diagram. As always, a hierarchical approach helps to reduce clutter by deferring details to lower-level diagrams.

The discussion of tasking within Chapter 4 used graphical methods to hide the syntax of the OS service calls. There, we represented OS services and objects as:

The same general scheme will be carried forward. However, we will stop writing out the coordination mode and similar auxiliary data as full English text. The same information will now be expressed using standard MTOS-UX notation.

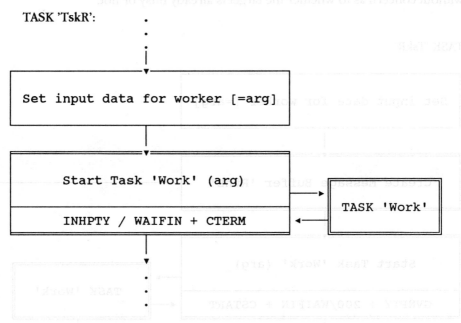

FIGURE 5-1:  Graphical Representation of Task Start

A graphical representation of the previous start of a worker is shown in Figure 5-1. The diagram has two lines between the start request and the target task to emphasize that the requester is blocked until the target terminates. Coordination mode **CTUNOC** would be shown with a single arrow from the service to the target.

## 5.6 MORE ON TASK START

For the initial start of SCAN and similar cyclic tasks, it was appropriate to select the inherent priority of the target task. For the case of a worker target task, however, normally the caller will wish to specify explicitly the priority at which the worker begins, instead of defaulting to the inherent value. If the computed priority value is contained in variable *prty*, the call would be:

start (wrktid,GVNPTY + prty,&arg,&result,WAIFIN + CTERM);

Not only does *prty* supply the priority with which the task starts, but it also determines the order in which start requests will be processed in case the target task is already running when *start* is issued. The OS maintains a queue of start requests, sorted in priority order. This permits a task to issue start requests without concern as to whether the target is already busy or not.

TASK 'TskR':

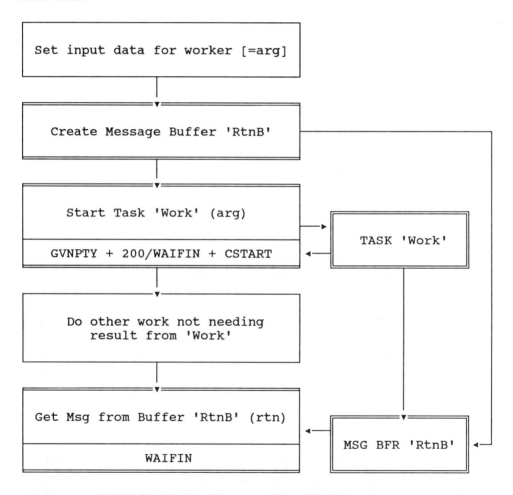

**FIGURE 5-2: Graphical Representation of Task Coordination**

Coordination mode **WAIFIN + CTERM** was suggested as a way to block the calling task (call it **TskR**) until the worker target task (**Work**) finished computing some output data. When the output data is available well before the termination of the worker, we may return the data prior to the termination of **Work** by including the identifier of a message exchange within the run-time parameters and changing the coordination to **WAIFIN + CSTART**:

<u>In header file common to tasks 'TskR' and 'Work'</u>

```
struct in_wrk_prm
  {
    long int in_arg_1;              /* input argument 1 */
    long int in_arg_2;              /* input argument 2 */
    long int ret_msb;              /* id of msg bfr to ret results */
  };

struct out_wrk_rtn
  {
    long int out_arg_1;            /* output argument 1 */
    long int out_arg_2;            /* output argument 2 */
  };

#define OWRSIZ sizeof(struct out_wrk_rtn)
```

<u>TASK 'TskR'</u> (Figure 5-2)

```
TsRent()
  {
    struct in_wrk_prm     arg;      /* parameter block sent to worker */
    struct out_wrk_rtn    *rtn;     /* addr of results block from worker */
    ...

    arg.in_arg_1 = 1;               /* set input data for worker */
    arg.in_arg_2 = 2;               /*  in parameter block */
    arg.ret_msb = crmsb (---);      /* create msg bfr in which to
                                         return results */

    start (wrktid,GVNPTY + 200,&arg,&result,WAIFIN + CSTART);
```

Now **TskR** is blocked only until **Work** starts. **TskR** can go on to do some other processing that does not require the return data. Finally, when the return data is required, **TskR** can wait at the message exchange for **Work** to post the return data.

```
          ...
     getmsw (arg.ret_msb,&rtn);           /* wait for return msg from worker */
          ...
   }
```

TASK 'Work'

```
    wrkent (prm)
      struct in_wrk_prm *prm;              /* addr of parameter block */
       {
         struct out_wrk_rtn *rb;            /* addr of results block */
           ...

         rb = (struct out_wrk_rtn *)alloc (OWRSIZ); /* allocate results block */
           ...

         rb->out_arg_1 = 10;                /* store return data in */
         rb->out_arg_2 = 20;                /*   parameter block */
         putmse (prm->ret_msb_1,&rb);       /* post return data to given
                                                msg buffer */
           ...                              /* continue with other work */
       }
```

In each of the examples shown **WAIFIN** was specified to block the request-ing task until the target starts, no matter how long that might take. In applica-tions where security and robustness are paramount, it is seldom proper to have a service that can block a task indefinitely. Thus, MTOS-UX permits the user to append a maximum wait time to all coordination specifications:

```
    if (start (wrktid,GVNPTY+prty,&arg,&result,WAIFIN+CSTART+500+MS)
       == TIMOUT) ...
```

If the target cannot even be started within the 500-ms limit, the request is automatically canceled and the function returns **TIMOUT**. For a successful start the return value is **NOERR** (= 0), while for a parameter error (such as *wrktid* not being a task identifier) the return value is **BADPRM**. The value **QUEFUL** (= −2) is returned in the unlikely case that there is not enough internal memory to process the start request.

For **WAIFIN** coordination (with or without a time limit), the value that is stored in the results buffer is also returned as the value of the request function. For **CTUNOC** and the other modes of coordination (to be introduced in sub-sequent chapters), the function value reflects the immediate processing, while the buffer value reflects the ultimate disposition of the request:

| Outcome | Function Value | Buffer Value |
|---------|----------------|--------------|
| immediate successful start | **NOERR** | * |
| eventual successful start | **NOERR** | * |
| no internal resources | **QUEFUL** | **QUEFUL** |
| bad parameter | **BADPRM** | **BADPRM** |
| timeout | **NOERR** | **TIMOUT** |

*NOERR if coordination is with start of target task, or "return argument" if coordination is with termination of target task (see Section 5.7).

The results value is stored in the buffer when the service is finally completed or times out. For all but coordination mode **WAIFIN**, that storage can be asynchronous with the current operation of the requesting task. Thus, the results buffer must be in an area that can tolerate asynchronous storage.

Various examples of *start* have been presented in this chapter to illustrate how the designer can very precisely control the priority of the target task, send that task a unique set of parameters for each task start, and coordinate directly with the target—all within a single service call. If any of these facilities had not been provided directly within the *start*, their effects would have to be simulated through subsequent calls. For example, if the priority of the target could not be set, the desired value would have to be stored within the run-time argument structure, and the target would have to issue a separate request to set its own priority to that value. This would be inefficient since extra service calls would be required. Furthermore, the priority queuing of the start requests could not be achieved.

## 5.7  TERMINATING A TASK

Terminating a task is the analog of returning from a procedure in the sense that each marks the logical end of a requested cycle of execution. Nevertheless, a procedure can be called directly without the imposition of the OS, while the OS controls entry to a task to guarantee that only one call (start) is processed at a time. As a result, terminating a task can involve several actions. The nature of the actions depends upon the options selected in the *start*. Let us explore some common cases.

Suppose task **T** was started by another task, **C**, and the start-task request specified coordination mode **WAIFIN + CTERM**. **C** would have been blocked as soon as it issued the *start*. When **T** completes its function and no longer needs to use a processor, it issues a termination request:

```
Task_T()
 {
  long int  rtn_arg     /* return argument */;
     ...

  rtn_arg = 100;
     ...

  exit (rtn_arg);
 }
```

Several actions ensue when *exit* is requested. First, the OS unblocks **C** and makes it ready to run again. Furthermore, *rtn_arg* is returned to **C** as the value of its *start* request.

The return argument (as *rtn_arg* is called) can be a simple integer or the address of a results structure. As with the run-time argument, the nature of the return argument must be known to **C** and **T**, but is immaterial to the OS. For the sake of clarity, however, values that can be returned by *start* for other reasons, such as −1 (**BADPRM**) and −2 (**TIMOUT**), should be avoided. The return argument is optional; *exit*() is a valid termination.

Next, if there is a start-task request for **T** already pending when it issues the *exit*, **T** restarts immediately using the priority and run-time argument of the highest-priority pending request. If there are no such requests, **T** goes Dormant.

Note that whenever a task written in C reaches its last curly bracket, it automatically issues an implicit *exit*(0). Thus, an explicit *exit* is not necessary unless a nonzero return argument is required.

An alternate form of termination request has already been introduced in Chapter 4. This request both terminates the current execution and specifies a restart after a given interval. If the restart is to be 1 second after the last scheduled STaRt TIMe, the request would be:

    trmrst (0L,1+SEC+STRTIM);

If the interval is to be added to the current (TeRMination) TIMe, the task would use:

    trmrst (0L,1+SEC+TRMTIM);

The first argument can be used to return a value to a starting task, as in *exit*. However, most tasks that terminate via *trmrst* were also started by a previous *trmrst*. Thus, the return argument is rarely used with *trmrst*.

Unlike most task-level requests, *exit* and *trmrst* do not return a value to the issuing task. If they are successful, they do not return at all.


## 5.8  CHANGING TASK PRIORITY

We have already seen in Section 1.5 that a task can set its own priority to a given value:

> #define mine 0L

> newpty = setpty (mine,USEVAL,125L);     /* set priority to 125 */

to a greater value

> newpty = setpty (mine,ADDVAL,10L);     /* increase priority by 10 */

or to a lesser one

> newpty = setpty (mine,ADDVAL,−10L);     /* decrease priority by 10 */

The new priority is clamped at the highest value (255) for increases and at the lowest value (0) for decreases. The new task priority is returned as the value of the request function.

It is common for a cyclic task that receives its input from a message to reset its priority to a level appropriate to the processing of the message. (A noncyclic task that is activated via *start* generally does not have to change its priority if the requesting task has already provided a proper value within the priority selection field of the start request.)

If the first argument of a *setpty* is the identifier of a task, **T**, instead of *mine*, the priority of **T** is changed:

> TsPrty = setpty (tskTid,ADDVAL,10L);     /* increase priority of T by 10 */

This feature permits a task that has previously started a target at a low priority to raise the priority when more urgent work arrives for the same target. As before, the new priority value is returned.

CY_1 (priority 110):

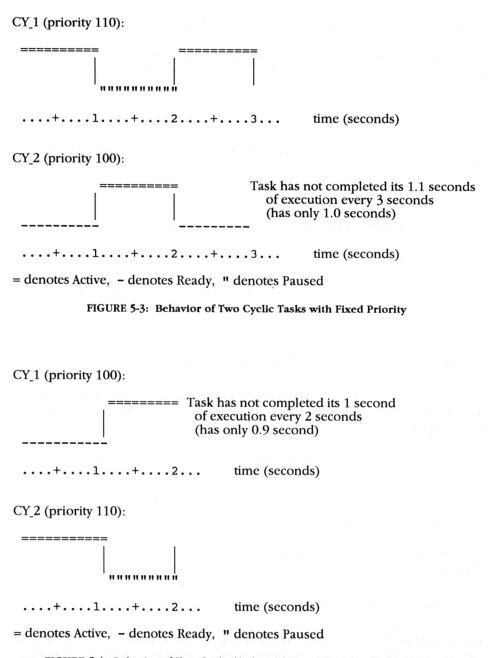

CY_2 (priority 100):

= denotes Active,  – denotes Ready,  " denotes Paused

FIGURE 5-3:  Behavior of Two Cyclic Tasks with Fixed Priority

CY_1 (priority 100):

CY_2 (priority 110):

= denotes Active,  – denotes Ready,  " denotes Paused

FIGURE 5-4:  Behavior of Two Cyclic Tasks with Fixed Priority, Order Reversed

### 5.9 A PROBLEM WITH PRIORITIES

The intuitive notion of a priority is that it measures the relative importance or urgency of the work performed by a task. We know what has to be done by each task in the application. By a combination of reasoning and experiment, we "tune" the priorities to give the system the desired dynamic behavior. Is this always possible? Mathematical analysis has uncovered a startling result: Even in simple cases, a fixed priority scheme cannot always provide satisfactory behavior [(Li73), (Sh87)].

By way of illustration, consider an application with just two periodic tasks, **CY_1** and **CY_2**. **CY_1** has a period of 2 seconds and needs 1 second of execution time (including OS overhead). **CY_2** has a period of 3 seconds and needs 1.1 seconds of execution time. Thus, the overall CPU needs in a 6-second interval are $(3 + 2.2 =)$ 5.2 seconds, for an 87% utilization. We should be able to meet the needs of each task, with time to spare.

First, let us assume that **CY_1** has the higher priority (110 verses 100 for **CY_2**). As Figure 5-3 shows **CY_1** does get its required execution time, but **CY_2** does not. Switching priorities (Figure 5-4) does not help, for now **CY_2** is satisfied, but **CY_1** is not. The problem is that in this case fixed priorities do not reflect reality; the urgency of a task really depends upon how close it is to the end of its period. We need to raise the priority of these periodic tasks toward the end of the period if they are still not completed. MTOS-UX permits this to be done.

Recall the "extra zeros" at the end of the *tcd* (Section 5.2). Three of these parameters are, respectively, a time interval, a priority change, and a priority limit. As a task is started MTOS examines the interval. If it is not zero, the OS starts an internal timer for the task. If the task has not terminated when the interval elapses, the OS automatically adds the specified (signed) change to the current priority, with a cap at the given limit. For the foregoing example, it is sufficient to raise the priority of **CY_2** from 100 to 120 after 2.5 seconds (25 hundred ms) of its 3-second period:

```
struct tcd  CY2tcd = {CY_2, ABS, -1, C, 100, 0, CY2ent, 1024, 0, 0,
                      25+HMS, 20, 120, 0};
```

With these changes, the requirements of each task are readily met (Figure 5-5).

### 5.10 DELETING A TASK

Real-time applications often have a static task structure. The tasks are all created during an initialization phase and then remain until the computer is turned off.  The state of the tasks varies with time, but not the tasks themselves. Permanence and durability of application tasks are characteristic of the real-time world.

CY_1 (priority 110):

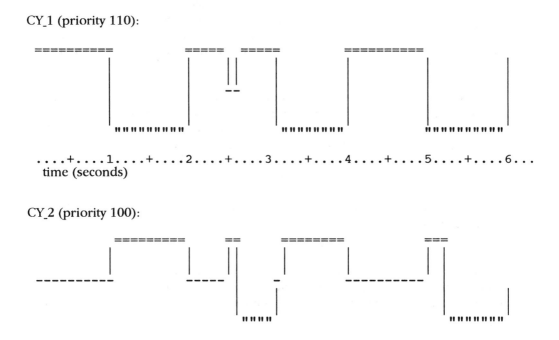

↑  priority raised to 120 (2.5 seconds after last start)

= denotes Active,  – denotes Ready,  " denotes Paused

FIGURE 5-5: Behavior of Two Cyclic Tasks with Timed Priority Change

In contrast, dynamic tasking is very common for nonreal-time computing. Tasks are created by the command line interpreter, shell, or job scheduler as requested by the users.  The tasks run to completion, terminate, and then cease to exist.  Transiency and expendability of application tasks are characteristic of the nonreal-time world.

Yet, even in an embedded real-time system there may be some tasks that are needed only for a while and so exist only for a while.  One example of a transient real-time task is a diagnostic or test program.  Another is a data analysis program that is needed only during test periods.  Even the majority of the tasks may be transient.  Suppose one of the production lines of a manufacturing plant makes different products from time to time while a second line continues to make a single product.  The control computer is constantly on line to service the single-product line. When it is time to make a new product on the variable line, the tasks for the old product are deleted and a set for the new product is created.

The request:

dltsk (rtn_arg);

terminates the requesting task and then deletes it. The return argument supports the termination, as in case of *exit*. Once a task is deleted, it is unknown to the OS; attempting to start it will result in an error.

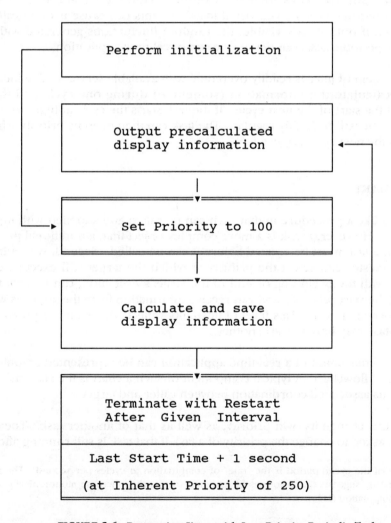

FIGURE 5-6: Preventing Jitter with Low-Priority Periodic Tasks

## 5.11 JITTER

The usual premise in scheduling a periodic task is that it is sufficient to have the task complete its designated function some time within the period of the cycle. Thus, if a task is to calculate and display some information every second, it is assumed not to matter when within that second the work is finished. Furthermore, it is common practice to assign priorities to periodic tasks so that the longer the cyclic period, the smaller the priority.[1]

As a result, a 1-second cyclic display task is likely to be given a relatively low priority and the point of display could vary dramatically from cycle to cycle (depending upon the work load from other periodic tasks and from asynchronous, aperiodic tasks). The visual instability this can cause is often called "jitter." Even if not directly visible, the random fluctuations generated within low-priority periodic tasks can destabilize some real-time applications.

The problem of jitter is readily overcome with available services. The idea is simply to calculate the information (sometime) during one cycle and then release it at the start of the next cycle. If the task starts the cycle at high priority the release time will be highly regular. The task can then drop its priority while it performs the next cycle (Figure 5-6).

## 5.12 SUMMARY

A task is like a procedure in that each can be called and supplied with input information. However, a task is a more complex object than a traditional procedure. First, a task must be created before it can be called. Second, with a task call the requester can select the priority at which the target will execute, can coordinate with the beginning or end of the target's execution, can control the queuing of the start requests, and can receive information from the target as well as pass information to it. This level of flexibility reflects the many purposes for which one task may have to start another.

The implementation of a real-time application can be represented graphically as a type of flowchart. A typical component of such a chart is the start task request, with its associated coordination between caller and target.

A task can change its own priority, as well as that of another task. The OS can also be asked to change the priority of a task if that task is still running after a

---

[1]The inverse of the cyclic period is the "rate" of computation in cycles per second. The rate monotonic theory suggests that priorities be assigned so that they increase monotonically with the rate of computation (Li73).

specified interval. This feature helps cyclic tasks meet their desired completion times. If necessary, a task can delete itself so as to liberate the task's resources.

## EXERCISES

**5.1** System tasks have keys that start '.SY'. For example, the Debugger has the key '.SYD'. Write a program that displays all exi. ting tasks that have such a key.

**5.2** Write a simple Command Line Interpreter (CLI) that starts a task whose key is supplied via Console input. Permit the user to specify the task priority and one line of ASCII text to be passed as a run-time argument. The CLI should wait until the selected task terminates and then repeat the process. Provide some way to terminate the CLI upon user command.

**5.3** Show in detail how to simulate task start when the only available services are send and receive a message via a message buffer and set task priority. Include the ability to specify the priority at which the target task runs and to transmit a run-time argument.

**5.4** Explain why the following code can lead to trouble if the task to be started is already running when the request is issued:

```
subpgm (trgt)
  long int  trgt;              /* id of task to be started */
    {
    long int  result;         /* result of request */

    start (trgt,INHPTY,0L,&result,CTUNOC);
    }
```

For what other coordination modes is there a potential problem with this coding?

# Chapter 6
## TIME AND TIME OF DAY

Real-time applications are concerned with physically real processes that proceed in terms of real-world clocks. Thus, such applications must be able to link up with real-world time, as opposed to CPU or other internal computer time.

Two aspects of time are involved: interval and time of day. Suppose we must send a stepping pulse to an electromechanical device. Such devices are very slow compared with computer operations; for the pulse to be effective, it must be on for at least, say, 50 ms. The requirements are thus:

> turn pulse on
> pause 50 ms
> turn pulse off

Suppose further that the stepping pulse toggles the AM/PM lamp on a display panel. The preceding sequence must be performed at noon and again at midnight. This requires not only the ability to generate a 50-ms interval but also the ability to place that interval at an exact time of day:

> while displaying time
>   {
>     wait until 12 AM (noon)
>     turn pulse on
>     pause 50 ms
>     turn pulse off
>
>     wait until 12 PM (midnight)
>     turn pulse on
>     pause 50 ms
>     turn pulse off
>   }

### 6.1 PAUSE FOR A GIVEN INTERVAL

A pause request efficiently delays task processing for a specified interval. During the pause, the CPU is automatically available for other work. In C, a typical request is:

pause (MS + 25);

In *pause*, as in all other requests that require an interval specification, the interval consists of two parts. The first chooses the time units, **MS** in the example. The include file MTOSUX.H defines the possible time units as:

| | |
|---|---|
| ms | MS |
| ten ms | TMS |
| hundred ms | HMS |
| seconds | SEC |
| minutes | MIN |
| hours | HRS |
| days | DAY |

To one of these is added the number of such units, 1 to 255. Thus, the range for intervals is 1 ms to 255 days.

When the interval is 0 there is no limit to the wait; the pause could last forever. As will be seen in a later section, however, a pause can be canceled by another task. Thus, *pause* (0L) really means "pause until canceled." The literal **NOEND** should be used instead of 0L to make this case explicit.

For success, the pause function returns **NOERR** when the specified interval ran to completion or **TIMCAN** when the pause was canceled (by *canpau*). The failure values are **BADPRM** when an illegal interval is given or **QUEFUL** when the service could not be rendered for lack of internal resources.

Some further examples of the pause function are:

```
status = pause (250 + MS);      /* pause for 250 milliseconds */
status = pause (SEC + 1);       /* pause for 1 second */
status = pause (NOEND);         /* pause until canceled */
```

## 6.2 REAL-TIME CLOCK

The OS maintains a tally of the number of milliseconds since the system was started to support time-dependent services, such as pause and terminate-with-future-restart. The physical source of this time base is a clock chip that generates an interrupt periodically. The clock period is installation-dependent, with 5 to 20 ms as the normal range. Fractional periods, such as 16 2/3 ms (60 Hz) or 1024 interrupts in 1000 ms can be easily accommodated. A real-time clock interrupt is often called a "tick" to remind us of its mechanical counterpart.

The period sets the "granularity" of the time base. (In reality, the OS is counting clock ticks, but keeping the tally in terms of ms.) Thus, with a period of 5 ms, the tally remains constant for 5 ms and then increases by 5. As a result, although a service request will accept an interval of, say, 3 ms, it could take as long as 5 ms to recognize that the time has elapsed.

Pause for a specified interval of time is a fundamental facility that is provided by all real-time operating systems. Alternate names are *delay* and *sleep*.


## 6.3  ALTERNATE REPRESENTATIONS OF TIME INTERVAL

The representation of time interval by the two-element structure:

> unit code;
> number of units;

is not unique to MTOS-UX. The proposed MOSI standard also specifies intervals in this way, but with a different set of unit codes (MOSI87, Section 2.5):

> implementation-dependent ticks
> microseconds
> milliseconds
> seconds
> minutes
> hours

In Ada (a language designed for real-time applications), intervals are measured in units of seconds, with a precision that is implementation-dependent. Thus, a 25-ms pause is:

> delay 0.025;

Some operating systems always measure interval in clock ticks; they do not offer any absolute time units. However, most physical events are known inherently in terms of real-world clock units, not arbitrary clock ticks. Thus, if we were to use clock ticks and (as could easily happen) the tick time had to be changed, all intervals in all tasks would have to be recomputed. Since there is a danger of missing some intervals, modern practice is to hide the tick time within the OS and have the tasks work with absolute time units.

## 6.4 PAUSE FOR MINIMUM TIME INTERVAL

In some real-time applications, there is a task that must run on every clock tick. Often that task has the job of sampling input data for changes.

A common structure for such a task is as an initialization section (which is entered just once) followed by a cyclic section. The cyclic section ends with a pause for a minimum interval and a branch back to itself:

```
samptsk ()
   {
       ...                    /* initialization section, if needed */
      while (1)
         {
             ...              /* cyclic section */
           pause (NXTICK);
         }
   }
```

The literal **NXTICK** produces **MS** + 1. Because of the granularity of the real-time clock, a 1-ms pause is always canceled at the next clock tick (for any value of the clock period). The value **MS** + 0 does not work, however, since for an interval of zero there is no pause at all.

Note that samptst could have been composed with *trmrst* instead of *pause*, as was done in task **PdSA** of Section 4.1.3. (A "first-time flag" would be needed to skip the initialization section after the first entry.) However, the overhead for pausing is always less than that for terminating and restart a task so that *pause* is preferable in this special case. In general, if the cycle time of the task is greater than every clock tick and the cycle time must be added to the last start time of the task, the cycle must be maintained by *trmrst* rather than *pause*.

## 6.5 SYNCHRONIZATION FOR EXACT TIME INTERVALS

It is sometimes necessary to separate two events, such as the generation of a pair of outputs, **A** and **B**, by a given interval, say, 250 ms. A straightforward approach would be output **A**, *pause*(250 + MS), output **B**. However, because of the granularity of the clock, the pause interval is usually shorter than expected. (On average, half the current clock period is already over when a pause is issued. Thus, the average pause is half a clock period too short.)

When accurate intervals are required, it is best first to synchronize to the start of a clock period by issuing a pause for 1 ms. The sequence would then be *pause*(NXTICK), output **A**, *pause*(250 + MS), output **B**.

When a pause ends, the task becomes ready to run, but the actual resumption of task execution may be further delayed if there are Ready tasks of higher priority. Consequently, if a task needs an exact interval, it also needs a very high priority.

## 6.6  CANCEL PAUSE

The primary purpose of *pause* is to block the requesting task for a given interval. Nevertheless, *pause* can also be an effective means to block a task until it receives a "go-ahead" command from some other task. The go-ahead is achieved by canceling the pause via a new service, *canpau*. Thus, the scenario for this mode of task-to-task coordination is:

| task **T** | task **C** |
|---|---|
| **pause** (NOEND) | ... |
| [task blocked] | < monitor application to decide when to continue T > |
| [task blocked] | **canpau** (tskTid) |
| [both tasks continue independently] | [both tasks continue independently] |

The argument of *canpau* is the identifier of a particular task. Thus, the coordination provided by pause/cancel_pause is always directed toward one specific target task. More general methods to coordinate with any number of tasks or with a task whose identity is not necessarily known will be given in later chapters.

By stipulating a finite interval for the pause, you can ensure a limit to the wait in case the expected event that the monitor task is seeking never occurs. Task **T** can use the value returned by *pause* to determine if **C** canceled the pause (value **TIMCAN**) or the maximum wait time was reached (value **NOERR**):

```
if (pause (250+MS) == TIMCAN)
    { /* task continued via cancel pause for coordination */
      ...
    }
else
    { /* task continued at end of maximum wait limit */
      ...
    }
```

The argument of *canpau* must be the identifier of an existing task. If not, the function returns a failure value **BADPRM**. Of course there is no guarantee that the target task is actually paused when the cancel is issued. To provide this information, *canpau* returns **NOERR** when the specified task was paused and **NOTOUT** when the task was not paused.

## 6.7  TIME OF DAY CLOCK/CALENDAR

Many applications must be aware of the real-world time and date. (The term "wall time" is often used to refer to the real-world time.) Time and date may be needed as tags on console messages or may be the key for storing data. Wall time may also be a factor in deciding what processing to do or how to do it. For example, a traffic control program may switch algorithms or parameters as predetermined periods of peak demand approach.

An OS must maintain clock and calendar information in either binary or ASCII-encoded form. For MTOS-UX, the information is kept as a time of day (TOD) clock/calendar string of the form:

DD MMM YYYY HH:MM:SS\0

where     DD      = day in month, starting at 01
          MMM     = abbreviated month name
          YYYY    = year
          HH      = hour, 00 to 23
          MM      = minute, 00 to 59
          SS      = second, 00 to 59

A sample string is:

"11 NOV 1918 11:00:00"

The month names are JAN, FEB, MAR, APR, MAY, JUN, JUL, AUG, SEP, OCT, NOV, DEC. Since the terminal null counts as a character, the string length is 21, not 20.

Ada provides an example of a binary encoding of clock/calendar information. As specified in package CALENDAR (LRM83, Section 9.6), the run-time support system for Ada must be able to supply the date and time as:

| subtype | YEAR_NUMBER | is INTEGER | range 1901 .. 2099 |
| subtype | MONTH_NUMBER | is INTEGER | range 1 .. 12; |
| subtype | DAY_NUMBER | is INTEGER | range 1 .. 31; |

```
subtype   DAY_DURATION     is DURATION    range 0.0 .. 86_400.0;
type      TIME             is private;

function CLOCK  return TIME;

procedure SPLIT ( DATE:        in    TIME;
                  YEAR:        out   YEAR_NUMBER;
                  MONTH:       out   MONTH_NUMBER;
                  DAY:         out   DAY_NUMBER;
                  SECONDS:     out   DAY_DURATION);
```

Function *CLOCK* returns a snapshot of the internal time in a format that is hidden from the task ("private"). That internal time can then be partitioned into its binary components with procedure *SPLIT*.

## 6.8  SET CLOCK/CALENDAR

The OS must have a source from which it can initialize or derive its TOD values. If the system has support hardware, such as a battery-backed clock/calendar chip, the OS can obtain TOD information without any task-level help. Commonly, however, the TOD is set by task request. When the TOD is encoded as a string, a typical request could be:

```
char  todstg[21] = " 4 JUL 1776 12:00:00";
settod (todstg);
```

The argument of *settod* is the address of a null-terminated string of the form just shown. If the format of the string is not valid (for example, if the month name does not exactly match one of the three-character abbreviations), the function fails and *settod* returns a value of **BADPRM**. A successful invocation returns a value of **NOERR**.

Once set, the string is automatically advanced each second. It is assumed that the *settod* is issued at the beginning of the given second.

The TOD string may be set and reset at will by any task. This has no effect upon outstanding pauses, timed restarts, and other interval-based time processing. (Such processing involves the millisecond counter, not the TOD string.)

## 6.9  GET (READ) CLOCK/CALENDAR

The current clock/calendar string may be read by issuing:

```
    gettod (todbfr);
```

The entire string (including the terminal null) is copied into the read-write buffer whose address is given by the argument. The string is guaranteed to be consistent; the clock/calendar is not permitted to change during the copy.

The following C task outputs the clock/calendar every minute:

```
    cctask ()
      {
          char ccstg[21];                       /* clock/calendar string */

          while (pause (MIN + 1) == 0)          /* pause 1 minute */
            {
                gettod (ccstg);                 /* get time */
                printf ("\n\r%s",ccstg);        /* output to console */
            }
      }
```

## 6.10 SYNCHRONIZATION WITH TOD

Certain tasks—typically those which produce periodic reports and summaries—must be synchronized with the clock portion of the TOD
clock/calendar string. MTOS-UX has a straight-forward mechanism to perform
this type of synchronization. For example, to pause until exactly 10:30, submit
the request:

```
    syntod ("103000");
```

The argument must be the address of a null-terminated string of the form
"HHMMSS". HH may be either a numeric value in the range '00' to '23' or '??
(match any). MM or SS may be '00' to '59' or '??'.

After invoking the service, the task is blocked until the given time string
matches the TOD clock/calendar. This is a simple pattern match. Thus, if a wait
for "103000" is issued at "103001", the task will wait until the next day. The string
"??1500" waits for 15 minutes after the hour, while the string "????00" waits for the
beginning of the next minute. The function returns a **NOERR** upon a successful
call.

The function *syntod* is often invoked at the beginning of the repeated section of a periodic task, as *pause* was used at the end of the cycle in the sample

task of Section 6.3:

```
reportsk ()
   {
    ...    /* initialization section, if needed */

   while (1)
      {
         syntod ("000000");          /* wait until midnight */
         ...                         /* prepare daily summary */
      }
   }
```

## 6.11  GET SYSTEM TIME

The tally of the number of milliseconds since the system was started is a 6-byte field of the form:

```
struct timer
   {
      short int   u2;   /* most significant 2 bytes of tally */
      long  int   14;   /* least significant 4 bytes of tally */
   }
```

It may be copied into a given user buffer via:

```
struct timer msbuf;

getime (&msbuf);
```

The function returns with **NOERR** unless there is a problem writing into the buffer. For write errors, the return value is **BADPRM**. The 6-byte value is guaranteed to be consistent, even if a clock interrupt occurs while the copy is being made.

Time intervals may be computed by capturing the time before and after an event and then subtracting. If the interval is under approximately 1200 hours (50 days), the number of milliseconds fits into an unsigned 32-bit integer:

```
struct timer          before,after;
unsigned long int     interval;
short int             test;
```

```
getime (&before);
    ...
getime (&after);
test = after.u2 - before.u2;
if (test == 0)
    interval = after.l4 - before.l4;
else if (test == 1)
    interval = 65536 + after.l4 - before.l4;
else ...                        /* overflow */
```

## 6.12  SUMMARY

The *pause* statement instructs the OS to block the requesting task for a specified interval of time (or "forever"). This permits a task to adjust its pace to the external physical world. During the pause the processor is available for work by other tasks.

A paused task can be restarted upon the request of another task. This provides a private means of coordination, targeted to a specific task and hidden from all other tasks. Since the pause cannot extend beyond the original pause interval, the target task can impose a limit to its wait for coordination.

The OS accepts a time of day clock/calendar string from any task and thereafter updates it every second. The current value of that ASCII string may be retrieved at any time. A task may also request to be blocked until it matches a given time of day pattern, with "match any" as a possibility for the hour, minute, or second fields.

## EXERCISES

**6.1** Write a set of tasks that print messages to the System Console at a given time. Any task should be able to submit a message having the following elements: ASCII message text, print time (hours, minutes, seconds), and flag indicating if the message is to be shown only once, or every day. Can these functions be performed with only one task?

**6.2** How might *syntod* be accomplished if the internal form of the clock/calendar were the number of seconds since January 1, 1986? What problems do leap years pose?

**6.3** Suppose a computer system were installed on a ship that regularly crossed time zones. Could *trmrst* or *pause* be used in a cyclic task that had to perform a certain function at exactly midnight of each day?

**6.4** Show how *getime* can be used to help optimize the following section of task code:

```
cvtuc (stg)
char *stg;  /* text to be converted to uc */
    {
        char temp;            /* temporary storage for character */

        while ((temp = *stg) != 0)
            {
                if ((temp > = 'a') && (temp < = 'z'))
                 temp + = ('A' - 'a'); /* convert to upper case */
                *stg++ = temp;
            }
    }
```

Optimization consists of determining the best storage class and type for *temp*, if *temp* is needed at all (**stg* could be used throughout the subprogram), and so on. The fastest running code is considered optimum.

For a complete discussion of the use of timers to optimize C code, see *Efficient C* by Thomas Plum and Jim Brodie (Pl85).

# Chapter 7
# EVENT FLAGS

===============================================================

Ideally, each task should be an independent program that is concerned with a specific aspect of an overall application. This simplifies all levels of the job: design, implementation, and maintenance. In practice, however, tasks often must be highly intertwined since they pursue a common overall objective, share the same hardware, respond to the same set of inputs, and control the same set of outputs. As a result, the most critical services provided by a real-time operating system are usually related to task coordination.

Broadly speaking, task coordination is the blocking of a task until the receipt of information transmitted by one or more tasks, or generated by the operating system. Often the coordination arises from a requested service, such as the allocation of memory or physical input/output. In these cases, the information is that the requested service has been completed and the task is coordinating with the operating system. No less important is coordination between different tasks.

Several specific methods of coordination have evolved to solve particular kinds of problems that commonly arise in real-time applications. In this chapter and the next three, we will discuss in detail the most important of these methods. Then, in Chapter 11, we will close the discussion by contrasting the individual methods and the underlying principles they embody. Our goal will be to provide some guidance in choosing an appropriate coordination scheme in individual cases.

## 7.1 COORDINATION VIA EVENT FLAGS

Event flags are binary variables that are maintained by the OS but contain information about discrete conditions within the application. For example, one event flag might indicate that a robot's left arm is fully extended, while another might show that a desired object has been located by its vision subsystem. In another application, each flag might indicate that one of the telephone lines being monitored is off-hook.

As we will see shortly, any task can create event flags as needed to support the application. However, the flags are not "owned" by the task that created them; they are owned by the application as a whole. This means that any task can set or reset a flag value, and can use the information for coordination. The task that created the flags has no special privileges. In fact, the identity of that task is not even preserved. The whole purpose of event flags is to establish an information structure that is *independent* of the tasks that use it, and thus need not be changed whenever tasks are added or deleted.

To simplify the services that refer to event flags, they are packaged into groups. Each event flag group (EFG) contains 16 flags; each flag can be independently set to 1 or reset to 0.

The main purpose of event flags is coordination. Any task can ask the OS to block it until a particular AND or OR combination of flags within a group is set. Furthermore, when flags are set, *all* tasks that have been waiting for those flags are continued.

The OS itself never spontaneously alters an event flag. All changes to flag values are in response to a specific request by a task.

## 7.2  CREATING A PUBLIC EVENT FLAG GROUP

Any task can create a public event flag group via *crefg*, with the key as the one argument. For example,

```
#define PMP1  0x504D5031

long int    pm1gid;      /* group identifier */

pm1gid = crefg (PMP1);
```

As with all creation requests, the service returns an identifier for success or **QUEFUL** for failure. For success, it does not matter if the group is created at this time or already existed. A newborn group has all of its bits cleared.

## 7.3  WAITING FOR EVENT FLAGS TO BE SET

A task can wait for *all* of a specified set of bits within an EFG to be set. For example, if a task needs to wait for bits 2, 3, *and* 4 within group PMP1, it would issue:

```
waiefg (pm1gid, EFAND+EF2+EF3+EF4, NOEND);
```

The special literal **NOEND** informs the OS that the task is willing to wait forever (if need be) for the flags to be set. Alternatives will be given shortly.

Another task might have to wait for *any* of a selected set of bits, such as bit 1 *or* 3. That task would use:

    waiefg (pm1gid, EF<u>OR</u> + EF1 + EF3, NOEND);

Since the latter wait ends when either bit 1 or 3 is set, it might be useful to know which bit (or bits) caused the task to continue. Thus, MTOS-UX returns a copy of the group value within the low-order word of the long-word function return value.[1] The group value shows the status of each flag—1 means set, 0 means reset. The literals **EF0** to **EF15** can be applied as masks to examine individual flags.

The high-order word indicates the overall result of the service call: **NOERR** for success or **BADPRM** for a parameter error. The previous call could be expanded to utilize the return information:

```
long int    pm1val;        /* result, group value */

pm1val = waiefg (pm1gid, EFOR + EF1 + EF3, NOEND);

if (pm1val > = 0L)
    { /* no error */
        if ((pm1val & EF1) != 0) ...        /* Flag 1 set */;
        if ((pm1val & EF3) != 0) ...        /* Flag 3 set */;
    }
```

In most applications, it is important to be able to specify the maximum time any task will be blocked. To satisfy this requirement, the user can add an optional wait limit in the same form as used in *pause* or any other time-dependent service. Thus,

    pm1val = waiefg (pm1gid,EFOR + EF1 + EF3,2 + SEC);

is guaranteed to return in 2 seconds or less. In case of time out, the high-order word is **TIMOUT**. In the unlikely event of having no internal memory available to form a timer, the high-order word will be **QUEFUL**. As with all other error codes, **TIMOUT** and **QUEFUL** are negative so that the sign test for failure is still valid.

With **NOEND** specified, the wait limit is "forever." **IMONLY** (immediate only) specifies a wait of 0: If the condition is already true, the high-order word is 0; otherwise, it is **TIMOUT**.

---

[1]Words are 16 bits; long words are 32 bits.

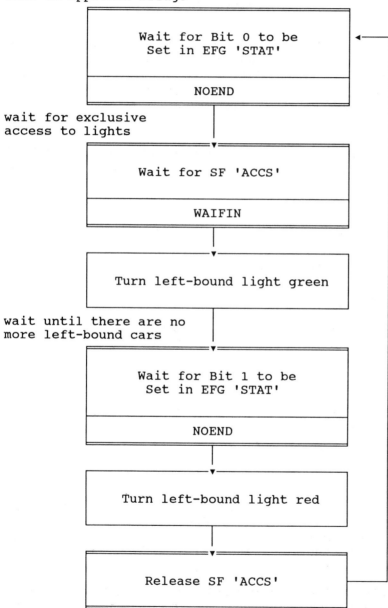

**FIGURE 7-1: Event Flag Coordination in Single-Lane Bridge Problem**

### 7.4 EVENT FLAG COORDINATION IN SINGLE-LANE BRIDGE PROBLEM

The single-lane bridge problem that illustrated some tasking concepts in Chapter 4 employed four flags within an event flag group (**STAT**) to indicate the status of the cars on or waiting for the bridge:

| Bit | Meaning |
|-----|---------|
| 0 | 1 or more left-bound cars waiting to cross bridge |
| 1 | no more left-bound cars on bridge or waiting to cross it |
| 2 | 1 or more right-bound cars waiting to cross bridge |
| 3 | no more right-bound cars on bridge or waiting to cross it |

There are three tasks that communicate via the EFG. A scanning task examines some peripheral sensors, keeps tallies on the number of cars on the bridge or waiting for it, and sets the bits within **STAT** to reflect the current status. The traffic light for each direction is maintained by tasks **C_LB** and **C_RB**, respectively. The general structure of each control task is sketched in Figure 7-1. The task is an endless loop. First, it waits for the event flag that indicates that a car is waiting for the bridge. There is no need to limit the wait. Upon continuing, the task must then wait for the semaphore that grants exclusive access to the lights in both directions. (A car could arrive from each direction simultaneously. Thus, the event flags by themselves are not sufficient to control traffic safely. Semaphores are discussed in Chapter 9.) Once the SF wait is over, the task is free to turn the light for its direction green. The bridge was assumed to have very little traffic. As a result, once the bridge is turned over to, say, left-bound traffic, that direction retains control until all left-bound cars have been serviced. That is implemented by waiting for a second event flag bit. After the second EFG wait, the light is turned red, access to the light data is released, and the loop repeats once more.

### 7.5 SETTING EVENT FLAGS

Any task that knows the identifier of a group of event flags can set or reset the individual flag bits. The following requests first reset all the flags in the PMP1 group, and then set bits 2 and 3:

```
srsefg (pm1gid, EFRST + EFALL);
srsefg (pm1gid, EFSET + EF2 + EF3);
```

Upon receipt of an *srefg* request, the OS immediately changes the selected flags, unblocks all tasks that are waiting for any flags that have been set, and returns the new group value to the task that issued the *srefg*.

A task can also instruct the OS to change a set of flags after a specified interval of time. Thus,

sgiefg (pm1gid, EF1 + EF7, 450 + MS);

sets flags 1 and 7 after 450 ms.

Flags that are to be set in the future are often called "alarm clock" bits. They have a variety of uses. For example, suppose a task must output an external signal for at least 500 ms while it simultaneously performs a calculation that could take between 200 and 700 ms. Assume that **EF0** of the **PMP1** group is free. The task turns the signal on, issues *sgiefg* (pm1gid, EF0 + 500 + MS), and then begins the calculation. When the calculation is done, it issues *waiefg* (pm1efg,EF0,NOEND). If more than 500 ms have elapsed, the flag is already set so the function returns immediately. Otherwise, the task is blocked for the remainder of the signal period. Upon continuing after the *waiefg*, the task turns the signal off.

An alarm clock can be reset by issuing another request targeted to the *same* flags in the *same* group. If the time interval in the second request is 0, the original request is canceled without starting a new timer.

Event flag values are not "consumed" by being used for coordination, that is, the OS does not automatically reset an event flag as it unblocks a task that was waiting for that flag. This is consistent with the view that EFGs represent real information whose validity transcends their use for coordination. As a result, if a task detects that the information carried by an event flag is no longer true, that task should reset the flag via *srsefg*.

There is a significant benefit for not having EF information consumed when a waiting task starts. Suppose task **WEF1** is already waiting for **EF1** when the flag is set. A moment later task **WEF2** issues a wait for the same **EF1**. **WEF2** is not blocked since **EF1** remains set. Thus, EF coordination is not sensitive to the prior use of the information by other tasks.

## 7.6  DELETING A PUBLIC EVENT FLAG GROUP

The ability to create objects (such as event flag groups) is a convenient way to make an application self-installing; in most cases, the objects are never deleted. Nevertheless, it is quite possible that an object might be transient, that is, needed only temporarily.  Such objects should be deleted to reclaim their (memory) resources.  The function:

    dlefg (gid);

deletes a public event flag group whose identifier is *gid*.  This function returns **NOERR** for success or **BADPRM** if *gid* is not proper.

A question always arises in deleting an object that is shared by several tasks: When has the last task finished with the object so that it can be removed? MTOS-UX has straightforward semantics for EFG deletion that seems to give highly satisfactory results.  *dlefg* does not immediately delete the group if there are either any tasks waiting for the EFG, or any outstanding timers ("alarm clocks").  If there are, the EFG is internally marked "deletion-requested."  Actual removal does not occur until there are no more tasks waiting or alarm clocks active.  In the interim, all EF functions may be applied normally.

## 7.7  LOCAL OR PRIVATE EVENT FLAGS

The event flags groups that can be created are called "global" or "public" to emphasize that they are not necessarily related to the organization of the tasks within the application.  This was done on purpose so that an EFG could be used to broadcast information to all tasks that may have a need to know.  When a task waits for an EFG, it does not have to know which task or tasks will provide an end to its wait; when a task sets a flag, it does not have to know which tasks are waiting for that information.

In addition to the global event flags, which must be created before they can be used, each task automatically possesses a private group of 16 local event flags. This is called "Group 0" since it can be accessed by using 0 in place of a group identifier in *srsefg*, *sgiefg*, or *waiefg*.  A local EFG is an inherent and permanent part of each task; Group 0 can neither be created nor deleted.

Local event flags evolved to facilitate coordination with the completion of a requested service.  We have already seen that a task can specify **WAIFIN** to indicate that it is to be blocked until a service is finished.  This was illustrated in Section 5.6, when Task **TskR** needed to coordinate with the termination of a worker task **Work** so that its return data would be valid:

    start (wrktid,GVNPTY+prty,&arg,&result,WAIFIN+CTERM);

Suppose instead that Task **TskR** has work that could be performed simultaneously by three other tasks, **WrkX**, **WrkY**, and **WrkZ**.  Rather than the single start of **Work**, we could have:

```
start (wkXtid,GVNPTY+prtyX,&wkXarg,&resultX,CLEF0+CTERM);
start (wkYtid,GVNPTY+prtyY,&wkYarg,&resultY,CLEF1+CTERM);
start (wkZtid,GVNPTY+prtyZ,&wkZarg,&resultZ,CLEF2+CTERM);
```

Coordination mode **CLEFn** instructs MTOS to continue the requesting task, but to set the specified local event flag when the target task terminates. Thus the three target tasks proceed in parallel. (This can be especially efficient when they are strongly I/O dependent or have other natural delays; recall Rule 4 of Chapter 4.) Task **TskR** can also proceed with any work that does not require the results of the worker tasks. Finally, **R** can coordinate with the completion of all three workers with a single invocation of *waiefg*:

```
waiefg (0L, EFAND+EF0+EF1+EF2, NOEND);
```

## 7.8 ALTERNATE IMPLEMENTATIONS

Some operating systems other than MTOS-UX have event flags. They are generally internal binary variables that may be set, read, or waited for by one or more tasks. Beyond that, the details vary with the implementation. To gain some perspective, we can examine how the proposed MOSI standard (Mo87, Section 8.6) treats event flags.

Under MOSI, each event flag is a single bit; there are no groups of flags. Consequently, there is no facility to wait for AND or OR combinations of bits. Each flag may be private (local) or shareable (public). In either case, the flag must be allocated (created) prior to use:

```
ALLOCATE_EVENT_FLAG (old_flag_id, shareable_flag)
```

*old_flag_id* is either null to allocate a new flag or is the identifier of an existing shareable flag to obtain permission to access it. The function returns the identifier whenever it allocates a new event flag.

The function:

```
READ_EVENT_FLAG (flag_id, flag_value)
```

returns the current value of the specified flag as *flag_value*.

```
SET_EVENT_FLAG (flag_id, flag_value)
```

forces the flag to the given value and continue any tasks that are waiting for it. The wait request:

WAIT_EVENT_FLAG (flag_id, flag_value, time_value, time_unit)

returns a time-out flag that indicates if the task continued because the flag reached the specified value, or the maximum wait time elapsed. Finally,

DEALLOCATE_EVENT_FLAG (flag_id)

removes a task's access to the given flag. If there are no more tasks with access to the flag, it may be deleted from the system. These proposed MOSI services may yet be changed before the standard is finally approved.

## 7.9  SUMMARY

Event flags are binary variables that are maintained by the OS, but contain information about discrete conditions within the application. Event flags are packaged in groups of 16 bits. These groups may be created and deleted by any task, but are the property of the application as a whole.

Event flags are used for coordination. Any task can ask the OS to block it until a particular AND or OR combination of flags within a group is set. Furthermore, when flags are set, *all* tasks that have been waiting for those flags are continued.

Any task can set or reset the individual bits within an event flag group. Furthermore, a task can ask the OS to set EF bits after a given interval. These "alarm clocks" enable a task to continue with other work and still determine when an interval has elapsed.

Each task inherently has a local EFG whose primary purpose is coordination with the completion of requested services. A task can issue several requests, such as to start each member within a list of tasks, and then coordinate with the completion of them all.

## EXERCISES

**7.1** Suppose there was no pause provided by the operating system. Show how pause could be achieved by a single EFG service call. What precautions are needed to be sure the pause does not end prematurely?

**7.2**  Show how the following problem could be solved: An output signal must be turned on when events A, B, and C are true and must be turned off when event D is true. However, the signal must not be on for more than 750 ms. Events A, B, C, and D are all detected by different tasks. How would the code have to be changed if the signal is also to be turned off in case event A becomes false?

**7.3**  A scanning task, which runs every 5 ms, is required to track a certain input bit and broadcast its on/off status. The bit is expected to stay on for 1 to 10 seconds. A second task is to determine the exact time the bit is on and keep a running average of the on times. A third task is to sound an alarm if ever the bit is on continuously for more than 25 seconds. Draw a flowchart for the three tasks that are involved in these functions. Hint: Use two event flags, one for the on status and another for the off status.

**7.4**  One of the disadvantages of using cancel pause (Section 6.4) to coordinate with a task is that the coordination information is lost if that target task has not yet paused. How might this problem be overcome?

**7.5**  Consider the following program in Ada:

```
procedure LUNCH is

    task PREPARE_SOUP;

    task body PREPARE_SOUP is

        ...   -- code for preparing soup

    end PREPARE_SOUP;


    task PREPARE_SANDWICH;

    task body PREPARE_SANDWICH is

        ...   -- code for preparing sandwich

    end PREPARE_SANDWICH;


    task PREPARE_TEA;

    task body PREPARE_TEA is

        ...   -- code for preparing tea

    end PREPARE_TEA;
```

**begin**   --start three tasks

PUT_LINE ("For lunch we are having soup, sandwich, and tea");

**end** LUNCH;   --all three tasks must complete before the program can exit

Show how this program could be implemented under MTOS-UX.

**7.6** Why is it important to design the packaging of event flags (i.e., to consider carefully which bits of application information will be assigned to each group)?

# Chapter 8
## MESSAGE BUFFERS AND MAILBOXES

======================================================================

We have already seen in discussing the overall organization of a real-time application that message passing is a fundamental method of coupling tasks (see end of Section 4.1.3). Normally, the coupling involves the passing of information, such as a packet of parameters for some work to be done, or the state of a job that is being performed in stages by a sequence of tasks. The coupling also involves coordination. For a receiver, this means the ability to wait for a message to arrive; for a sender, this means the ability to wait for a message to be received. Thus, even if the content of the message is empty (0 bytes long), message passing can still be used to coordinate the activity of tasks.

An event flag can also couple tasks, but with the information restricted to a single bit. In the limit, a message without content also carries a single bit of information: It is present at an exchange or not. Even so, coordination via event flags and messages is essentially different. When an event flag is set, *all* tasks that are waiting for that event continue, and the event flag still *remains set* for any tasks that come later to examine it. With a message, the task that receives it *consumes it*; if there are two tasks waiting for a message, *only one* continues while the other remains waiting.

In designing the OS, each message exchange could have been permanently tied to its parent task, as was done with the local event flag group. Were this to have been done, sending a message to an exchange would have been tantamount to sending it to a designated receiving task. But such an arrangement is too limiting. Real-time applications often require the sharing of work among multiple, equivalent tasks. This sharing can be especially important if there are multiple processors in the system so that separate pieces of work can be processed simultaneously. Load sharing can even be beneficial for single processor systems when each piece of work may be suspended because of I/O or other inherent delays. (Recall Rule B of Figure 4-1: Try to keep the processor (or processors) always busy with productive work.)

Within MTOS, the arrangement for message passing is the analog of the bank queue with one line and (possibly) multiple servers. Each exchange is a separate object, distinct from the tasks that send and receive the messages. In principle, any task can send a message; any task can receive a message. (Of course, application designers usually impose task-level restrictions, but these are outside of the operating system.) Thus, if two tasks can perform a given type of processing, each will seek the *next available* message from a common exchange. The mes-

sage exchange is thus an implementation of the multiple producer/multiple consumer model of intertask communication (Figure 8-1).

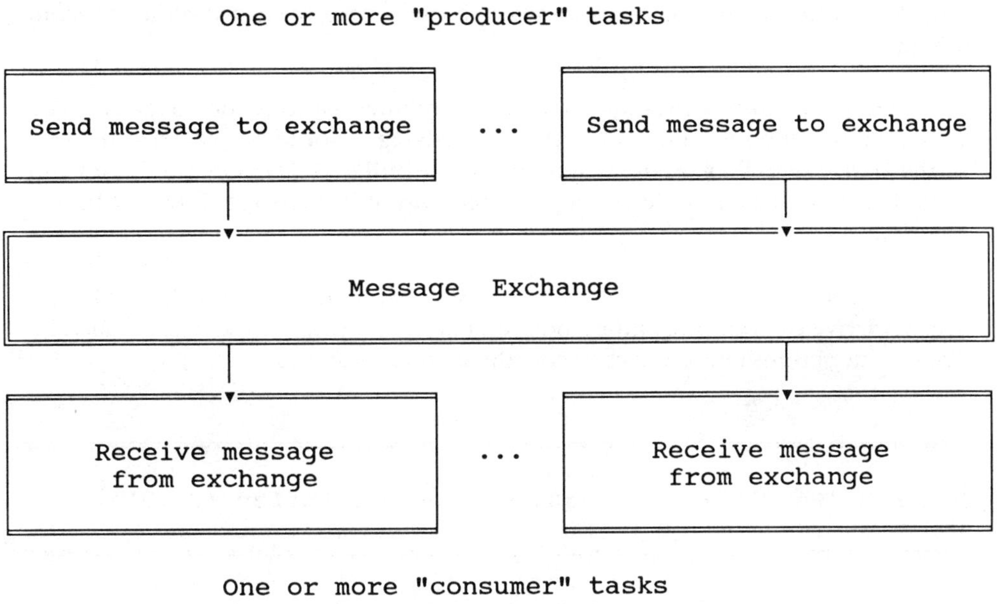

One or more "producer" tasks

```
┌─────────────────────────────────┐       ┌─────────────────────────────────┐
│                                 │       │                                 │
│   Send message to exchange      │  ...  │   Send message to exchange      │
│                                 │       │                                 │
└─────────────────────────────────┘       └─────────────────────────────────┘
            │                                          │
            ▼                                          ▼
┌─────────────────────────────────────────────────────────────────────────┐
│                                                                           │
│                        Message    Exchange                                │
│                                                                           │
└─────────────────────────────────────────────────────────────────────────┘
            │                                          │
            ▼                                          ▼
┌─────────────────────────────────┐       ┌─────────────────────────────────┐
│                                 │       │                                 │
│      Receive message            │  ...  │      Receive message            │
│      from exchange              │       │      from exchange              │
│                                 │       │                                 │
└─────────────────────────────────┘       └─────────────────────────────────┘
```

One or more "consumer" tasks

FIGURE 8-1: Multiple Producer/Multiple Consumer Model of Intertask Communication


Message exchange plays a central role in many real-time applications. As a
result, MTOS-UX provides two different realizations of an exchange: a message
buffer and a mailbox. The message buffer is the quickest and simplest mechanism for passing messages. It will be described first. The mailbox provides additional facilities and will be covered later in this chapter.

A message buffer (MSB) is a place to which a message may be sent and from
which a message may be received. The number of MSBs and the kinds of messages transferred are completely determined by the application; the OS imposes
no restrictions of its own.

An MSB message is always the size of a single pointer variable (6 bytes for
the 80386; 4 bytes for all of the others). Often the message is the address of a
structure containing the parameters of some work to be done. However, the
content of the message is not significant to the OS; the value is transferred
without regard to its possible meaning.

A message buffer is a storage device; when there is no receiver immediately available, the 4- or 6-byte message is copied into the buffer. The maximum number of messages is specified when the buffer is created. A task that attempts to post a message to a full buffer is given a failure return value of **QUEFUL**. Similarly, when a task receives a message the 4 or 6 bytes are removed from storage.

After a task posts a message, it always continues without coordination. The only option at the send end is whether the message should be placed at the end of the buffer (FIFO) or at the beginning of the buffer (LIFO) in case there is no task already waiting to receive the message. An MSB message does not have a priority.

A task seeking a message at an empty MSB can either wait for the next message to arrive or continue and be notified that no message is currently available. These wait options enable tasks to coordinate their activities.

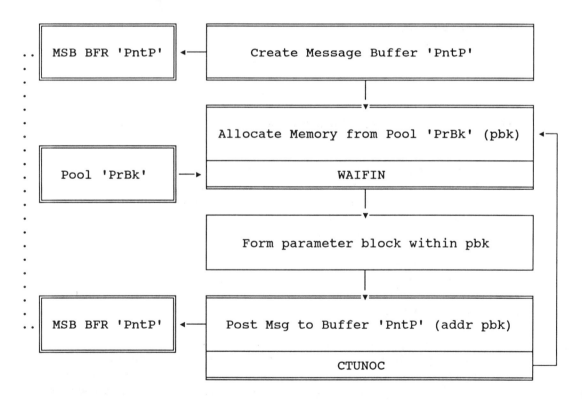

**FIGURE 8-2: Typical Producer Task: Using Message Buffer**

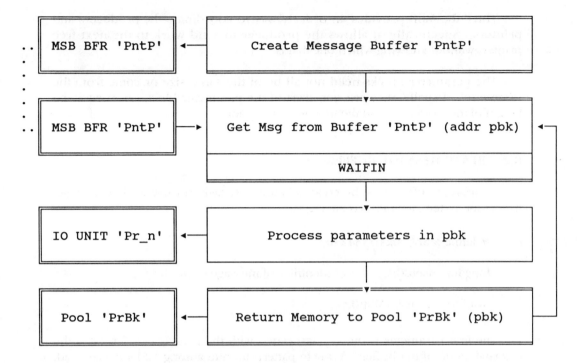

FIGURE 8-3: Typical Consumer Task: Using Message Buffer

## 8.1 TYPICAL USE OF MESSAGE BUFFER

As an illustration of the utility of message buffers, consider an application in which there are three tasks that produce blocks of parameters. Each block must be expanded into a formal report that is to be output to one of two identical printers. It is not important to specify the printer to be used for a given report. It is important that a printer not be idle while a block of parameters is available.

Each producer task allocates a work area from a memory pool, builds a parameter block in the area, and then sends the address of the area as a message to a certain MSB (Figure 8-2). The producer does not wait for the message to be received and thus is immediately available to prepare the next block (Figure 8-3).

Two tasks do the report generation and printing. Each task executes the same reentrant code, but has its own dedicated printer. A printer task seeks the address of a parameter block as a message from a common MSB. (If there is no message queued, the task waits.) When the printing is completed, the printer task deallocates the work area and then seeks the next message in an endless loop.

Thus, the MSB provides an orderly way to coordinate the producers and printers. Specifically, it allows the producer to send work to the next free printer, without knowing which one that is.

The parameter blocks need not all be of the same size or come from the same pool. Usually, they are not. Part of the parameter block can specify the length of the work area and the identity of the pool.


## 8.2  CREATE MESSAGE BUFFER

A message buffer must be created before any task can use it. For a single-processor system, a typical create call is:

```
#define MSB0  0x4D534230

long int  msbid0;          /* identifier of message buffer 0 */

msbid0 = crmsb (MSB0,50L);
```

The first parameter is the key associated with the message buffer. It is the external name of the buffer. A 4-byte pattern unique among MSBs is required. The second parameter indicates the maximum number of messages that can be stored. The low-order 13 bits are used so that the highest value is 8191.

If an MSB with the given key does not already exist, it is created by this request. The only return values are the MSB identifier for success and **QUEFUL** or **BADPRM** for failure. The successful return value does not distinguish an MSB that already existed from one that was just created. An MSB is created empty.

The buffer is created within a memory pool known as the Transient Program Area (see Section 12.7). For a single-processor (SP) system, there is only one TPA. For a multiprocessor (MP) system, there is one global TPA and one local TPA per processor. Thus, with MP the designer can specify the TPA by adding a term to the size parameter. The choices are **MSBGBL** (for a global buffer), **MSBLC0** (for a buffer local to processor 0), . . . , **MSBLCF** (for a buffer local to processor 15).

Some further calls are:

```
#define MSB1  0x4D534231
#define MSB2  0x4D534232

long int  msbid1,msbid2;   /* identifier of message buffers 1,2 */
```

```
msbid1 = crmsb (MSB1,MSBGBL+200);

if ((msbid2 = crmsb (MSB2,MSBLC2+500)) == QUEFUL) ...
```

A local message buffer must be created, used, and deleted on the processor specified in the second parameter of *crmsb*. The advantage of a local buffer is reduced traffic over the backplane. The advantage of a global buffer is universal access by all tasks.

The task that creates a message buffer automatically receives the identifier. Any C task that knows the key can also determine the identifier via:

```
long int  id2;

id2 = getmsb (MSB2);
```

Upon return, *id2* either has the identifier of the buffer with key **MSB2** or **BAD-PRM** if no such buffer exists.


## 8.3  POST MESSAGE TO BUFFER

Once a task knows the identifier of a buffer, it may post messages to that buffer. If there is already an unfulfilled get-message request queued, the message fulfills the request and unblocks the receiver. If there is no receiver immediately available, the message is stored (unless the buffer is full). In either case, the task that posted the message continues on.

Since a message buffer will store messages until they are claimed, it is important to control the manner in which storage occurs. Normally, a task posts a message to the *end* of a buffer. The request:

```
putmse (msbid,msg);
```

posts a message contained in variable *msg* to the end of the buffer whose identifier is given by *msbid*. If all messages are posted this way, the buffer becomes a pure first-in, first-out storage device.

In some parts of an application, last-in, first-out might be more desirable. For example, the printing of error messages sometimes needs this rule. The request to post a message to the *beginning* of the buffer is:

```
putmsb (msbid,msg);
```

You are free to mix both types of requests, even within a given buffer: Send most messages to the end, but occasionally force a highly important message into the front of the queue. Both posting functions return **NOERR** for success, **BADPRM** if the target is not a message buffer, or **QUEFUL** if storage is needed, but the buffer is full.

Note that the message buffer facility has been designed primarily for speed. Thus, there are no provisions for message priority or coordination at the send end. Applications needing these features can find them in the mailbox services that are described later in this chapter.


## 8.4  GET MESSAGE FROM BUFFER

The OS provides a pair of C functions to get a message from a buffer:

```
long int  msbid;          /* identifier of MSB */
long int  *msg;           /* message */
long int  result;         /* result of request */

result = getmsw (msbid,&msg);

result = getmsn (msbid,&msg);
```

Parameter *msbid* must be the identifier of an MSB; otherwise *result* is **BADPRM**. The address of the variable to receive the message is given by the second parameter.

With the first function, the task will be blocked until a message is available. With the second, if no message is already queued, the return value is **MBEOF**. Thus, *getmsw* is get-a-message-with-wait and *getmsn* is get-a-message-with-no-wait. For *getmsw*, tasks waiting for a message are queued first-come, first-served. This seems to be a fair rule since it is hard to conceive of a case in which the receiving tasks are not all equivalent. There is no limit to the number of tasks that may be queued waiting for a message.


## 8.5  DELETE MESSAGE BUFFER

A message buffer may be deleted by invoking:

```
    result = dlmsb (msbid);
```

If *msbid* is not the identifier of a buffer, the function returns a failure value of **BADPRM**. The value for success is **NOERR**.

Usually, the MSB is not being used when it is deleted. However, if there are any queued messages or pending receive requests, then the buffer is marked "deletion pending," but it is not removed until activity ceases. New requests will still be honored while the buffer is awaiting deletion.

## 8.6 ACHIEVING MUTUAL EXCLUSION WITH A MESSAGE BUFFER

Commonly, tasks that share alterable data must be sure that access is limited to one task at a time. As will be explained in the next chapter, semaphores are the traditional mechanism to achieve the required exclusive access. Nevertheless, a message buffer can be a viable alternative. A buffer is created and then "primed" by sending it one dummy message. Thereafter, whenever a task needs access to the variables, it would request to receive that message, with wait. Since there is only one message, only one task at a time could proceed; all others queue up at the buffer. Sending the message back to the buffer enables the next task to proceed.

The idea is easily generalized for cases that can permit access by more than one task at a time. To give a concrete example, suppose there are four independent and equivalent channels on a certain piece of equipment. Several tasks wish to use a channel, but do not care which one is provided. A buffer is created to handle the assignment of channels. The creating task initially fills the MB with four messages, each containing a channel number (say, 0 to 3). Now a task waits for a message granting it permission to use one of the channels and eventually returns the message to release the channel to the next user.

## 8.7 MAILBOXES VERSUS MESSAGE BUFFERS

While message buffers are versatile enough to solve many problems that arise in real-time applications, there are often cases in which a stronger facility is required. MTOS-UX mailboxes provide full coordination at both the send and receive ends, arbitrary message length, unlimited queuing, and 256 levels of message priority.

As with a message buffer, a mailbox (MBX) is a place to which a message may be sent and from which a message may be received. The number of mailboxes and the kinds of messages transferred are completely up to the designer.

A mailbox message, however, can be a record containing any number of characters. The content of the record is not significant; the bytes are transferred as an unstructured string. Thus, a record may be a block of text to be processed, a set of data to be reduced, or even the address and length of "the real text or data," as stored in a memory pool.

A task receiving a mailbox message may specify an input buffer shorter than the incoming message. This is considered normal. The message is truncated, with the excess text discarded. In any case, receiving a message always "consumes" it, that is, removes it completely from the MBX.

After a task sends a message, it has the option of continuing, or waiting until the message is received. Similarly, a task seeking a message at a mailbox that presently has no messages can either continue or wait for the next message to arrive. These wait options enable tasks to coordinate their activities.

MBX messages have a priority. If there is no receiver waiting, more important (higher-priority) messages are stored in a queue ahead of less important ones. For messages of equal priority, it's first-in, first-out.

There is no corresponding priority for receivers. When a task waits for an MBX message, it's strictly first-come, first-served. It is assumed that all receivers are identical so that there is no need for priority ordering of the wait queue.

Although a mailbox is a storage device, it holds only the *parameters* of unfulfilled send or receive requests. The *content* of a message is not copied until a receiver is available, and then the transfer is made directly into the receiver's buffer. The sender may choose to dispatch a message and then continue without waiting for a task to receive it. Nevertheless, because there is no internal storage of text, the sender cannot alter the area containing the message until it is transferred to the receiver.

The differences between a message buffer and a mailbox are summarized in Figure 8-6.

## 8.8  OPEN/CREATE MAILBOX

A mailbox must be opened before it can be utilized. The open specifies both the external name (the usual 4-byte key) and the intended manner of access (the "mode"). The mode is either **MBRCV** for receiving or **MBSND** for sending. A task may make both types of open (without any requirement for an intervening close) if it intends to both send and receive messages with the same target MBX:

```
#define MB03 0x4D423033
```

```
long int  mb3id;          /* identifier of MBX 3 */

mb3id = opnmbx (MB03,MBRCV);

opnmbx (MB03,MBSND);
```

If a mailbox with the given key does not already exist, it is created by this request. The only return values are the MBX identifier for success and **QUEFUL**
for failure. The return value does not distinguish a mailbox that already existed
from one that was just created. A mailbox is created empty (no senders or
receivers waiting).

Each time a mailbox is opened, a tally within the control data for the MBX is
incremented, and each time the MBX is closed the tally is decremented. There
are separate tallies for send and receive opens. However, the identity of the task
making the request is not saved. As a result, it is not necessary for each task that
uses a mailbox to have opened it. All that is required is that the current tally of
opens minus closes be greater than zero for the corresponding mode.

### 8.9  SEND MESSAGE TO MAILBOX

A mailbox message can be represented as a C structure containing a
mandatory 4-byte text length followed by any number of bytes of text:

```
struct msg
  {
    long int     msgs;            /* size of text, in bytes */
    char         msgt[20];        /* typical text */
  };
```

Occasionally, dummy messages (that is, ones having 0 length and hence no
text) are sufficient when the MBX is employed for pure coordination without any
transfer of information. More often, the text is some set of parameters, such as:

```
struct msg
  {
    long int     msgs;            /* size of text, in bytes */
    short int    mtyp;            /* type of msg */
    long int     mprm1[20];       /* parameter 1 */
       ...
  };
```

The simplest way to send a message to a mailbox is with no priority (0L) and wait-forever coordination (**WAIFIN**):

```
struct msg      msg1;        /* message */
long int        result;      /* result of request */

sndmbx (mb3id,&msg1,0L,&result,WAIFIN);
```

In this case, *mb3id* must point to a mailbox that has been opened for sending and not subsequently closed.

When a message priority is appropriate, it is entered as the third parameter:

```
sndmbx (mb3id,&msg1,100L,&result,WAIFIN);
```

For proper alignment, the priority must be a long word, even though the range is 0 to 255.

For coordination mode **WAIFIN**, *sndmbx* does not continue until the service is completed. Thus, *result* contains the same information as is returned by the request function itself. Possible values are **NOERR** for successful transfer of message, **BADPRM** for failure due to bad parameter, or **QUEFUL** for failure due to lack of internal resources. For other coordination modes, such as:

```
long int        instat;      /* initial status of request */

instat = sndmbx (mb3id,&msg1,100L,&result,CLEF0 + 100 + MS);
```

*sndmbx* returns immediately with the initial status of the request (**NOERR, BAD-PRM**, or **QUEFUL**). When the service is completed, *result* contains the final status: **NOERR, BADPRM, QUEFUL**, or **TIMOUT** for failure due to not having a receiver within the specified maximum wait time.

We can take advantage of the deferred coordination modes, such as **CLEFn**, to do work while "waiting" for a message to be received. A typical sequence would be:

```
sndmbx (mb3id,&msg1,100L,&result,CLEF0 + 100 + MS);

    ...      /* do other work */

waiefg (0L,EFOR + EF0,NOEND)  /* now wait for end of send */;
```

```
if (result != NOERR)
    ...        /* process error */;
```

When sending a message to a mailbox, it is not necessary that any task currently have the box opened for receiving.


## 8.10  RECEIVE MESSAGE FROM MAILBOX

The request to receive a message mirrors the one to send, except that there is no priority among the receivers. A typical receive sequence is:

```
struct msg     rec1;                        /* received message */

rec1.msgs = sizeof(struct msg) – 4;          /* set size */

rcvmbx (mb3id,&rec1,&result,WAIFIN);
```

As with the send message, the first four bytes of a receive message are reserved for the size of the text. Often, the messages are of fixed size, so that the *msgs* component can be set initially and never change. When the size can vary, it is customary to set *msgs* to the largest possible value (and be sure the text portion is correspondingly large enough). The OS limits the actual transfer to the smaller of the size of the message text and the size of the receiving text area. The actual number of bytes transferred is stored in the first four bytes of the receiving area, overwriting the original maximum size. If the receiving area is longer than the message, the unused portion of the receiving area is not cleared. If the message is longer than the receiving area, the unused portion is discarded. Neither case is considered an error. A text length of 0 is valid and provides coordination without text transfer.

Coordination for *rcvmbx* is similar to that for *sndmbx*. One difference is that all receivers are assumed to have equal priority so that the wait queue is strictly FIFO. Another is that while no coordination (**CTUNOC**) is often appropriate when sending a message, it makes little sense when receiving one.

Examples: receive up to 12 bytes into *rec1*--

```
rec1.msgs = 12;
```

with a maximum wait of 4 seconds:

```
rcvmbx (mb3id,&rec1,&result,WAIFIN + 4 + SEC);
```

without limit, but continue and set LEF 15 when done:

    rcvmbx (mb3id,&rec1,&result,CLEF15);

If there is a message available when the receive is issued, the function returns immediately with status **NOERR**. Otherwise, the task is expected to wait or not as specified in the coordination qualifier. However, when the MBX is acting as a private conduit ("pipe") between tasks, it is important to be able to distinguish a mailbox that is temporarily empty from one that is permanently in that state. In the first case, it makes sense to wait for a message; in the second it does not. Toward this goal, when a receive request is made to an empty mailbox, the OS checks if the MBX was once opened for sending and is currently not opened in that mode. In that special case, the receive request returns immediately with "at end of file" (**MBEOF**) status. In all other cases, an unfulfilled receive request is queued. This applies for all four basic coordination modes (**WAIFIN**, **CTUNOC**, **CLEFn**, and **CSIGn**).

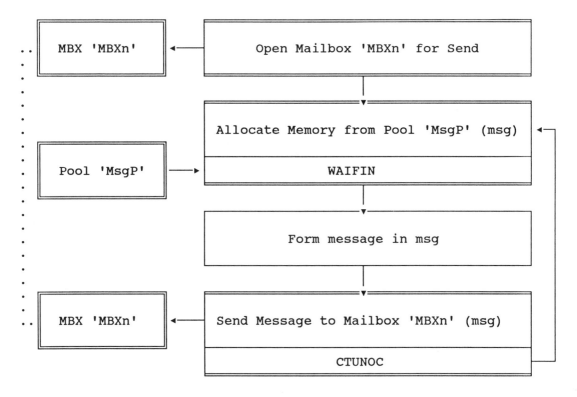

**FIGURE 8-4: Typical Producer Task: Using Mailbox**

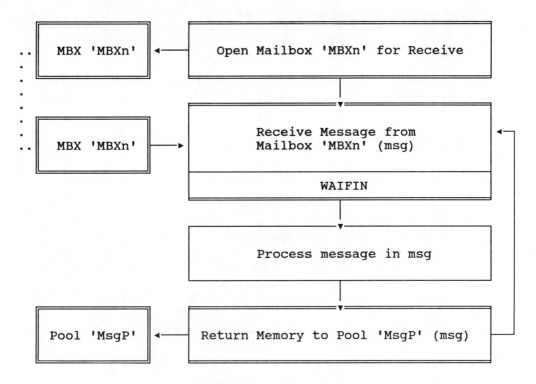

FIGURE 8-5:  Typical Consumer Task: Using Mailbox

## 8.11  CLOSE AND DELETE MAILBOX

Very often a task that communicates via a mailbox is organized as an endless loop, as shown in Figures 8-4 and 8-5.  For such tasks the mailbox exists for the entire life of the application.  Nevertheless, there are provisions to close and to delete a mailbox, if need be.  The functions:

result = clsmbx (mb3id,MBSND);

result = clsmbx (mb3id,MBRCV);

close the given mailbox in the send and receive mode, respectively.

A valid close decrements the opens-remaining tally for the given mode.  If the new tally is still 1 or more, the function returns **NOTFRE** to indicate that there are other opens still outstanding.  If there are no more opens left for the given mode, the function returns **NOERR**.

The mailbox may be deleted by invoking:

result = dlmbx (mb3id);

If the argument is not the identifier of a mailbox, the function returns a failure value of **BADPRM**.  The value for success is **NOERR**.

| MESSAGE BUFFER | | MAILBOX |
|---|---|---|
| size of address | length of message? | any |
| yes | stores message? | no |
| yes | maximum number? | no |
| no | message priority? | yes |
| none | coordination for send? | general |
| WAIFIN | coordination for receive? | general |
| faster | speed? | slower |

FIGURE 8-6:  **Message Buffers Versus Mailboxes**

## 8.12  USING A MAILBOX AS A PIPE

A "pipe" is a connection between two tasks, arranged so that the output of one task becomes the input to the other.  Under UNIX a pipe is implemented via the file system; under a real-time OS a pipe can be achieved using a mailbox. The following suggests one method to create a mailbox pipe.  Many variations are possible.

A sender task (**S**) issues a *opnmbx* with mode **MBSND**.  When **S** wishes to output some text, it issues *alloc* (Section 12.8) to obtain a pool area large enough to house the text.  (Typically the area is larger than needed because of the granularity of a pool allocation.)  The text is stored.  **S** then posts a message containing the address and length of the allocated area to the pipe MBX.  The priority is 0 so that messages proceed FIFO.  No-coordination is selected; **S** continues.  When there is no more output, **S** closes the MBX.

A receiver task (**R**) issues a corresponding *opnmbx* with identical key and mode **MBRCV**.  **R** seeks a message from the pipe MBX with unlimited wait.

When **R** continues, it has either the address of the pool area or the **MBEOF** status. In the former case, it processes the text, deallocates the pool area, and then repeats the loop. In the latter case, it also closes the MBX to delete it.

## 8.13  DANGLING REFERENCES

The OS services to send and receive a message from a mailbox can be performed synchronously by choosing coordination mode **WAIFIN**. In this context, "synchronously" means that the requesting task does not continue running until the message is transferred. However, the OS also permits asynchronous communication via the deferred coordination modes **CSIGn** and **CLEFn** and the uncoordinated mode **CTUNOC**. With these last three asynchronous modes, the task continues to execute while the message transfer takes place.

In principle, a task that participates in asynchronous communication is free to execute any of its code and thus may be at any point within its code space when the message is finally transferred. Therein lurks a danger. Unless this freedom is carefully controlled, there is a significant potential for trouble.

A simple example can demonstrate the difficulty. A task enters a subprogram. Upon entry, it allocates some space for local variables, including a message buffer. The task builds a message in the buffer, sends the message to a mailbox with deferred coordination, performs other work, and then exits the subprogram. The exit code automatically reclaims the storage allocated for the local variables.

Usually there is no problem—by the time the "other work" is finished so is the transfer of the message. However, every so often the transfer is delayed so that the other work finishes first. In this case, while the message is waiting to be received, its memory is reallocated for other purposes. The OS cannot know that it is preserving an address that is no longer valid; when the receiver seeks a message, it gets whatever happens to be stored in the buffer at that moment. In general, preserving a pointer to a variable that no longer exists is known as a "dangling reference." Among the candidates for a dangling reference are the receive buffer of *rcvmbx*, the run-time argument of *start*, the return argument of *exit* or *dltsk*, and the results buffer of any asynchronous service.

Several solutions are possible. The simplest is to always specify **WAIFIN** for a service that involves a local variable. Alternately, choose **CLEFn**, but wait for the event flag to be set before exiting the scope of the local variable. (The *scope* of a variable is that portion of the code in which the variable exists.) Yet another alternative is to avoid local variables altogether by always utilizing static areas. That however is often not convenient for dynamically composed messages. In these cases, you can avoid the troublesome automatic deallocation that occurs with local variables by having the sending task explicitly allocate the message area from a fixed block or common memory pool.  A preamble or header within the message supplies the allocated address, plus the pool identification and allocation size, unless these are known by convention:

Message structure

```
┌─────────────────────────────────────────────────┐   ◄─────┐
│                                                   │         │
│  size of message text (header + content)          │         │
│                                                   │         │
├─────────────────────────────────────────────────┤         │
│                                                   │         │
│  text header: address of this allocated structure │─────────┘
│                                                   │
│              (pool from which allocation was made) │
│                                                   │
│              (size of allocated area)             │
│                                                   │
├─────────────────────────────────────────────────┤
│                                                   │
│  text content: ...                                │
│                                                   │
└─────────────────────────────────────────────────┘
```

The receiving task then does the deallocation.


## 8.14  SUMMARY

Message exchanges are a convenient way to connect tasks that feed information to each other.  As with an event flag group, a message exchange is a free-standing object, separate from the tasks which use it.  This permits any number of "producer" tasks to send messages to an exchange and any number of "consumer" tasks to receive them.  Furthermore, the transfer of a message can be a point of coordination, with both the sender and the receiver waiting for the transfer.

Nevertheless, coordination based on message transfer is inherently different from coordination based on event flags.  A task that receives a message removes it from the exchange.  Thus, if two or more tasks are waiting for a message, only one gets it and the others continue to wait.  (Recall that all waiting tasks continue when an event flag is set.)

Over the years, two different types of message exchange have evolved to permit the designer to opt for speed when complete generality is not needed.

The first type, message buffers, are the faster of the two, but accept only messages that are the size of a pointer (4 or 6 bytes). These messages can have only two levels of urgency (i.e., messages can be posted to either the front or the back of the queue.) Furthermore, the sender can only post a message without coordination, while a receiver can only coordinate using the equivalent of **WAIFIN** or **IMONLY**.

The second type of exchange is the mailbox. It is fully general. Messages can be of any length and can be assigned any of 256 levels of priority. All coordination modes and options are available to both the sender and receiver.

## EXERCISES

**8.1** Draw a flowchart for a text spooler task. The task must be able to accept ASCII text from any other task and print them in priority order. The priority is that of the sending task.

What changes would have to be made to employ the size of the text as the priority (with the fewer the number of 1K blocks of text, the higher the priority)?

**8.2** Show in detail how to achieve the following type of 2-task rendezvous: Task **S** must send a message to Task **R** and then wait until both the message is received and an answering message is produced. Task **R** must wait until it receives a message from **S**. **R** then processes the message and sends a reply back to **S**. **S** knows the identity of **R**, and vice versa. The rendezvous must work no matter which task arrives at the message exchange first.

**8.3** Generalize the rendezvous so that any task can send a message to **R** and wait for a reply.

**8.4** Construct a UNIX-type ASCII pipe between two tasks using a message buffer. The sending task must be able to send an arbitrary, null-terminated string of ASCII characters. The string may be generated dynamically, so that its final length may not be known when the first characters are sent. It is acceptable for the sender to retain part of the string, in case the buffer is full.

# Chapter 9
## SEMAPHORES AND CONTROLLED SHARED VARIABLES

In most applications, tasks must share sets of data, such as a table that is read by one task and updated by another. A second example of shared data are the global variables within a non-reentrant procedure that could be called by different tasks.

A segment of code in which a task is accessing some shared resource is often called a "critical region" with respect to that resource. Not every reference to shared data forms a critical region, however. Accessing a fixed data table would not qualify. A region is critical only if there could be harmful interactions because of the sharing of the resource. For data, this means that the variables are both *shared* and *alterable*. More general resources, such as a printer or console, engender critical regions only when it is undesirable to intermix the output from different tasks on the same page or screen.

Shared resources must be protected against the potentially harmful interactions by permitting only one task at a time to enter a critical region. In the first example, while the data is being read, the update task must be blocked; while the data is being updated, the reader task must be blocked.

In real-time applications, a critical region can be so small that its existence is easily overlooked. Suppose that a certain memory-mapped byte (call it *lamps*) is used to control eight lights: a 1 in bit **i** turns the i[th] light on; a 0 turns it off. Initially all lights are off. At some point task **TskA** turns light 7 on by OR-ing with 0x80. A higher-priority task, **TskB**, turns light 0 on by OR-ing with 0x01. Most of the time this works. But occasionally, because of an ill-timed task switch, the two tasks are in the critical region for *lamps* at the same time:

| TskA | lamps | TskB |
|------|-------|------|
| lamps = > reg | 0x00 | blocked |
| OR reg with 0x80 | 0x00 | blocked |
| preempted by TskB | 0x00 | lamps = > reg |
| preempted by TskB | 0x00 | OR reg with 0x01 |
| preempted by TskB | 0x00 | reg = > lamps |
| preempted by TskB | 0x01 | ... |
| reg = > lamps | 0x01 | blocked |
| ... | 0x80 | blocked |

In this case, the final value is 0x80 instead of 0x81. Problems such as these are insidious since they arise from subtle timing relations.

Critical regions must be protected by guaranteeing one-task-at-a-time access. MTOS-UX provides two different facilities to achieve such mutual exclusion: the semaphore (SF) and the controlled shared variable (CSV). Since the SF is the simpler, it will be described first.

A semaphore is an operating system object that is created by task request. In most applications, a separate SF is created for each critical region. (One could utilize a single SF to protect several regions, but this usually leads to excessive contention delays.) Prior to entering a critical region, every task must invoke *waisem* to wait for the corresponding SF to be free. If another task already has taken that SF, the new task waits. Queuing is based on the current priority of the waiting tasks. Upon exiting a critical region, a task must relinquish control to the next waiting task:

task A:  request SF, enter critical region, ...,   release SF

- - - - - time - - - - ->

task B:    request SF,   < blocked for SF >    enter critical region, ..., release SF

A simple way to protect critical procedures is to make the first statement a wait-for-SF and the last statement before returning a release-SF. This places all control aspects completely within the procedure. As a result, a caller does not have to know that the procedure is critical.

## 9.1 CREATE SEMAPHORE

A typical call to create a semaphore is:

```
#define SF34 0x53463334

long int  s34id;              /* sample semaphore */

s34id = crsem (SF34);
```

The argument is the external name associated with the semaphore. If a semaphore with the given key already exists, the function just returns the identifier. Otherwise, the OS creates the SF and returns the identifier. Only in the unlikely case of not having any internal resources remaining does *crsem* fail. The value returned upon failure is **QUEFUL**.

## 9.2  WAIT FOR SEMAPHORE

Every task that wishes to enter a critical region protected by semaphore **SF34** must first issue a wait-for-semaphore-to-be-free request. In most cases, the call would specify wait-forever (**WAIFIN**) coordination:

        long int  result;              /* result of request */

        waisem (s34id,&result,WAIFIN);

The first argument must be the identifier of an existing SF, as provided by *crsem*. Otherwise, the function returns a failure value of **BADPRM**. Failure values are also stored within the results buffer addressed by the second argument. As usual, a maximum wait time can be added to the coordination mode. Thus,

        waisem (s34id,&result,WAIFIN + 10 + SEC);

waits up to 10 seconds for the SF, while

        waisem (s34id,&result,CLEF2 + 1 + MIN);

waits no more than 1 minute for that SF and sets local event flag 2 as a completion indicator. The variable *result* receives the final status when the request is completed: **NOERR**, for success; **BADPRM**, **TIMOUT**, or **QUEFUL** for failure.

Each SF either is free or is "owned" by a task that issued a *waisem* without a corresponding release. Ownership is not permanent; once the release is given, the SF becomes free again to be owned by another task.

With some operating systems, the SF has just two states: free and in-use. ("In-use" means owned by some task, but the identity of the owner is not necessarily retained.) These are called binary semaphores. With a binary SF, any task, including the current SF owner, must wait if it issues a wait-for-semaphore request and the target SF is already in-use.

MTOS-UX provides counting, not binary semaphores. The difference is that a task does not wait if it issues *waisem* targeted to a semaphore that it currently owns. The SF has an internal use-count that is incremented by 1 each time the owner issues a wait request and is decremented by 1 each time the owner issues a release. Note that the use-count is 0 when the SF is first created and when the SF is free.

There is value in providing counting semaphores, as opposed to just binary ones. In a complex application, it may be necessary for a task to make *nested* entries into critical regions for the same variables, say, in the main body of the code, and in some utility procedures. Each region separately needs the protection of the SF. With only a binary SF, it would be necessary for the task to know if it already has reserved the SF, and when it is safe to release it. With a counting SF, each critical region is bracketed by *waisem* and *rlsem* (release semaphore). Upon exiting from the last of these nested brackets, the SF count returns to 0, and the SF is automatically freed.

There is an essential difference between event flags and semaphores, even though both are used to achieve coordination between concurrent tasks. If several tasks are waiting for the same EF and it is set, then *all* those tasks continue simultaneously. If several tasks are waiting for the same SF and it is released, *only one* task (the one with the highest priority) continues; the others continue to wait.

The semaphore provided by MTOS-UX is similar to, but not exactly the same as, the semaphore proposed by Dijkstra [(Di65), (De84, Section 4.11)]. MTOS's *waisem* is close to Dijkstra's **P** or **wait**; MTOS's *rlssem* is close to Dijkstra's **V** or **signal**. The difference is that when a Dijkstra semaphore is created, a nonnegative number **s** is assigned to the SF. Thereafter, **s** can increase or decrease (down to 0) via **P** and **V**. The action of **P** is:

if (s > 0) then --s else block task on SF

The action of **V** is:

if (any tasks are blocked on SF) then release 1 task else ++s

A Dijkstra SF need maintain only the use-count, **s**, and the list of tasks waiting for the SF; it need not record the current owner of the SF. Furthermore, the release **V** may precede the wait **P**, and the task that issues the release need not be the one that performed the wait. A Dijkstra semaphore permits **s** tasks to proceed into a critical region. These could be **s** different tasks, the same task **s** times, or any other combination that sums to **s**. MTOS-UX permits the same task to proceed any number of times, but blocks all other tasks.

Possession of a semaphore does not guarantee that a task cannot be interrupted by a task of equal or greater priority. Preemption is always permitted. However, having the SF does guarantee that a preempting task will not be allowed past a *waisem* for that SF.

## 9.3  DEADLY EMBRACE

There is no limit to the number of semaphores that a task can reserve and the number of *waisem* requests it can have outstanding.  Thus, a task may wait for one SF while it has reserved another.  But beware the "deadly embrace."  To illustrate this phenomenon, suppose that task **D** has reserved SF **SFN1** and seeks SF **SFN2**.  Task **E** already has SF **SFN2** and seeks SF **SFN1**.  Deadlock.

In principle, the solution is easy: Have all tasks that seek multiple semaphores always seek them in the same order.  In complex cases, this may not be easy to arrange.

Deadly embraces can also arise from other combinations of limited resources.  For example, a task that has a semaphore and is seeking a memory pool allocation can deadlock with a task that has a large portion of the memory and is waiting for that SF.

To reduce the effects of a deadly embrace, avoid unlimited waits.  Use **WAIFIN + 10 MS**, rather than just **WAIFIN**.  And when you fail to obtain one of the needed resources, relinquish other limited resources and then try again.  Furthermore, use different time limits in different tasks.  In that way it is unlikely that the same deadly embrace will reappear on each cycle of retry.

## 9.4  RELEASE SEMAPHORE

The request:

    result = rlssem (s34id);

decreases the use-count of the given semaphore and releases it to the next user if the count becomes 0.  If the argument is not a semaphore currently held by the calling task, the function returns a failure value of **BADPRM**.  Two values represent success: **NOERR** means that the SF was released and is now free, while **NOTFRE** means that the SF is still held since the count has not been reduced to 0.

For best overall performance a semaphore should be released immediately upon exit from the critical region.

## 9.5  DELETE SEMAPHORE

In a dedicated real-time application it is likely that control objects, such as semaphores, would be created by an initialization task and then remain "forever." In contrast, the semaphores created by transient (temporary) tasks are not likely to be permanent. Thus, the OS provides a mechanism to delete a semaphore once it is no longer needed:

    result = dlsem (s34id);

If the argument is not the identifier of a semaphore, the function returns a failure value of **BADPRM**. The function returns **NOERR** for success.

    Usually, the SF is not in use when it is deleted. If it is in use, the delete request is discarded, and the function returns the warning value **NOTFRE**. Each task that accesses a non-permanent SF should delete the SF before it exits.

## 9.6  CONTROLLED SHARED VARIABLES

    As already noted, it is common in real-time applications for a set of tasks to share a group of alterable variables. The semaphore facility permits the OS to grant each task exclusive access to the variables to prevent possibly harmful interference.

    In some cases, however, a task does not simply want exclusive access to the variables; it wants that exclusivity only after a certain relation exists among variables in the group. Until then the task must be blocked. For example, suppose the group contains 32 binary variables akin to event flags. The task might have to be blocked until a given set of these variables are all equal to 1. Thus, the task might have to leave the critical region so that other tasks can access and change the variables, but then reenter the critical region when the desired relation is true [see conditional critical regions in Per Brinch Hanson's *Operating System Principles* (Br73)]. MTOS-UX includes five service calls that make it efficient to handle this type of coordination:

    *crcsv*    create a group of controlled shared variables

    *usecsv*    wait for exclusive access to a group of controlled shared variables

    *waicsv*    wait for given function of controlled shared variables to be TRUE

    *rlscsv*    release exclusive access to a group of controlled shared variables

    *dlcsv*    delete a group of controlled shared variables

## 9.7  CREATE A GROUP OF CONTROLLED SHARED VARIABLES

The first step toward establishing a group of controlled shared variables is defining their structure. To illustrate the creation and use of CSVs, let us assume that we are interested in maintaining multiple windows on a CRT screen. The supporting data is:

```
#define NW  4                    /* maximum number of windows */

struct mw
  {
    long    int  wid[NW];        /* width */
    long    int  len[NW];        /* length */
    short   int  avl[NW];        /* 0 = available */
      ...                        /* position and other data */
  };
```

We can create a set of controlled shared variables having this structure via the sequence:

```
#define WNDO        0x574E444F
#define MWSIZ       sizeof (struct mw)

struct mw *wndgid;      /* identifier of group = addr of first variable */

wndgid = (struct mw *) crcsv (WNDO, (long) MWSIZ);
```

The first argument (*WNDO*) is the usual key associated with the group of variables. The second argument (*MWSIZ*) is the overall size of the variables, in bytes. If a group with the given key already exists, the group identifier is returned as the value of the function when the current and original lengths match. When they do not match, **BADPRM** is returned. For a new key, the OS attempts to create the group. If successful, again the identifier is returned. If there is not enough internal memory currently available to do the creation, the function returns the error code **QUEFUL**.

The group identifier is also the address of the first variable. The group is created with all variables initialized to 0.

## 9.8  WAIT FOR EXCLUSIVE ACCESS TO CONTROLLED SHARED VARIABLES

For tasks to share the variables successfully, all users must wait until the OS grants exclusive access. (This is the implication of the term "controlled.") If the task needs exclusive access with no preconditions having to be met, it would invoke the unconditional form of the wait request. For example,

>usecsv (wndgid,NOEND);

provides a wait without limit, while

>usecsv (wndgid,100 + MS);

sets a maximum of 100 MS to the wait. If the group does not exist, *usecsv* returns **BADPRM**. If the requesting task already has exclusive access to the group, the return value is **DUPTSK** (duplicate task request). If the group is available or becomes so during the specified interval, the return value is **NOERR**. Finally, if the group remains unavailable during the given interval, the request is canceled and the return value is **TIMOUT**.

Once exclusive access is granted, the task may freely and safely read and write the group variables. Recall that the group identifier is also the address of the first of the variables. Continuing the example just introduced,

```
if (usecsv (wndgid,100 + MS) == NOERR)
  {
    printf ("Size of window #1 is %lx by %lx\n\r",
      wndgid->wid[0],  wndgid->len[0]);
    .
    .
    .
  }
```

## 9.9  RELEASE CONTROLLED SHARED VARIABLES

When a task no longer needs its exclusive access to a group of CSVs, it must issue a release request:

>rlscsv (wndgid);

The argument identifies the group. Once the group is released, the task must not alter any of the group variables, even though the OS does not have the ability to enforce this rule.

Calls to *waicsv* and *rlscsv* mark the entry into and exit from the critical region for the group, in a way analogous to *waisem* and *rlssem*.

## 9.10  WAIT FOR FUNCTION OF CONTROLLED SHARED VARIABLES TO BE TRUE

If only unconditional waits for access are needed, it is easier and faster to implement the variables as a task-level, public structure and protect the structure with an ordinary semaphore. The strength of CSVs arises when a task wishes to enter a critical region only when a certain condition is met among the variables. Alternatively, a task which is already within a critical region may wish to leave it until a condition is met.

The C function to wait for a certain relation among CSVs to be true is formally defined as:

```
int waicsv (gid,bfun,interval)
   long int  gid,interval;
   int    (*bfun) ();
```

The first argument identifies the variables group, the second argument supplies the address of the evaluation function, and the third argument indicates the maximum time to wait before returning from *waicsv*. If the interval is **NOEND**, the service can never time out. Possible return values are **NOERR** (for success), **TIMOUT** (if *bfun* is never TRUE during the specified interval), **QUEFUL** (if the timer cannot be allocated), or **BADPRM** (if the group does not exist).

When it is called, *bfun* is presented with a pointer to the group variables as its only argument. The function must return an integer value of TRUE (nonzero) if the task is to be blocked or FALSE (zero) if the task is to be continued. No task-level service calls (SVCs) are permitted within *bfun*.

The wait service call may be made either as a way into the critical region or as a way to exit the region until *bfun* is TRUE. In either case, *waicsv* does not return successfully until both *bfun* is TRUE and the task has been given exclusive access to the variables.

The *bfun* evaluation function is called immediately after *waicsv* is invoked if the requesting task already has exclusive access to the variables or the variables are free. If the task is to be blocked, *bfun* will be called again each time a task leaves the critical region via *rlscsv* or *waicsv*. Whenever more than one task could be unblocked because its evaluation function is TRUE, only the highest-priority task will be continued at that point. The others will have to wait until the variables are available again.

To complete the example already started,

```
static int  idx;                    /* index of available window */
static int  mwid;                   /* min width of available window */
static int  mlen;                   /* min length of available window */

int testw ();                       /* test value function */

waicsv (wndgid,testw,5 + MIN);      /* wait for testw to be TRUE */
       .
       .
       .

testw (data)                        /* sample function */
   struct mw *data;
     {
       register int i;              /* search index */

       for (i = 3; i > = 0; --i)
         {
           if ((data->avl[i] != 0) &&
             (data->wid[i] > = mwid) && (data->len[i] > = mlen))
             {
               data->avl[i] = 1;    /* take window */
               idx = i;             /* note which one */
               return (1);          /* end wait */
             }
           return (0);              /* keep waiting */
         }
     }
```

Whether or not a task had exclusive access to the group originally, it loses this privilege while it is blocked and regains it when the task becomes unblocked because the evaluation function was satisfied. However, it does not have access upon a time out or other unsuccessful return. Thus, the application must have the following overall structure:

```
if (waicsv (wndgid,testw,5 + MIN) == NOERR)
   {
       .
       .
       .
     rlscsv (wndgid);
   }
```

## 9.11  DELETE A GROUP OF CONTROLLED SHARED VARIABLES

When a group of controlled shared variables is no longer needed by any task, it may be deleted by invoking:

result = dlcsv (wndgid);

The function returns **NOERR** for success and **BADPRM** for failure.

The same problem arises in deleting a group of CSVs as in deleting a group of public event flags: how to know when the last task is finished with the group so that it can be removed. The same solution is used. Thus, *dlcsv* does not immediately delete the group if there are any tasks waiting because of *waicsv*. If there are, the group is internally marked "deletion-requested." Actual removal does not occur until there are no more tasks waiting. In the interim, all CSV functions may be applied in their normal manner.

## 9.12  PRIORITY INVERSION

Once the OS grants task **LP** a semaphore, group of controlled shared variables, or any other exclusive-access object, the OS is not free to take the object back and give it to another task. (That would defeat the whole purpose of providing exclusive-access objects.) As a result, if a higher-priority task (**HP**) seeks the same object, it must wait until **LP** releases the object. But, because **LP** is a low-priority task, it may take a very long time for it to execute. Thus, a low-priority task can block a higher-priority one for an indefinitely long period. This is known as priority inversion.

Equivalent forms of priority inversion can occur when a task:

   is blocked waiting to restart another task that is executing at a low-priority,

   is blocked waiting to communicate with a partner that is executing at a low priority,

   needs memory or another shared resource that is held by a low-priority task,

among other cases. This is not the same as a deadly embrace (Section 9.3) since in principle the high-priority task does get to run eventually.

In very simple cases, it is tempting to have the OS temporarily raise the priority of task **LP** to that of **HP** to break the inversion. However, because of the many and subtle ways in which priority inversions can occur, and the complexity of nested blockages, there is no easy way to avoid inversions completely. These problems are actively being investigated at the Software Engineering Institute of Carnegie-Mellon University (Lo88) and other places.

## 9.13 SUMMARY

A "critical region" is a segment of code in which alterable variables or some other resource is being shared by two or more tasks. The resource must be protected against potentially harmful interactions by enforcing one-task-at-a-time entry into any critical region for that resource. Semaphores and controlled shared variables can provide the required mutual exclusion.

A semaphore is sufficient to protect a set of shared alterable variables when all entries into their critical regions are unconditional, that is, do not depend upon the current values stored in the variables. A semaphore is created for the set of variables. Before every task enters a critical region, it requests temporary ownership of that SF by issuing *waisem*. The OS allows only one task to proceed; it blocks all others. When a task leaves the critical region, it releases the SF by issuing a *rlssem*. If there are no tasks waiting for the SF, the SF is set free. Otherwise, only the highest-priority task is unblocked.

Controlled shared variables are a further refinement of the idea of semaphore protection. The request to enter a critical region can contain a condition function. Now the task may be blocked until both exclusive access can be granted and the function (evaluated with respect to the variables) returns TRUE. The same service also permits a task that is already in a critical region to exit until the same two criteria are met.

## EXERCISES

**9.1** Show how to protect a non-reentrant floating point library without requiring the individual users to know the details of the protection scheme.

**9.2** How could the Dijkstra counting semaphores, as described at the end of Section 9.2, be achieved under MTOS-UX?

**9.3** At times an application needs coordination somewhat weaker than total mutual exclusion. Suppose several tasks are sharing data. Some tasks alter the data and thus must have exclusive access. However, other tasks only read the data. The readers, as a group, can share the data, provided the entire reader group and each individual writer exhibit mutual exclusion. How can this be achieved? Hint: Introduce a mode variable (0 = free, −1 = altering data, any other value = number of readers).

Is there a way to prevent a succession of readers from effectively locking out a writer?

**9.4** MTOS-UX has a service call that allocates one element from a linked list of fixed length areas and a corresponding service call to return one element to the list (Sections 12.3 and 12.4). Show how these services, as well as the creation of the linked list (Section 12.1), could have been provided at the task level using other available facilities (such as mailboxes, semaphores, or controlled variables). Comment on the relative efficiency of such a task-level simulation of kernel services.

Repeat the exercise when *n* elements at a time are to be allocated for each request. (The request would remove **n** elements from the pool and return the address of the first of these. The *n* − 1 others would be linked to the first. For deallocation, the user would return the head of a linked list of elements to be returned.)

**9.5** The following is a version of the "dining philosophers" problem posed by Dijkstra and discussed by Ben Ari (Be82). Five tasks must each perform a similar operation that requires exclusive control over two shared resources, F[i] and F[i+1]:

| | | | |
|---|---|---|---|
| TSK0 needs: | F[0] | F[1] | |
| TSK1 needs: | | F[1] | F[2] | |
| TSK2 needs: | | | F[2] | F[3] |
| TSK3 needs: | | | F[3] | F[4] |
| TSK4 needs: | F[0] | | | F[4] |

Each task arrives at the point at which it must perform its operation asynchronously with respect to the other tasks. Devise a scheme that permits each task to perform its operation as soon as its resources are available. Resource **F** is initially completely free; no other tasks are concerned with the resource.

**9.6** Task **BATC** has four operations it can perform depending upon the equipment available to it:

| Operation | | | |
|---|---|---|---|
| | 1, lowest priority | needs | A, C |
| | 2 | | E (only) |
| | 3 | | B, C, D |
| | 4, highest priority | | A, D, E |

The equipment is shared with other tasks, each of which needs exclusive control while it is using a piece of equipment. **BATC** is cyclic; after performing the highest-priority operation available to it, it releases control over the equipment and seeks another operation.

Outline the control aspects of task **BATC**, including the creation of any needed structures. Encoding the availability of **A** to **E** is part of the problem.

**9.7** MTOS-UX evaluates the unblocking function of a group of controlled shared variables within the context of the OS, not the task that issued the *waicsv*. For a CPU with protected modes, this means that the *bfun* executes with the privileges of kernel code. Discuss possible advantages and disadvantages of this mode of execution upon:

**a.** the efficiency with which a task-level user could create communication and coordination mechanisms beyond those built into the OS.

**b.** the ease of incorporating local task data into the unblocking function.

**c.** the security of internal OS data.

**9.8** The trial MOSI standard includes a function (SUSPEND_PROCESS) that blocks a given task until a corresponding RESUME_PROCESS is issued (MOSI87, Section 7.4.1). Do you foresee any potential problems with this type of asynchronous suspension?

# Chapter 10
## TASK COORDINATION AND COMMUNICATION VIA SIGNALS

===============================================================

The major mechanisms for task-to-task interaction that have been described so far (event flags, messages, semaphores, and controlled shared variables) all use public objects that are accessible to all tasks. There is no sense of a private communication targeted to a specific task. Signals fill this gap by permitting one task to send information to a designated recipient.

A signal is a software interrupt that may be handled at the task level. There are four modes of use:

♦**intratask coordination**: A task may elect to have a signal sent to itself as the completion indicator for a requested service (coordination modes **CSIGn**).

♦**intertask coordination/communication**: A task can send a signal to another task, or to a group of tasks, as a means of coordination or communication.

♦**error recovery**: The OS automatically sends signal (26) to a task when the task generates an error exception, such as an arithmetic overflow. For many processors, error exceptions are also caused by a reference to a nonexistent address and an attempt to execute an unimplemented instruction.

♦**debugging**: A signal is sent after the execution of a breakpoint, which is implemented as an illegal instruction or a software interrupt instruction. A different signal is sent after the execution of any instruction for which the trace flag is set in the task's status or flags register. Normally, these signals invoke the Debugger.

This chapter concentrates on the coordination and communication aspects of signals. The role of signals in error recovery and debugging is described in Chapter 16.

There are 32 signals in total, but only 0 to 15 and 31 are available for task-to-task interaction. (The remaining 15 signals are reserved for error recovery and debugging.)

Signals differ from other coordination mechanisms in that the receiving task may either wait for a signal to arrive (akin to waiting for a message or event flag) or may receive a signal asynchronously, that is, while it is carrying out other ongoing activities. Furthermore, each task can decide how it will respond to each separate signal. The choices are: (1) ignore the signal, (2) perform a specified task-level procedure, (3) be blocked until continued by the Debugger, or (4) be forced to terminate. Signal 31 (the "kill" signal) is usually reserved for the forced termination. The response to intertask signals is commonly to perform a task-selected procedure (choice 2).

The signal mechanism is inherent within the operating system. Signal facilities may neither be created nor destroyed. All a task can do is change its response to a given signal.

## 10.1 SIGNALING AS AN END-OF-SERVICE INDICATOR

In previous chapters, we have discussed two ways in which a task can determine that a requested service is completed:

1. It can wait so that the request function does not return until the service is completed (mode **WAIFIN**).

2. It can continue immediately and have a specified local event flag set upon completion of the service (mode **CLEFn**).

There is also a third mode, **CTUNOC**, in which the task continues without any coordination.

The fourth possibility is to have the task continue, with a signal in the range 0 to 15 sent when the service is completed. This mode is specified by the literals **CSIG0** to **CSIG15** in the coordination field of the service. The following "word diagram" illustrates how the signaling mechanism can be put to advantage:

1. Allocate a work area from a pool; save the address.

2. Build a message in the work area.

3. Set the response to, say, Signal 3 to be procedure *done3* ().

4. Send the message with **CSIG3** as coordination mode.

5. Continue with other work.

6. When the message is transferred, Signal 3 is sent to the task. The ongoing "other work" is interrupted and procedure *done3* is performed.

*done3* () deallocates the work area whose address was saved and then returns. This automatically resumes the interrupted other work.

Thus, the benefit of signal coordination is that it permits some task-level operations to be performed upon the completion of a service, without having to wait directly for that completion.

## 10.2  SET RESPONSE TO SIGNAL

When a task is first created, the default response is to ignore Signals 0 to 15 and terminate for Signal 31. (If the optional Debugger task has been installed, then the default for the error signals, 15 to 30, is to become blocked and start the Debugger to unblock it. If the Debugger is not present, the default is to print an error message on the System Console via the Error Logger task, if present, and then terminate the errant task.)

The function *setsig* resets the response to a prescribed list of signals. The C definition of the function is:

```
int setsig (sigmsk,resp)
    long int  sigmsk;
    int  (*resp) ();
```

The signals of interest are selected by *sigmsk*, using one bit per signal, left to right. A value of 0x80000000 selects only Signal 0. The literals **SIG0** to **SIG31** may be combined to select the appropriate bit or bits. **SIGALL** means all signals. (The coordination mode literals, **CSIG0** to **CSIG15**, may not be used.)

The desired response is indicated by *resp*. Four literals are recognized: **SIGIGN** (ignore), **SIGBLK** (become blocked if the Debugger is present; terminate if not), **SIGTRM** (terminate), and **SIGDFL** (reinstate the default). Any other value is assumed to be the address of a function to be executed upon receipt of the signal.

**NOERR** is returned for a successful call of *setsig*. **BADPRM** indicates that the change was rejected because the function was not executable (for example, started on an odd address for the 680xx family).

Some examples of the call are

to reset the response of all signals to the default:

```
      setsig (SIGALL,SIGDFL);
```

to set the response to Signal 3 to procedure *done3*:

```
      int done3();        /* define done3 as a procedure */

      setsig (SIG3,done3);
```

to set the response to Signals 1, 2, and 5 to ignore the signal:

```
      setsig (SIG1+SIG2+SIG5,SIGIGN);
```

## 10.3  SIGNAL RESPONSE PROCEDURE

The structure of a signal response procedure is identical to that of a task: It is a procedure having a single argument. The argument is the address of a structure that is built by the OS when the signal is sent. The structure contains the signal number, plus the context of the task at the point of interruption. While the latter may not be of interest for communication and coordination signals, it is vital for error signals.

The signal response procedure executes at the task level and can issue any OS requests that the task could. The procedure acts completely as though it had been called by the task. It inherits the priority of the interrupted task and any task-level objects that the task had at that point. It can access any static data that the interrupted task could, but cannot see any local data. (This is generally true of a called procedure in C.) Correspondingly, any changes the procedure makes to the priority, task-level objects or static data are the same as though the interrupt task itself had made them.

Normally, the procedure returns by reaching the last curly bracket of its code. In that case, the task continues from the point of interruption. Nevertheless, the procedure is free to terminate the task itself by issuing *exit* or *trmrst*.

Because the procedure acts as an extension of the task, the procedure may not execute immediately upon the arrival of the signal. For example, if the target task is blocked waiting for a previous service to be completed, the signal processing is held off until the task becomes Active. Furthermore, while a task is executing a procedure invoked by a communication or coordination signal, the OS will not preempt that processing to handle another signal of the same type. The OS records any pending signals for a task and then processes them as soon as it is appropriate to do so.

## 10.4  TASK-TO-TASK COMMUNICATION VIA SIGNALS

One task can send a signal to another task, thus invoking whatever response the receiver currently has in force. The request specifies both the receiving task and the signal number:

```
    sndsig (tskRid,15L);          /* send signal 15 to task R */
```

Normally, the first argument is the identifier of the target task. (It is not an error for a task to send a signal to itself.) For the special value 0, the signal is sent to all other application tasks in the system. This might be used to terminate all tasks prior to shutting down the computer:

```
    sndsig (0L,31L);
```

One advantage of the signal for task-to-task communication is that the receiver can be interrupted to perform some signal-specific activity via a response procedure and then return to continue the interrupted "main" line of execution. Let us illustrate this with a task (**HU**) that handles unusual conditions detected by a pair of scanning tasks (**SD** and **SM**). The individual scanning tasks have neither the time to evaluate the unusual conditions they find nor the overall information to take proper action. Thus, when a scanning task detects something that needs closer scrutiny, it sends a signal to **HU**.

For **SD**, the "somethings" are discrete events that can be represented by integers 0 to 14. Thus, **SD** just sends the corresponding signal:

```
    if problem "i" is suspected then send signal "i" to task HU;
```

The problems detected by **SM** are more complex so that further information must accompany the signal. **SM** transmits the auxiliary data in a mailbox message:

```
    if problem is suspected then
        {
        send message with problem parameters to mailbox 'PPHU';
        send signal 15 to task HU;
        }
```

The main activity for **HU** is to handle any problems that have already been identified. The arrival of a signal interrupts that activity so that a potentially more important new problem can be included in the overall solution. When there are no outstanding problems, **HU** issues a pause-until-signal-arrives. This blocks the task until a signal is sent.  Thus, **HU** would have one of the common task organizations: once-through initialization followed by a repeat-forever loop (Figures 10-1 and 10-2).

TASK HU():

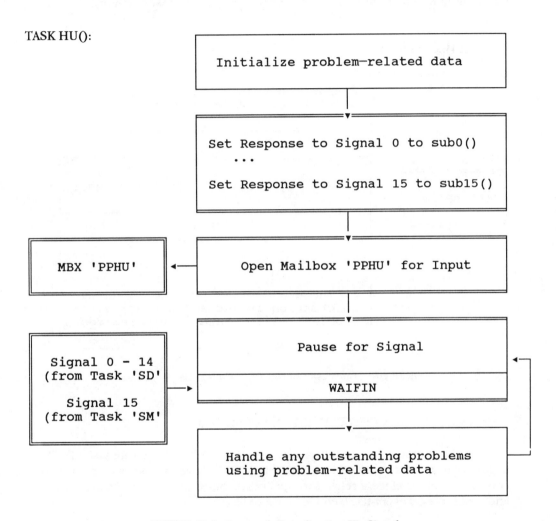

**FIGURE 10-1:  Intertask Coordination Via Signals**

If Signal 0 arrives while *sub15* is executing, that new signal is simply latched (stored internally).  When *sub15* returns, *sub0* automatically begins.  The OS keeps track of which signals have arrived and clears the corresponding latch as each signal response completes.  Nevertheless, there is only 1 latch per signal; if Signal 15 arrives during *sub15*, the second signal is lost. (In this respect, signal software interrupts are equivalent to hardware interrupts.)  Not to worry, the loop in *sub15* will make sure **HU** sees all its messages.  Furthermore, if **HU** runs at higher priority than **SD**, there is no danger of a message arriving just as **HU** has decided to return from *sub15* (at least in a single processor system).

TASK HU(), continued

subi(): **i** = 1 to 14

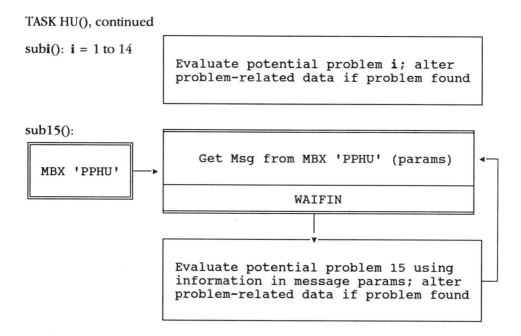

FIGURE 10-2:  Intertask Coordination Via Signals

## 10.5  TASK-TO-TASK COORDINATION VIA SIGNALS

Simple intertask coordination can be achieved by having one task (**TskT**) pause for a signal that is sent by another task (**TskC**) when **TskC** wants **TskT** to continue.  This is closely related to the coordination pairs pause/cancel-pause and wait-for-local-event-flag/send-local-event-flag.

The pause-for-signal request specifies a maximum wait time.  The time can be a specific interval:

      pausig (100+MS);

or can be "forever":

pausig (NOEND);

The first signal to arrive cancels the pause to continue the task, even if the response is to ignore the signal. Normally, *pausig* returns the signal number (0 to 31). However, if a signal does not arrive within the given interval, *pausig* returns with a value of **TIMOUT**. An invalid time interval is indicated by the value **BADPRM**.

## 10.6  SEND SIGNAL AFTER GIVEN INTERVAL

A task can have a specified signal sent to itself after a given interval:

sgisig (3L,2+MIN);

The signal to be sent is specified by the first argument. Proper values are 0 to 15 and 31. The interval is given in the usual way.

Often, the response to a signal sent by *sgisig* is the execution of an asynchronous procedure. In this way, a single task can carry out a primary activity and periodically perform some auxiliary work (via the signal-invoked procedure).

As a simple example, suppose a task must perform a very long calculation, say, one that takes about 5 minutes. It is desired to show that the calculation is in progress by outputting a '>' every 10 seconds. This can be accomplished easily through *sgisig*:

```
int showp ();               /* define showp as a procedure */

setsig (SIG0,showp);        /* set response to signal 0 */

sgisig (0L,10+SEC);         /* send first signal 0 */

do long calculation

setsig (SIG0,SIGIGN);       /* reset response to signal 0 */

...

showp ()
  {
   putchar ('>');           /* output in-prograss character */

   sgisig (0L,10+SEC);      /* send next signal 0 */
  }
```

## 10.7  SUMMARY

A signal is a software interrupt that may be handled at the task level.  Signals provide a mechanism for asynchronous coordination and communication as well as for synchronous error recovery and debugging.  (Synchronous or asynchronous indicates whether or not the arrival of the signal directly correlates with the current activities of the receiving task.)

There are 32 different signals.  Each task may select its own response to each separate signal.  The primary response is to perform a preselected, task-level procedure and then return to the ongoing task activity.  Alternate responses are: (1) to ignore the signal, (2) to terminate the task, and (3) to halt the task and start the Debugger.  A task can determine its current response to any signal and can dynamically change that response.

The OS automatically sends a corresponding signal when it detects a task error, such as an arithmetic fault or a bad parameter within a service call.  A task may elect to have the OS send a signal when a requested service is completed or a given time interval has elapsed.  A task can also send a selected signal to one given task, to a group of tasks, or to all the application tasks.  Finally, a task can pause until a signal arrives from any of the aforementioned sources.


## EXERCISES

**10.1**  Task **TskS** must send a message to six tasks, **R1** to **R6**.  The message is very long, but essentially the same content applies to each receiver's version.  Thus, the message is sent first to **R1**.  After that task has finished with the message, it must notify **TskS**, which has proceeded to other work in the meantime.  **TskS** must then modify the text and send it on to the next task, **R2**.  In like manner the message is passed to each **R** task.  Show in detail the service calls that accomplish this part of the application.

**10.2**  Show how a single task can use signal services to determine how much idle time there is in an application.  At what priority should that task run?

**10.3**  Signal 26 is automatically sent to a task whenever the OS detects a bad parameter within a service call.  If the task's response is to call a procedure, that procedure is invoked with a pointer to structure *scf* as its one argument:

```
sig26s (sigblk)
  struct scf *sigblk;
    {
      ...
    }
```

For the 680xx family, the data in the *scf* is:

```
struct scf
{
    short   fsn;        /* signal number */
    long    tid;        /* task id */
    long    drg[8];     /* D0 - D7 */
    long    arg[7];     /* A0 - A6 */
    long    sp;         /* sp (A7) */
    short   sr;         /* sr */
    long    pc;         /* pc */
    ...
}
```

Use this information to provide a general "bad parameter" display facility. Since the task key is generally of greater interest than the task identifier, you may want to invoke *getkey (tid)*, which returns the key corresponding to task identifier *tid*.

# Chapter 11
## TASK COORDINATION: SPECIFIC METHODS, GENERAL PRINCIPLES

========================================================================

Task coordination is a fundamental and essential part of a real-time application. In principle, each task is an independent program that is capable of running asynchronously with respect to all other tasks. In practice, tasks are highly inter-related; they work in unison. Specifically, most tasks act upon the same body of current data. Some tasks bring fresh data into the body, others transform the data, and finally, some output a product or response based on the data. In every case, tasks feed data to each other, with producers and consumers coordinating to be sure that transformations are performed with consistent values.

In the last few chapters we described several different types of coordination that have evolved over many years and hundreds of applications. People have discovered that there is no one universal method that solves all coordination problems easily and efficiently. But they have also discovered that just a small set of basic techniques and methods does suffice for the vast majority of real-time applications.

In essence, coordination is the blocking of a task until some specified condition is met. Often, the condition is a function of information that is produced by one or more tasks and maintained by the operating system. But this need not be the case. With pause/cancel-pause, for example, coordination is achieved without any transfer or permanent storage of information.

The specific methods of coordination that were described in the previous chapters differ significantly in both the nature of the unblocking condition and the type of information involved. These internal differences, in turn, lead to corresponding differences in the user-level characteristics and capabilities of the methods. As a result, the application designer can usually choose a scheme that is exactly right at each point for which coordination is needed.

Nevertheless, to make a proper choice of coordination scheme, the designer must understand what the underlying differences are and how they appear at the task level. In this summary chapter, we attempt to classify the various methods and to diagram the relations among them. This is an expanded version of a classification scheme that the author originally published in 1983 (Ri83).

Many alternate diagrams could be drawn, each of which represents a valid classification. Our goal is to find a classification that will guide in the selection

142

process.  The end product is essentially a decision tree: If you need this characteristic, choose this branch.


## 11.1  SINGLE-SIDED VERSUS DOUBLE-SIDED COORDINATION

The first division (Figure 11-1a) separates those methods in which only one partner can be held for coordination from those in which both partners are coordinating with each other.  *Single-sided* methods are totally asymmetric: One task issues a wait for a certain condition to be true; another task sets the condition that ends the wait.  However, the second task itself cannot be blocked while setting the condition.  Furthermore, with most single-sided coordination methods, it is possible that no task waits since the end-wait condition may already have been set before the wait request is issued.  Event flags always provide single-sided coordination.

Coordination can also be *double-sided* to provide a greater degree of symmetry between the partners.  With double-sided methods there is a mutual coordination between both partners; either partner can wait for the other.  Specifically, the first task to issue a coordination request always waits for the second task to issue a matching request.  One task always waits; there is no sense of presetting the end-wait condition.  The pair send-message-to-mailbox-with-wait-for-transfer/receive-message-from-mailbox-with-wait-for-transfer produces this type of synchronization.  However, unless both requests include the optional "with-wait-for-transfer," coordination via a mailbox will not be double-sided.

Since most coordination methods are single-sided, we will follow that path first and then return later to analyze the double-sided methods.


## 11.2  SINGLE-SIDED COORDINATION

For lack of better terms, we will refer to the partners in single-sided, task-to-task coordination as the *coordinator* (C) and *target* (T), respectively.  The target issues the wait; the coordinator sets the end-wait condition to continue the target.

Referring again to Figure 11-1a, the next division separates those single-sided methods for which the identity of the target task must be specifically known to the coordinator and those for which such knowledge is not necessary.  Consider, for example, the coordination that can be produced by the services *pause* and *canpau* (cancel-pause).

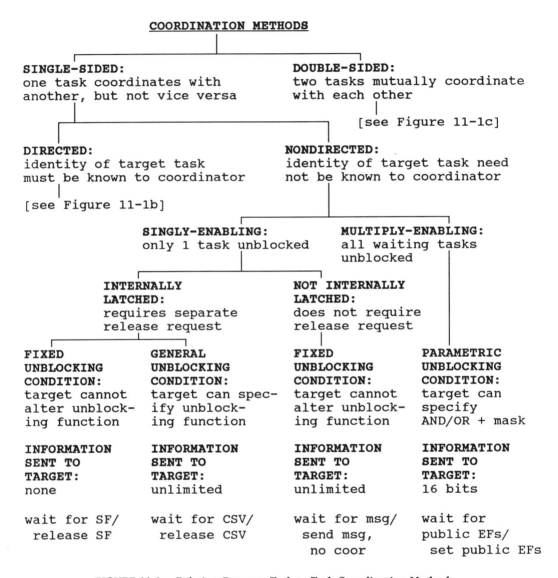

**FIGURE 11-1a:** Relation Between Task-to-Task Coordination Methods

Task **T** pauses (for a given maximum time interval, or "forever"):

pause (200+MS);

When task **C** wants **T** to continue, it cancels that pause:

canpau (tskTid);

The cancel-pause is always directed at a specific task. Thus, the identity of the target inherently must be known. Furthermore, only that one target task is unblocked, and no message or other information is transmitted from **C** to **T**.[1]

We will use the term *directed* to refer to those coordination methods for which the identity of the target task inherently must be known to the coordinator. In contrast, coordination based on event flags or messages is *nondirected*. The task that supplies the unblocking information need never know the identity of the target task or tasks, if any.

Use directed methods whenever you need direct control over one specific task. Use nondirected methods whenever the coordination is not with any given task, but with any that may be interested or with the next task that has requested coordination. Among the non-directed schemes, public event flags provide broadcast, that is, coordination with any task that may be interested; message exchanges maintain multiple-server queues for coordination with the next available task.

In this discussion, we are making the separation based on inherent or necessary knowledge. In any given application, there could be only one task waiting for a particular public event flag or at a particular message exchange. Thus, there could be *a priori* knowledge of the coordination target even with public event flags or message exchanges. But this knowledge is not necessary to coordinate via public event flags or messages. With pause/cancel-pause, target identity is an absolute necessity.

## 11.3 NONDIRECTED METHODS

At the next lower level in the diagram, nondirected methods can be split further into those which never unblock more than one task upon a change in coordination data and those that unblock all waiting tasks that meet some function of the data. We will call the first class *singly-enabling*, the second *multiply-enabling*. Public event flags are multiply-enabling. Multiply-enabling methods are used mainly for the broadcast of binary coordination data.

Singly-enabling coordination methods can be subdivided even further into those which are *internally latched* by the operating system and those that are not. With latched methods, there is an internal busy/free flag (the latch) that is

[1]Strictly speaking, when the pause is for limited duration (rather than with **NOEND**), one bit of auxiliary information is sent: Did the pause end because the time elapsed or was it canceled early for coordination?

maintained by the operating system as part of the coordination data. A target task **TskA** makes a request to wait until a certain facility (such as a semaphore) is free. When **TskA** is permitted to proceed, the OS sets the flag busy. While the flag is set, the OS will not permit any other target task (**TskB**) to proceed. **TskA** must issue a specific release request to unlatch the facility to permit **TskB** to continue. (In this special case, each task is first the target and then the coordinator for the next target.)

Latched coordination methods provide mutual exclusion, that is, one-task-at-a-time access. Examples are semaphores and controlled shared variables. The major difference between these methods is the amount of auxiliary information that is associated with the coordination mechanism and the flexibility of the un-blocking condition.[2] SFs work only with the busy/free latch, the identity of the current owner of the latch and the wait queue; this is all the unblocking function can depend upon. In contrast, CSVs permit complete freedom to maintain any amount of auxiliary information and to use that information in any arbitrary way via the unblocking function.

A message exchange is not inherently latched and hence does not necessarily lead to mutual exclusion. If there are 10 messages available at the exchange, then 10 tasks will be permitted to proceed. Dijkstra's **P/V** coordination works the same way.

Of course, a designer can force a message exchange to be effectively latched by permitting only one message to be posted. The message becomes an external (task-level) latch. Whichever task has been given the message at a given moment has also been granted permission to continue.

## 11.4  DIRECTED METHODS

We now turn our attention to single-sided, directed methods (Figure 11-1b). In selecting among these schemes, it is important to decide if the end-wait condition supplied by the coordinator should be *stored* or *transient*. Transient means that the end-wait information is lost if the target is not already blocked. The coordination provided by pause/cancel-pause is transient. So is pause-for-signal/send-signal. (With this mechanism, for pure coordination without "side effects," the response of the target should be to ignore the signal.) Of the two, pause/cancel-pause requires less internal overhead and thus is recommended if no auxiliary data needs to be sent to the target. Since the target task is told which

---

[2]We cannot say that the auxiliary information is transmitted directly from the coordinator to the target, in the same sense that a mailbox message is transmitted. The auxiliary information is associated with the coordination mechanism as a whole, not with any single act of coordination. Thus, the CSVs that the target receives may have been set by several tasks, or by one task at several different times.

of the 32 signals ended the pause, pause-for-signal/send-signal inherently transmits five bits of auxiliary data. Nevertheless, the OS does not retain those five bits after coordination is achieved. If the target doesn't save the information, it is lost.

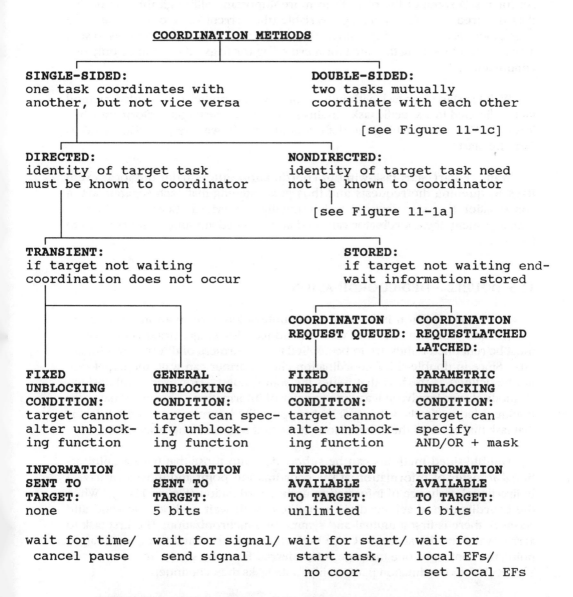

## COORDINATION METHODS

**SINGLE-SIDED:**
one task coordinates with
another, but not vice versa

**DOUBLE-SIDED:**
two tasks mutually
coordinate with each other

[see Figure 11-1c]

**DIRECTED:**
identity of target task
must be known to coordinator

**NONDIRECTED:**
identity of target task need
not be known to coordinator

[see Figure 11-1a]

**TRANSIENT:**
if target not waiting
coordination does not occur

**STORED:**
if target not waiting end-
wait information stored

**COORDINATION
REQUEST QUEUED:**

**COORDINATION
REQUESTLATCHED
LATCHED:**

| | | | |
|---|---|---|---|
| **FIXED UNBLOCKING CONDITION:** target cannot alter unblocking function | **GENERAL UNBLOCKING CONDITION:** target can specify unblocking function | **FIXED UNBLOCKING CONDITION:** target cannot alter unblocking function | **PARAMETRIC UNBLOCKING CONDITION:** target can specify AND/OR + mask |
| **INFORMATION SENT TO TARGET:** none | **INFORMATION SENT TO TARGET:** 5 bits | **INFORMATION AVAILABLE TO TARGET:** unlimited | **INFORMATION AVAILABLE TO TARGET:** 16 bits |
| wait for time/ cancel pause | wait for signal/ send signal | wait for start/ start task, no coor | wait for local EFs/ set local EFs |

FIGURE 11-1b: Relation Between Task-to-Task Coordination Methods

Use local event flags if you need directed coordination with storage of the unblocking data. Up to 16 bits of data are available per task. However, although the target receives a snapshot of the 16 event flag bits, they are not strictly information transmitted from the coordinator to the target; other tasks may have set (or reset) some of the bits. Even more important, although the unblocking data is stored, it is held in a single variable (the current value of the local event flags); there is no sense of queuing. Thus, if more than one task attempts to start a given target by setting the same local event flag (or flags), there will be only one continuation.

Wait-for-start/start-task-without-coordination is another single-sided method that is directed to a specific task. In this special case, the target is Dormant while it waits. Without stretching the definition too much, we interpret "Dormant" as "wait-for-start."

Wait-for-start/start-task-without-coordination differs from the local event flags by queuing the requests and thus guaranteeing that each separate act of coordination (i.e., start request) will eventually be serviced. Because of the run-time argument, the coordinator can send an unlimited amount of information to the target.

## 11.5 DOUBLE-SIDED COORDINATION

Next, our attention is focused on double-sided coordination. The terms "target" and "coordinator" that were introduced for single-sided coordination must be redefined if they are to be applied to the partners of double-sided methods. Since in double-sided coordination either partner can wait, the target cannot be defined as the task that issues the wait request. However, double-sided methods always involve at least one transfer of information. The coordinator for double-sided methods is that task that supplies the information and the target is that task that receives the information (at the first transfer if there are two).

Double-sided methods can be subdivided into those that have a unidirectional transfer of information at the coordination point and those that have a bidirectional exchange of information upon coordination (Figure 11-1c). When the coordination is achieved via a mailbox (with wait on both the send and receive), there is first a mutual and symmetric synchronization: The first task to arrive waits for the second. Once both tasks have reached the coordination point, the content of one message is transferred from the sender to the receiver. That ends the coordination partnership; both tasks then continue.

In contrast, with the pair wait-for-start/start-task-with-wait-for-termination, there are two transfers of information, one into the target and another into the coordinator. The target is the task being started. It is either already at the coordination point by being Dormant (waiting for start) or arrives there by issuing a termination request (which is equivalent to wait for restart). The coordinator issues the start request with wait for termination. If the target is not Dormant, the coordinator waits until the target terminates and thus becomes available for restart. In either case, there is an initial mutual synchronization of the two partners. Next, the run-time argument is transferred from the coordinator to the target, and the target continues (restarts at its entry point). However, the coordinator does not continue. It takes a second event, the termination of the target, to continue the coordinator. At that second event, there is another transfer of information, this time a transfer of the return argument from the target back to the coordinator. We can characterize this type of coordination as stimulus/response. The simple ADA rendezvous (Chapter 17) is also of this type.

```
                    COORDINATION METHODS
                             |
          ┌──────────────────┴──────────────────┐
SINGLE-SIDED:                       DOUBLE-SIDED:
one task coordinates with           two tasks mutually coordinate
another, but not vice versa         with each other
          |                                    |
[see Figure 11-1a]                             |
                       ┌───────────────────────┴──────────┐
DUAL SYNCHRONIZATION WITH             STIMULUS/RESPONSE:
UNIDIRECTIONAL TRANSFER OF            after meeting at coordination
INFORMATION:                          point only target continues;
after meeting at coordination         coordinator waits until target
point, one partner sends infor-       sends acknowledgement
mation to other, then both
continue
          |                                    |
NONDIRECTED:                          DIRECTED:
identity of target                    identity of target task
task need not be                      must be known to
known to coordinator                  coordinator
          |                                    |
INFORMATION                           INFORMATION
SEND TO TARGET:                       SEND TO TARGET:
unlimited                             unlimited

INFORMATION                           INFORMATION
SEND TO COORDINATOR:                  SEND TO COORDINATOR:
none                                  unlimited

wait to recv msg/                     wait for start/start task,
  wait to send msg                      with wait for termination
```

FIGURE 11-1c:  Relation Between Task-to-Task Coordination Methods

The two double-sided coordination methods that have evolved happen to have another significant difference: Start task is directed, mailboxes are not. In choosing between these two methods, this difference can be decisive, especially if there are many transactions to perform by any of several equivalent tasks. If mailboxes are chosen, the parameters of the transaction can be queued as a message. When one of the equivalent consumer tasks becomes available, it seeks the next message from the mailbox. Thus, with the work queue maintained via a nondirected mailbox, there can never be both an available transaction and an available consumer task. In contrast, when the transaction parameters are sent to a specific consumer via a start-task run-time argument, we have no simple way to distribute the work equitably. We could have some consumers idle (Dormant) while others have a long queue of restart requests. To help balance the scales, start task has the advantage of bidirectional transfer of information, whereas the mailbox has only a unidirectional transfer.

In some cases, we have to decide if it is more important to have automatic load leveling (which favors mailbox coordination) or more important to be able to coordinate with the completion of the transaction (which favors start-task). When both features are required, it is necessary to combine two different methods of coordination. For example, a mailbox can be used to receive the transaction parameters. Included with the parameters is the identity of the task that produced the transaction. After depositing the parameters at the mailbox, the producer issues a wait for one of its local event flags. A consumer task receives the parameters, completes the transaction, and then sets the local event flag to continue the producer. Thus, we have achieved nondirected, double-sided coordination with two coordination points, but at the expense of extra service calls.

## 11.6 EQUIVALENCE OF COORDINATION METHODS: SIMULATING ONE METHOD WITH ANOTHER

Are the methods diagrammed in Figure 11-1 a fundamental set of coordination primitives? Or can the coordination they provide be achieved by an even smaller set? Three issues will be considered: (1) the extent to which the attributes of one class of methods can be simulated by restricting or limiting the use of another class, (2) the degree to which the unblocking function used in one method can be simulated using different methods, and (3) the efficiency, clarity, and vulnerability of such simulations.

### 11.6.1 Altering Attributes by Restricted Use

As we have already noted, nondirected coordination can always be reduced to a corresponding directed method by permitting only one task to be the target. Thus, if only one task ever waits at a given message exchange, any task sending a message to that exchange is, in effect, sending it to that specific task. However, this restriction is imposed by the application designer; it is not enforced by the OS.

Similarly, the mutual exclusion that results from internal latching can be achieved with message exchange, by providing external latching. Suppose a given exchange is primed initially with a single message. That message may be taken from the exchange and put back, but no other message is allowed to be posted. In this case, the message becomes the latch; the exchange functions as a (binary) semaphore.

Generally, singly-enabling coordination becomes multiply-enabling when each task immediately releases the facility to any other task that may be waiting. For example, suppose we need a "big" event flag group, say, one 128 flags long. We could use controlled shared variables to create the group and submit the address of correspondingly big AND and OR unblocking functions in the *waicsv* requests. Then, all we have to do is always follow the *waicsv* calls by *rlscsv* to make the big EFG multiply-enabling.

Thus, we see that the inherent attributes of certain coordination methods can be simulated by imposing task-level restrictions on the use of more general (and hence slower) methods. It remains to be seen if the unblocking functions themselves can be simulated.

### 11.6.2  Synthesizing Unblocking Functions with CSVs

With a sufficiently general primitive, such as controlled shared variables, it is easy to synthesize the deblocking function of a wide range of other coordination methods. To illustrate, we will make a priority-enqueued message exchange.

First, we define a message structure, *msg*, that has a header (used to queue and control the message) and some text (shown as a nominal single character):

```
struct msg
    {
        /* common header */
        struct msg    *nxt;    /* pointer to next message, if any */
        short int      pty;    /* message priority */
        short int      len;    /* text length, if needed */
        /* content */
        char           text;
    };
```

```
#define msgptr  struct msg *  /* pointer to this type of message */
```

If all messages are of known fixed length, *len* could be omitted; if the queue is first-in, first-out, *pty* could be omitted.

At the task level, the message exchange would be a group of controlled shared variables that contain a pointer to the first message and a pointer to the last message in the queue.  Both are 0 when the exchange is empty:

```
struct mx
  {
     msgptr  first;              /* pointer to first message */
     msgptr  last;               /* pointer to last message */
  };

#define mxlen     sizeof(struct mx)     /* size of exchange */
#define mxid      struct mx *           /* identifier of exchange */
```

We will synthesize four basic functions:

```
mxid    create_x ();            /* create (empty) message exchange */
int     send_x ();              /* send to message exchange */
int     receive_x ();           /* receive from msg exchange */
int     delete_x ();            /* delete message exchange */
```

Create entails just a direct call of *crcsv*:

```
mxid create_x (key)             /* create (empty) message exchange */
   long int key;                /* key of message exchange */
    {
      return ((mxid) crcsv (key, (long) mxlen));
    }
```

For example,

```
#define MEX1  0x4D455831

mxid  mex1;                     /* id of message exchange */

mex1 = create_x (MEX1);        /* create message exchange */
```

The delete follows a similar pattern.

The procedure to add a new message first waits for exclusive access to the exchange variables, inserts the new message, and then releases access. For efficiency, two special cases are recognized. The first is an empty exchange. In this trivial case, both exchange pointers are set to the new message. In the second special case—an incoming message with 0 priority—the message is immediately placed at the end of the queue. In the general case, the program must traverse the message queue.

```
send_x (xid, smsg)                      /* send to message exchange */
    mxid    xid;                        /* id of message exchange */
    msgptr  smsg;                       /* ptr to message */
    {
        int         result;            /* result of OS service call */
        msgptr      prev;              /* ptr to previous messages */
        msgptr      next;              /* ptr to next messages */
        short int   npty;              /* priority of new message */

    /* wait for exclusive access */

        if ((result = usecsv (xid, WAIFIN)) != NOERR)
            return (result);            /* failure */

    /* add new message to priority chain */

        if (xid->first == 0)
            { /* exchange is empty */
                xid->first = xid->last = smsg; /* new msg is only msg */
                smsg->nxt = 0;          /* new msg is end of chain */
            }

        if (smsg->pty == 0)
            { /* 0 priority: place new msg directly at end */
                next = xid->last;       /* get current last */
                next->nxt = smsg;       /* chain new msg to last */
                xid->last = smsg;       /* new msg is last msg */
                smsg->nxt = 0;          /* new msg is end of chain */
            }
        else
            { /* find proper place based on priority */
                npty = smsg->pty;       /* get priority of new message */
                prev = xid->first;      /* get current first on chain */
                if (npty > prev->pty)
                    { /* new message is to be first */
                        xid->first = smsg;  /* new msg becomes first msg */
                        smsg->nxt = prev;   /* connect msg to chain */
```

```
                }
            else
                {
                while (((next = prev->nxt) != 0) && (next->pty > = npty))
                    prev = next;            /* continue down chain */
                    prev->nxt = smsg;       /* connect msg to chain */
                    if ((smsg->nxt = next) == 0)
                        xid->last = smsg;   /* new msg is new last msg */
                }
            }

    /* release access */
        return (rlscsv (xid));
        }
```

Typical use would be:

```
    struct msg msg1;                        /* test message */
        ...

    send_x (mex1, &msg1);                   /* send messages to exchange */
```

The receive procedure waits for the exchange to be nonempty and then dequeues the first message:

```
    int not_emp ();      /* unblocking function */


    int receive_x (xid, dmsg, dur)          /* receive from msg exchange */
        mxid    xid;                         /* id of message exchange */
        msgptr *dmsg;                        /* ptr to message buffer */
        long int dur;                        /* max wait time */
        {
            int    result;                   /* result of OS service call */
            msgptr prev;                     /* ptr to previous messages */
            msgptr next;                     /* ptr to next messages */

    /* wait until there is a message */

        if ((result = waicsv (xid, not_emp, dur)) != NOERR)
            return (result);                /* timeout or failure */

        *dmsg = xid->first;                 /* deliver current first on chain */
        if ((xid->first = (*dmsg)->nxt) == 0)
```

```
            xid->last = 0;                    /* exchange now empty */


    /* release access */
        return (rlscsv (xid));
    }



  int not_emp (xid)
     mxid    xid;      /* id of message exchange */
        {
          if (xid->first == 0)
              return (1);                    /* not empty: unblock */
          else
              return (0);                    /* empty: keep waiting */
        }
```

A sample receive call is:

```
    msgptr  buf;  /* buffer for addr of test messages */
    ...

    result = receive_x (mex1, &buf, 1+SEC); /* receive msgs from exchange */
    printf ("Receive: result = %x, text = %c\n", result, buf->text);
```

By similar techniques the task-level programmer can fabricate a message exchange with whatever priority or nonpriority queuing algorithm is desired. The problem is efficiency. Every task waiting for a message has the same *not_emp* calculation performed every time the exchange is released. Say, there are four tasks waiting for a message at an empty exchange. A message is added. As a result, the same *not_emp* calculation is performed four times: once (successfully) upon release after the message is added, and then three times (unsuccessfully) after the first task takes the message and releases the exchange. However, we know by the inherent nature of an exchange queue that *not_emp* must succeed the first task and must fail for all remaining ones. Thus, we could build this knowledge into the specific send and receive request functions of an OS-level exchange and completely avoid the overhead of *not_emp*. But, for a task-level exchange, we cannot do this. The generality of the CSV primitive requires that we compute the unblocking function each time, since in principle, the result could be to block or unblock.

In addition, every message transfer with a task-level exchange requires four OS services: two to get the controlled shared variables and two to release them. An equivalent OS-level exchange uses only half that many calls and thus has only half that many context switches. As always, the penalty for generality is loss of efficiency. In real-time applications, the loss of efficiency is often disastrous to overall system performance.

### 11.6.3  Synthesizing Unblocking Functions with Mailboxes

Only MTOS-UX provides controlled shared variables. With most other real-time operating systems, the mailbox is the only general primitive with which all coordination is to be done. Can various unblocking functions be formed from just mailboxes?

A technique for simulating semaphores with mailboxes has already been described. Beyond that, the road becomes long and treacherous. To take one example, let us simulate the AND unblocking function of an event flag group using only mailboxes. To make it even simpler, we are willing to forgo the maximum wait limit; waits can be forever.

We define a public variable to house the value of the group:

    extern short int  values;          /* value of simulated EFG */

and control access to that variable through a mailbox (MB1) that acts as a semaphore. MB1 is primed with a dummy initial message. A trivial implementation of *waiefg* would then be:

```
    short int curval;              /* local copy of EFG */
    short int mask;                /* AND mask for EFG */
    long int  access;              /* zero-length message for access to EFG */
    long int  stabuf;              /* status of service call */

    access = 0;                    /* make length of access message 0 */

    do
      {
        rcvmbx (MB1,&access,&stabuf,WAIFIN);       /* gain access to EFG */
        curval = values;                           /* capture value */
        sndmbx (MB1,&access,0L,&stabuf,CTUNOC); /* release access */
      }
    while ((curval & mask) != mask);
```

This method fails as soon as no task can use the group. At that point, the access message remains in the mailbox causing the **do** loop to be repeated constantly.

To avoid such repetition, after one unsuccessful test we do not repeat the loop until some task has used and released the group. For this, we need a second mailbox. MB2 receives a dummy "group was released" message and is initially empty. The simulated *waiefg* now becomes:

```
rcvmbx (MB1,&access,&stabuf,WAIFIN);        /* gain access to EFG */
curval = values;                            /* capture value */
sndmbx (MB1,&access,0L,&stabuf,CTUNOC);     /* release access */

if ((curval & mask) != mask)
   { /* condition not immediately satisfied: wait for change */
     do
       {
          rcvmbx (MB2,&access,&stabuf,WAIFIN);       /* wait for change */
          sndmbx (MB2,&access,0L,&stabuf,CTUNOC); /* release change msg */

          rcvmbx (MB1,&access,&stabuf,WAIFIN);       /* gain access to EFG */
          curval = values;                           /* capture value */
          sndmbx (MB1,&access,0L,&stabuf,CTUNOC); /* release access */
       }
     while ((curval & mask) != mask);
   }
```

The function to set some of the bits (corresponding to *srsefg*) is:

```
rcvmbx (MB1,&access,&stabuf,WAIFIN);        /* gain access to EFG */
values &= onbits;                           /* set some bits */
sndmbx (MB1,&access,0L,&stabuf,CTUNOC);     /* release access */

sndmbx (MB2,&access,0L,&stabuf,CTUNOC);     /* indicate change */
rcvmbx (MB2,&access,&stabuf,WAIFIN);        /* cancel change */
```

While this is a proper simulation of an event flag, it is terribly slow. The work performed by a single *srsefg* requires four separate calls in the mailbox simulation. Since most of the processing time of any service call is in the context switch and similar fixed overhead, the time required to do *sndmbx* or *rcvmbx* is about equal to that required for *srsefg*. Thus, the simulation of *srsefg* runs about four times slower. The simulation of *waiefg* is even worse. When *waiefg* is fabricated at the task level, it takes four mailbox calls **per waiting task** to do the unblocking calculations. This costs four context switches per task. When the same unblocking calculations are performed within the OS as part of *srsefg*, there are no additional context switches, no matter how many tasks are waiting for the event flags.

A mailbox simulation of an event flag is also subject to a serious side effect. After a task **C** changes the flag values, all waiting tasks must be continued via **MB2** so that they can perform their coordination condition tests. While these tests are going on, **C** is blocked waiting for the access message to be passed from task to task. It is not until the last task has seen the change and returned the message to **MB2** that **C** can continue. But if even one of the tasks that must see the change message is relatively low in priority, it can take indefinitely long for that message to work its way back to **C**. Thus, with a simulated event flag group, a high-priority task can become blocked for reasons unrelated to it and beyond its control. However, when the OS does the unblocking, the calculations are performed directly and immediately so that there cannot be any uncontrolled delays.

High overhead and undesirable side effects are typical whenever one attempts to simulate a specific coordination method at the task level using general coordination primitives. To answer the question we posed at the beginning of Section 11.6: Yes, you can have a simple OS with just a few coordination primitives, but the application suffers as a result.

## 11.7 SUMMARY

Coordination is the blocking of one or more tasks until some specified condition is met. Over the years, various methods of coordination have evolved to solve the specific kinds of problems that arise in real-time applications. These methods are fundamentally different in their attributes and effects (Figures 11-1 and 11-2). For example, some methods require that the identity of the coordination partner be specifically known, while others work with total anonymity. Another basic difference is in the amount of auxiliary information transmitted during the act of coordination or associated with the coordination scheme.

In this chapter we have analyzed and classified the major coordination schemes. The goal was to help guide the selection of the most appropriate technique, based on the desired coordination properties and communication requirements. The classification rests upon the following dichotomies:

**single-sided** versus **double-sided**. Double-sided schemes are symmetrical; whichever task gets to the coordination point first waits for the other. Thus, two tasks are mutually coordinating with each other. In contrast, single-sided schemes are asymmetrical. One task coordinates with another, but not vice versa. The roles of the coordinator and target tasks are always distinct.

**directed** versus **nondirected**. In directed methods the identity of the target task must be specifically known to the coordinator. In nondirected methods, the identity of the target is hidden.

| Method | Keys | | | | | | |
|---|---|---|---|---|---|---|---|
| | 1 | 2 | 3 | 4 | 5 | 6 | 7 |
| pause (=wait for time)/ cancel pause | SS | DI | SE | NL | FC | TR | none |
| wait for signal/ send signal | SS | DI | SE | NL | FC | TR | signal number |
| wait for local EFG/ set local EFG | SS | DI | SE | NL | PC | ST | group value |
| wait for start/ start task without coordination | SS | DI | SE | IL | FC | ST | run-time argument |
| wait for semaphore/ release semaphore | SS | ND | SE | IL | FC | ST | none |
| wait for CSV/ release CSV | SS | ND | SE | IL | GC | ST | variables |
| send msg with wait/ receive msg without wait or recv msg with wait/ send message without wait | SS | ND | SE | NL | FC | ST | message |
| wait for public EFG/ set public EFG | SS | ND | ME | NL | PC | ST | group value |
| wait for start/ start task with wait | DS | DI | SE | IL | PC | ST | run-time argument |
| send msg with wait/ receive msg with wait | DS | ND | SE | NL | FC | ST | message |

Keys
1) SS = single-sided,  DS = dual-sided
2) DI = directed, ND = nondirected
3) SE = singly-enabling, ME = multiply-enabling
4) IL = internally latched, NL = not internally latched
5) FC = fixed unblocking condition (uc), PC = parametric uc,
   GC = general uc
6) ST = unblocking condition stored, TR = unblocking condition
            transient
7) Amount of information transferred

FIGURE 11-2: Attributes of Task-to-Task Coordination Methods

**singly-enabling** versus **multiply-enabling**. Singly-enabling procedures permit only one task at a time to proceed when more than one is waiting for coordination. Multiply-enabling procedures release all tasks that satisfy the coordination condition.

**transient** versus **stored**. With a stored mechanism, the OS retains the coordination information until it is needed. With a transient mechanism, if the target is not waiting for coordination, the continue-task information is lost.

**unidirectional** versus **bidirectional**. When coordination is accompanied by an exchange of information, the flow of that information can be in one or two directions.

In some cases, the properties of one coordination method can be constructed from another (often more general) scheme. For example, a non-directed mechanism reduces to a directed one if (by the design of the application) only one task is ever allowed to be the waiting target. Furthermore, controlled shared variables are sufficiently general to enable the task-level programmer to build almost all the other coordination mechanisms. Nevertheless, such task-level constructions are very inefficient compared with OS-level services.

## EXERCISES

**11.1** Synthesize a 128-bit global event flag group using controlled shared variables. Show the code for set, reset, and wait.

**11.2** Show how a task can wait for a message at more than one mailbox at a time. What is the maximum number of mailboxes that can participate in such a scheme? Does this expansion of the wait-for-mailbox facility alter its coordination attributes so that its position on Figure 11-1 would have to be changed?

**11.3** A task can reserve a peripheral unit so that a series of input or output operations can be performed without interference by other tasks (Section 13.3). Release frees the unit for other tasks to use. Place reserve/release on Figure 11-1.

**11.4** What types of coordination facilities, other than those shown in Figure 11-1, might be useful in real-time applications? Can they be fabricated from existing services?

**11.5** Can the MTOS-UX counting semaphore be synthesized from other task-level facilities? (Recall that *waisem* must not block a task if it is the current user of that SF.)

# Chapter 12
## MEMORY POOLS

The cost of memory has fallen dramatically over the past several years. Nevertheless, in most real-time systems, it is still not economically feasible to include all the memory that every task might ever need under its worst case peak load. Fortunately, one doesn't have to.

The general level of activity in many real-time applications is governed by the rate at which input arrives, or at which input variables change value. A sudden burst of new input information causes a corresponding demand for work that propagates from task to task. Often such bursts in the rate of new input are followed by long periods of relative calm. Thus, demands for work, and for the memory and other resources with which to perform the work, normally flow like ripples after a sudden disturbance. As a result, the systemwide requirements for resources are much more stable than are the spasmodic needs of any one task or processing stage.

These observations have led to the notion of resource sharing, in particular, of memory sharing. While it may not be feasible to assign permanently to every task its worst case needs, it is practical to have large amounts of memory available for temporary allocation to the few tasks that need it at any moment. Such shared memory is taken from a memory pool.

A pool is a contiguous area in memory that is logically divided into fixed-length subunits called blocks. Individual blocks may be dynamically allocated and deallocated. A task submits a create-pool request specifying the address and length of the area and the size of the block. The OS builds the required support structures and returns the identifier of the new-born pool. Thereafter, any task that knows the identifier can allocate blocks from the pool.

A pool may be global or local depending upon the physical location of the underlying memory area. A global pool exists in global memory and is thus accessible by every task. A local pool exists in the local memory of a particular CPU board. It is accessible only by tasks running on that board.

MTOS-UX provides two types of pools. The first permits a task to allocate only one block per request. Because of this limitation, allocation is very fast. A pool for which the allocation unit is fixed at 1 block is called a Fixed Block Pool (FBP). Services related to FBPs will be described first. The second type of pool is called a Common Memory Pool (CMP). It permits allocations of any number of contiguous blocks, up to the whole available pool area. The price of this complete flexibility is greater internal processing time.

## 12.1  CREATE FIXED BLOCK MEMORY POOL

Pool specifications normally arise from an analysis of expected maximum demand. For example, suppose that blocks 124 bytes long are needed for a certain type of parameter-passing message. Since only one block need be obtained at a time, a fixed block organization is satisfactory. Worst case analysis shows that no more than 160 such blocks are ever needed, including those messages that are held in queues waiting to be processed. The area starting at 0xB0000 is available. The request to create such a pool and label it with the external name (key) 'FBP0' is:

```
#define FBP0  0x46425030

long int  fbp0;        /* pool identifier */

fbp0 = crfbp (-1L,FBP0,0xB0000,160L,124L);
```

For a single-processor system, the first parameter is not relevant since all memory is equivalent. For multiple processors, it indicates whether the memory is global (-1) or local to a specific processor (0 to 15).

The remaining parameters are the key, base address, number of blocks, and block size in bytes, respectively. The minimum block size is four bytes. If the base address is odd it is rounded up to the next even value, while if the size is odd it is rounded up to an even value. For optimum performance on most 32-bit processors, the base address and block size should be a multiple of four.

For the MTOS implementation of a fixed block pool, there is no "hidden overhead"; that is, the operating system does not reserve any portion of an allocated block for its own purposes. Thus, the overall size of the pool is exactly 160 * 124 = 19840, or 0x4D80 bytes. The area starting at 0xB4D80 is available to create another pool if need be.

Each FPB must have a its own 32-bit key. However, the remaining parameters need not be unique. In fact, with multiple processors, it is common to have identical local pools on each of the processor boards:

| on processor 0 | on processor 1 |
|---|---|
| #define FBP0  0x46425030 | #define FBP1  0x46425031 |

```
long int fbp0;  /* pool id */            long int fbp1;  /* pool id */

fbp0 =                                   fbp1 =
  crfbp (0L,FBP0,0x20000,160L,124L);       crfbp (1L,FBP1,0x20000,160L,124L);
```

Here, we are using address 0x20000, which is local to each board. The creation request for a local pool must be issued on the processor on which the pool is to reside.

If a pool with the given key already exists, the function just returns the pool identifier. For a new pool, the OS checks the parameters. If any are bad, such as a block length of 0, the function returns a failure value of **BADPRM**. If there are no internal resources remaining to create a pool, the return value is **QUEFUL**. For a successful creation, the function returns the pool identifier.

## 12.2  GET IDENTIFIER OF FIXED BLOCK POOL

The task that creates an FBP obtains its identifier from the create request. A task that is sharing the pool can determine the identifier via:

```
fbp0 = getfbp (FBP0);
```

If there is no pool with the given key, the function returns a value of **BADPRM**. As an alternative to calling *getfbp*, the task that creates the pool can send the identifier to the other users as an ordinary long word (pointer) variable.

## 12.3  ALLOCATE A BLOCK FROM AN FBP

A task that cannot proceed until it obtains a block from an FBP might allocate a new block with:

```
int *blkadr;           /* buffer for addr of allocated block */

alofbp (fp0id,&blkadr,WAIFIN);
```

The first argument must be the identifier of an FBP as returned by *crfbp* or *getfbp*. A parameter error is generated if the pool does not exist. The second argument must point to a buffer into which the address of the start of the allocated area can be stored. For the 80386, the buffer receives a 6-byte (far) address.

If all blocks have already been allocated, the task waits until a block is
returned for reuse. In general, an unsatisfied allocation request is stored internally until memory becomes available. The queue is ordered by the current
priority of the requesting task, with first-come, first-served for requests of equal
priority. If the internal facilities needed for queuing are exhausted, the function
returns immediately with *blkadr* set to **QUEFUL**. Queue exhaustion is normally
a rare event.

In the first example, the wait until a block is available is unlimited. To guarantee that the task will not be blocked for more than 15 seconds, the request
changes to:

    alofbp (fbp0,&blkadr,WAIFIN + 15 + SEC);

With a wait limit imposed, the task should check to see if the allocation suc-
ceeded or timed out. The test could be performed on the value stored in
*blkadr*:

    if ((long int) blkadr == TIMOUT)
        {
        ...   /* timeout code */;
        }

To be completely safe, the task may also test for the failure value of **BADPRM**:

    if (((long int) blkadr & 0xFFFFFFF0) == 0xFFFFFFF0)
        {
        ...   /* failure code */;
        }

## 12.4  RETURN A BLOCK TO A FIXED BLOCK POOL

An allocated block is returned to the pool when it is no longer needed:

    result = dalfbp (fbp0,blkadr);

The task that returns the block need not be the one that allocated it. Commonly, a task (**A**) allocates a block and then partially fills it with information.
Next, **A** passes the address of the block on to another task, **B**, for further processing. The block may eventually pass down a long chain of tasks. The last task
calls *dalfbp*. Unless the pool does not exist, *dalfbp* always returns **NOERR**.
Notice that the second argument supplies the address of the block being

returned directly; there is no indirection for deallocation, as there must be for allocation.

Once a block has been deallocated, all previous users are honor-bound not to reference its contents.

## 12.5 DELETE FIXED BLOCK POOL

An FBP may be deleted by the command:

result = dlfbp (fbp0);

Deleting a pool releases the internal support structures and makes them available for other uses. Any pending requests for allocation are terminated with the value **DLTPND** (deletion pending). After a pool is deleted, its memory space can be reformed into another pool.

## 12.6 CREATE COMMON MEMORY POOL

Fixed block pools are most appropriate in applications that share areas of just a few different sizes. In such cases, it is feasible to have a pool for each possible size and take advantage of the speed of FBP services.

As the number of different sizes increases, it soon becomes impractical (or at least inefficient in terms of memory use) to have so many pools. Rather, such applications would need a pool that permits a more general type of allocation scheme. The Common Memory Pool (CMP) provides the required generality.

A CMP is still organized in blocks, but a task can now allocate a contiguous area that spans several blocks. In effect, an allocation can be for any size, up to the full capacity of the pool.

Creation of a CMP follows the same pattern as with a fixed pool. The request still stipulates the key, base address, global/local specifier, block size, and overall pool size. The only differences are that the pool size is now the total number of bytes available within the pool, and the block size must be a power of 2. The latter is enforced by making the create parameter the logarithm (base 2) of the block size. The permissible range is 1 to 30.

A typical call to create a CMP is:

#define CMP0  0x434D5030

```
long int  cmp0;        /* pool identifier */

cmp0 = crcmp (-1L,CMP0,0xB0000,20480L,6L);
```

In this case, the pool is 20480 bytes long, beginning at global address 0xB0000. Blocks are 64 bytes each.

MTOS-UX allocates memory within a CMP using a first-fit search algorithm. It reserves one bit per block at the beginning of the pool area to know which blocks are allocated. As a result, the larger the value of the block size, the less pool area that is taken for control and the faster the allocation search for a given number of bytes. However, if the block size is too large, the allocated area may often be much larger than needed, since allocations are always in terms of whole blocks. Thus, the block size is a compromise between speed of allocation (for which large blocks are advantageous) and waste of memory (for which small blocks are advantageous). Popular values are 6 (64-byte blocks) to 10 (1024-byte blocks).

For a successful creation, the function returns the pool identifier. For failure, the return value is **BADPRM** when a parameter is out of the accepted range or **QUEFUL** when there are no internal resources remaining to create a pool.

If the base address is odd, it is rounded up to the next even value, while if the pool length is odd it is rounded down to an even value. As usual, any task that knows the key can determine the identifier:

```
cmp0 = getcmp (CMP0);
```

**BADPRM** indicates that there is no CMP with the given key.


## 12.7 TRANSIENT PROGRAM AREA

Most pools are created for the exclusive use of the application tasks. When the OS needs memory for its own internal needs, it generally takes it from private, dedicated areas. However, there is one set of pools that is shared by both tasks and the OS. These are the Transient Program Areas (TPAs). There is always a global TPA. For a multiple-processor system, there is normally also one local TPA per processor. The keys for these special CMPs are '.GTA' and '.LT0' to '.LTF'.

Task stacks are always formed within a TPA. Tasks that are created dynamically from relocatable files are built within a TPA. In addition, space for message buffers and controlled shared variables is taken from a TPA. Even so, a TPA is just a CMP; it is available to any task that wants to use it.

## 12.8 ALLOCATE MEMORY FROM CMP

A request to allocate memory from a CMP requires not only a selection of the pool and coordination information, but the length of the desired area as well:

        int *alobf;            /* buffer for starting addr of allocated area */

        alloc (cmp0,256L,&alobf,WAIFIN + 150 + MS);

will wait no more than 150 ms for 256 bytes. The request:

        alloc (cmp0,100L,&alobr,WAIFIN + IMONLY);

will allocate 100 bytes, but only if it is immediately available. Finally,

        long int  msgsiz;      /* (maximum) message size, bytes */

        alloc (cmp0,msgsiz,&alobf,CLEF3);

will allocate the number of bytes given in variable *msgsiz*, without time limit, and set local event flag 3 when the allocation is completed.

Usually, the first argument is the identifier of a CMP as returned by *crcmp* or *getcmp*. However, as a convenience shorthand, the argument may also be −1 to designate the global TPA, or 0 to 15 to designate a local TPA. A parameter error is generated if the pool does not exist.

The number of *bytes* to be allocated is specified in the second argument. (If the number is not a multiple of the block size, it is automatically rounded up to the next multiple.) The request always fails immediately if the allocation exceeds the entire capacity of the CMP.

As with *alofbp*, the last argument must point to a buffer into which the OS can store the address of the allocated memory. Since for **CLEF** and **CSIG** coordination, the allocation address buffer is the only means by which the task can determine the fate of the request, error values are also stored. An allocated area is not initialized. If two separate requests are made, the two allocated areas are not likely to be contiguous.

## 12.9  DEALLOCATE MEMORY

The system call:

    result = dalloc (cmp0,256L,alobf);

deallocates a contiguous pool area 256 bytes long, starting at the address supplied by *alobf*. (If the length is not a multiple of the block size, it is automatically rounded up to the next multiple.) Note that *alobf* contains the address directly; it is not a pointer to the address. As with *alloc*, the first argument is either a pool identifier, −1 or 0 to 15.

The function returns with **NOERR** if successful and with **BADPRM** if not. Failure occurs if the area being returned was not taken from the given pool, or if it is not marked internally as being currently allocated.

The task that does the deallocation need not be the one that made the original allocation. For example, suppose that a task obtains 256 bytes for a message buffer. The task then passes the address of the buffer on to another task which acts on the message and then deallocates the message buffer. The ability to share areas freely among tasks is one of the strengths of the pool facility.

Furthermore, an allocated area need not be deallocated in total; it can be released in parts. In the foregoing example, suppose that the task obtained 256 bytes because that is the maximum message size. While forming the message (say, based on input text), the task determines that only 192 bytes are actually needed and releases 64 bytes. After processing the message, the recipient task decides to deallocate 128 bytes immediately and retain 64 bytes for a summary record. Finally, at the end of the day, the last 64 bytes are released to complete the deallocation.

## 12.10  DELETE COMMON MEMORY POOL

Any CMP, other than a TPA, may be purged by a delete command:

    result = dlcmp (cmp0);

Unsatisfied allocation requests are terminated with the value **DLTPND**.

Some applications benefit by collecting all or most of the spare memory into the global TPA. For example, suppose there is a half-million-byte random-access memory (RAM) board in the system. Approximately 200K bytes are needed for permanent storage. The remaining 300K bytes are placed in the global TPA. At some point, a set of tasks need, say, 100 buffers of size 36 bytes for temporary storage during one phase of their work. The task can allocate that area from the TPA:

    alloc (−1,3600L,&alobf,WAIFIN);

It can then have the OS form that allocated TPA area into another pool:

    tmpf = crfbp (−1L,TMPF,alobf,100L,36L);

from which the tasks can obtain 36-byte buffers as needed. When that phase of the work is completed, the temporary pool is deleted, to return the area to the TPA:

    dlcmp (tmpf);

## 12.11  UNIX-LIKE STORAGE ALLOCATION FUNCTIONS

UNIX includes a general-purpose memory allocation package that is described under **malloc (3C)** in the System V documentation. MTOS-UX library **ALOLIB.C** has a corresponding set of functions, implemented in terms of *alloc* and *dalloc*. Storage is taken from the Global TPA; coordination is **WAIFIN**. The four functions are:

| | |
|---|---|
| long *calloc* (num, siz) | allocates space for *num* items, each of which is *siz* bytes long. The allocated space is initialized to 0. The function returns a pointer to the space if successful or 0 if not. |
| int *free* (adr) | deallocates space pointed to by *adr* that was obtained by a call to *calloc*, *malloc*, or *realloc*. Under MTOS, the function returns **NOERR** if successful or **BAD-PRM** if not. Note that UNIX does not return a value so that success or failure cannot be determined. |
| long *malloc* (nb) | allocates *nb* bytes. The allocated space is not cleared. The function returns a pointer to the space if successful or 0 if not. |
| long *realloc* (adr, nb) | changes the size of a previously allocated block to *nb*. The contents of the block are unchanged up to the smaller of the new and old size. The function |

returns a pointer to the space (which may have moved) if successful, or 0 if not. Upon failure, the old space remains allocated.

In terms of these functions, an allocation of 256 bytes would be:

alobf = malloc (256L);

or

alobf = calloc (1L,256L);

## 12.12 STORAGE MANAGEMENT TECHNIQUES

The chief advantage of a fixed block pool is that it permits the OS to maintain the pool with very efficient techniques. When the pool is created, the given area is formed into a linked-list of blocks, that is, a chain in which each block contains the address of the next block. An internal pointer leads to the first available block. Allocation requests are then satisfied by removing the first block from the start of the list. Similarly, deallocation is performed by adding the returned block back into the chain. Since no searching is ever involved, the time required for both allocation and deallocation does not depend upon the number of blocks remaining in the pool.

Unfortunately, a linked list of fixed-size blocks cannot be easily extended to the more general needs of a common memory pool. A CMP permits a task to allocate an area of any arbitrary size. Consequently, the OS must be able to find a sequence of N *contiguous* blocks whose combined size satisfies the request. (N = requested size/block size, rounded upward.) Simply taking the first N blocks does not work since they are not likely to be contiguous.

Several general storage techniques are available for the internal management of a CMP. MTOS-UX happens to employ an internal array in which the status of each allocatable block is represented as a single bit. (The bit is set when the block is allocated and reset when it is returned.) Allocation involves searching the bit map for N consecutive zeros. Special techniques are employed to make the bit map search fairly efficient. Nevertheless, the search time does vary with the fragmentation of the pool: the number and distribution of currently available blocks. For deallocation the bits are reset by direct computation without any searching.

In some alternate allocation schemes, the OS maintains a linked list of allocatable areas, each of which may extend over more than one block. Allocation still involves searching, but over areas rather than their component blocks.

When a large enough area is found, the allocated space is removed from the area, and the reduced area is put back on the list. With this technique, deallocation requires either placing the returned space on the list as a separate new area or combining it with an existing area. In addition, the returned space may fill the gap between two existing areas so that two list elements merge into one.

The details of how the OS maintains a pool are generally hidden from the task that makes allocation requests. Nevertheless, the statistical properties of allocation processing often cannot be ignored in real-time programming. Nor can the possibility of finding no memory available at the time it is needed. It is common to preallocate some reserve memory in very critical applications. Although this somewhat defeats the purpose of having a shareable pool, if not overdone it can be a prudent technique.

With MTOS, when memory is deallocated it is immediately returned to the pool and possibly given to a task that had already queued an allocation request. This is normally done in real-time systems. In other environments, the return of deallocated areas is sometimes deferred until there is little or no memory left in the pool. At that point, the OS must do significant processing to reclaim the accumulated returned space and reconstitute the pool. This processing is known as "garbage collection." It is generally to be avoided in real-time applications since it introduces an unpredictable and possibly lengthy interruption to task work. While garbage collection is being done by the OS, even the most important task is blocked.

## 12.13  SUMMARY

A pool is a contiguous area in memory that is logically divided into fixed length subunits called blocks. Individual blocks may be dynamically allocated and deallocated. A task submits a create-pool request specifying the address and length of the area, and the size of the block. The OS builds the required support structures and returns the identifier of the new-born pool. Thereafter, any task that knows the identifier can allocate blocks from the pool.

A pool may be global or local depending upon the physical location of the underlying memory area. A global pool exists in global memory and is thus accessible by every task. A local pool exists in the local memory of a particular CPU board. It is accessible only by tasks running on that board.

MTOS-UX provides two types of pools: fixed block pools and common memory pools. A fixed block pool (FBP) delivers exactly one block per request. Because of this restriction, allocation is very fast. A common memory pool (CMP) permits allocations of any number of contiguous blocks, up to the whole available pool area. The price of this complete flexibility is greater internal processing time.


## EXERCISES

**12.1** Show the steps required to create a fixed block pool large enough for 1000 records, each 64 bytes long, taking the storage from the TPA via purely MTOS calls. Recode using the UNIX library to obtain the storage.

**12.2** A task allocates 1000 bytes from a CMP whose block size is 64 bytes. Later, it finds that only 200 bytes are needed. Code (a) the initial allocation, (b) the deallocation of the excess portion, and (c) the final deallocation. Hint: Deallocations must be on block boundaries.

**12.3** The possible permanent loss of pool blocks could be prevented by an automatic deallocation upon termination of the task that did the allocation. Why is this not a good idea?

# Chapter 13
## PHYSICAL INPUT/OUTPUT

===============================================================

Real-time applications need both physical and logical input/output (I/O). In physical I/O, the user selects a particular console, printer, disk, or other device and indicates the hardware details of the operation to be performed. For example, for a disk write, the programmer selects the starting logical block address and number of blocks, as well as the source data address and mode of coordinating with the completion of the transfer.

For logical I/O, the user deals in terms of a file on a given volume (disk or portion of a disk). The programmer has no control over the placement of the file within particular physical blocks. Such details are handled by the file system component of the OS. Furthermore, the coordination mode is commonly fixed at the unlimited wait until the service is completed.

This chapter is concerned primarily with physical I/O. The file system is described in the next chapter.


### 13.1 PERIPHERAL UNITS

Physical I/O is always targeted to a specific peripheral device. Electrically, the device is connected to the computer through an interfacing chip or set of chips. Computationally, the device is connected to the application through an operating system support structure called a *peripheral unit*. Peripheral units are dynamic objects. Thus, they have two names: a 4-byte key selected by the programmer and a long integer identifier selected by the OS when the unit is created.

Most real-time applications utilize a terminal for routine communication with an operator, as well as for error logging and debugging. The unit that corresponds to this terminal is called the System Console. Its key is 'SYSC'. The System Console may be the only byte-oriented I/O device available. Similarly, there may be a System Printer (with key 'SYSP') and System Disk (with key 'SYSD'). Even though system units are common, they are not required; the OS can run in the absence of all such units, even the System Console.

Normally, the units for standard devices are created during system start-up. As a result, they are immediately available to every task.

## 13.2  STANDARD CONSOLE

The standard UNIX-like I/O library functions, such as *printf* and *getchar*, perform their I/O on the "STandard Console" (**STC**) for the requesting task. This console can vary from task to task; it need not be the System Console.

    printf ("This line goes to the task's Standard Console\n\r");

When a task is created, its **STC** is set to that of the creating task. Thereafter, each time the task is started via a *start* request, the **STC** of the requester becomes the **STC** of the target. For a task started in response to unsolicited input on a console, that console becomes the new **STC**. (This is very convenient for a command line interpreter, debugger, or other task that can be invoked from more than one console.)

A task can always change its **STC** to any unit for which the identifier is known. Thus, if a task wishes to output to the System Printer via *printf*, it can first get the identifier of the printer:

    #define SYSP  0x53595350

    long int  SYPid;        /* id of SYstem Printer */

    SYPid = getuid (SYSP);

And then install that unit as the task's Standard Console:

    setstc (SYPid);

The two service calls may also be combined into a single line of code, without bothering to save the identifier:

    setstc (getuid (SYSP));

    printf ("This line goes to the System Printer\n\r");

For *getuid*, the response **BADPRM** means that there is no unit with the given key; for *setstc*, **BADPRM** means that the argument is not the identifier of a peripheral unit.

A task may ask for the identifier of its current Standard Console:

    int  mySTC; /* unit id of STandard Console */

    mySTC = getstc ();

    Putting all these ideas together, the following sequence prints one line on
the Standard Console, switches to the System Printer for two lines, and then
reverts to the original Standard Console:

    printf ("This line goes to the task's Standard Console\n\r");

    mySTC = getstc ();              /* save current STC */

    setstc (getuid (SYSP));         /* change to System Printer */

    printf ("This line goes to the System Printer\n\r");

    setstc (mySTC);                 /* reinstate saved STC */


## 13.3  PHYSICAL I/O REQUEST

    The components of the I/O library, including *printf*, are written as task-level
C functions.  They, in turn, invoke an OS service, *pio*, to do the actual physical
operations.  The formal definition of this service call is:

    int  pio (uid, fun, prty, parms, stabfr, qual)
      long int  uid, fun, prty, *parms, stabfr[], qual;

The first parameter, *uid*, specifies the unit to which the request applies.  The
specific operation (function) is encoded by *fun*.  All devices are capable of the
first two of the following operations; most can perform all four: **PIORSV**
(reserve), **PIORLS** (release), **PIOWRI** (write), and **PIOREA** (read).

    **PIORSV** reserves the given unit.  While a unit is reserved, no other task can
use it (except by preemption).  Requests by other tasks are queued.  **PIORLS**
releases the unit.  The exclusivity provided by reserve/release is especially important for shared units, such as the System Console and System Printer.  Unless
this feature is invoked, the lines of text from two or more reports or messages
can become intermixed.

    A preemption specifier, **PREEMP**, may be added to each operation code
other than  **PIORSV** and **PIORLS**.  In this case, the normal reserve restrictions
are disregarded and the unit is treated as though it was unreserved.  Furthermore, a preemptive request is performed ahead of any normal request on the
unit's wait queue.  However, any request currently being processed on the unit

is allowed to complete. Preemption is intended mainly for emergencies so that critical communications can proceed even if the communications unit is reserved.

The *pio* parameter *prty* specifies the priority of the request. The range is 255 for the most urgent requests to 1 for the least urgent. The special value 0 selects the current priority of the requesting task. Normally, *prty* is 0.

Any supporting parameters for the function are supplied via *parms*. This argument is normally the address of a structure whose components vary with the type of unit. The details are given later. If there are no parameters (as is true for **PIORSV** and **PIORLS**), *parms* should be 0.

The last two parameters are the address of the results buffer and the value of the coordination qualifier, respectively. The qualifier is the usual coordination-mode-plus-optional-wait-limit. The results buffer is an array consisting of *two or more* long integers. Upon the completion of the function, the first will contain the overall results indicator: **NOERR**, **BADPRM**, **TIMOUT**, **QUEFUL**, **RSVERR** (reserve/release error), or **PHYFLR** (physical failure). The second long integer will contain the number of characters input. For output, this tally will be 0. For those units that report controller status information, such information is returned starting at *stabuf*[2].

The following sequence reserves a unit, outputs one line, inputs one line, and then releases the unit. The priority of the requesting task is used in each call:

```
long int  scuid,stabuf[2];

pio (scuid,PIORSV,0L,(long *)0,stabuf,WAIFIN+1+MIN);
pio (scuid,PIOWRI,0L,&st1msg,stabuf,WAIFIN);
pio (scuid,PIOREA,0L,&st2msg,stabuf,WAIFIN);
pio (scuid,PIORLS,0L,(long *)0,stabuf,CTUNOC);
```

The details of the I/O parameter block (*st1msg, st2msg*) will be given shortly.

## 13.4  DRIVERS

Physical I/O encompasses such basic operations as input, output, and formatting. These functions are performed by a special program called a *driver*. Drivers are specific to the type of hardware involved. Thus, there is a driver for consoles interfaced via an MC68901 MFP and a different program for consoles using a Z8530 SCC.

The following names have been established for common drivers:

**CONDRV:** for CRT, TTY or printer/keyboard consoles

**SKBDRV:** for memory-mapped screen/keyboard consoles

**DSKDRV:** for hard or floppy disks

**MDKDRV:** for disklike structures implemented in memory

**SPRDRV:** for printers with serial connections

**PPRDRV:** for printers with parallel connections

**UNXDRV:** for communications with UNIX (terminal emulator)

**MEMDRV:** for contiguous memory without disk structure

The list of drivers is open-ended; it is easy for a programmer to write and install a driver for a device not already supported in the standard library.

## 13.5 CONSOLE DRIVERS

The organization of the parameter block pointed to by the *pio* argument *parms* depends upon the driver that controls the target unit. To simplify using various drivers, the parameter blocks have been arranged so that an entire class of drivers can share the same structure. The classes defined so far are byte-oriented devices (**CONDRV, SKBDRV, SPRDRV, PPRDRV, MEMDRV**) and block-oriented, random-access devices (**DSKDRV, MDKDRV**). There is also a special set of parameter blocks just for the UNIX terminal emulator driver (**UNXDRV**).

Any individual parameter block has a very simple structure with just a few components. However, because of the large number of combinations of drivers and functions, a full explanation of all of them is beyond the scope of this guide. By way of illustration, we will present some aspects of the most common driver, that for a console (**CONDRV** or **SKBDRV**).

### 13.5.1 Generalized Parameter Block

The following parameter block supports all current functions for the console drivers, as well as other byte-oriented devices:

```
struct bodiop
  {
    char      *aub;      /* addr of main user bfr */
    long int   lub;      /* len of main user bfr */
```

```
char      *axb;      /* addr of auxiliary bfr */
long int  spl;       /* timeout for read, or special data */
};
```

The meaning of individual items depends upon the function.


### 13.5.2 Functions and Features

Console drivers **CONDRV** and **SKBDRV** provide one write and three read functions. **PIOWRI** outputs the given text to the CRT screen or printing mechanism. The text can be in read-write or read-only memory. The address of the text is given in *aub*, and its length is in *lub*. However, the write ends when the first NULL (0) is found in the text. (The NULL is not output.) As a result, it is common to set the length arbitrarily high and let a NULL terminate the text. None of the other members of structure *bodiop* are used.

As an example, the fixed parameter block to output up to 250 characters from the null-terminated string *mytext* would be:

```
char  mytext[250];

struct bodiop st1msg = {mytext, sizeof (mytext), 0, 0};
```

During the write, the driver accepts certain unsolicited input characters, including X-OFF (control-S, 0x13), X-ON (control-Q, 0x11), ESCAPE (0x1B), and control-D (0x04). X-OFF suspends the output; X-ON continues it. These command characters permit the operator to hold a section of text for prolonged examination. (Otherwise, the text might be pushed off the screen by subsequent lines of output.) An unsolicited control-D starts the Debugger, if it has been created and is currently Dormant. Similarly, an unsolicited ESCAPE starts a task that is specified when the unit is created. This could be a command line interpreter or other operator-query task.

**PIOREA** inputs ASCII text into a given buffer, with limited editing capability. The parameters are the address of the input buffer (*aub*), the maximum number of characters to be read (*lub*), and the maximum time the driver will wait for the entire text to be input (*spl*).

The maximum number of characters includes the mandatory CARRIAGE RETURN that terminates the read. The maximum wait time starts when the driver is entered; it does not include any time spent waiting to enter the driver. The time is specified in the same way as the pause interval. Thus, to create a fixed parameter block that inputs up to 80 characters into *mybfr*, with a 2-minute time out:

    char mybfr[80];

    struct bodiop st2msg = {mybfr, sizeof (mybfr), 0, 2 + MIN};

For this function, the driver first outputs the default prompt "? " and then expects the input text to be entered. The read ends when a CARRIAGE RETURN (CR, 0x0D) is entered. Since the buffer is not cleared by the driver, upon return from *pio*, the buffer will contain the input text, the CR, and any remnant of the original content.

Each character typed is echoed to the screen or printer portion of the console. A control character, other than a CARRIAGE RETURN, LINE FEED (0x0A), or BELL (0x07), is echoed as a '^' followed by the corresponding uppercase letter. Thus, ENQUIRE (0x05) echoes as "^E." If a non-CR is typed when there is only one byte left in the input buffer, the driver responds by echoing a BELL. This alerts the operator that the buffer is full. The non-CR character is discarded.

DELETE (0x7F) may be typed at any time prior to the terminating CR. It deletes the last character, provided the number of input characters left in the buffer is not 0. For a CRT, the DELETE blanks out the last character echoed and moves the cursor back one position.

CONTROL-X (0x18) resets the fill pointer back to the beginning of the buffer, but does not clear out any text already entered. (Subsequent text overwrites whatever is left in the buffer.) For a CRT, CONTROL-X moves the cursor back to the prompt. The display is blanked as the cursor travels leftward.

PIOREP inputs ASCII text into a given buffer, with the same editing capability and parameters as PIOREA. However, PIOREP permits the caller to specify the prompt string (*axb*). Thus, this function is a write-then-read as a single service. The prompt must be terminated by a null. The example given within the previous section would become:

    char myprompt[] = "\n\rEnter up to 80 characters, incl. CR: ";

    struct bodiop st3msg = {mybfr, sizeof (mybfr), myprompt, 2 + MIN};

when using *myprompt*, instead of the default prompt. Since the write and read are treated as one request, it is not possible for another task to interpose I/O between the prompt and corresponding response.

The third console read function, **PIORE1**, is provided to support *getchar*. There is no prompt. The first character input satisfies the request; there is no terminal CR. The input is not echoed as part of this function (but is likely to be printed via a separate request).

For **PIORE1**, the parameter *aub* points to the address of the input buffer and *spl* specifies the maximum wait time. No other part of *bodiop* is involved. Thus, the following code will input a line of text and echo it in uppercase:

```
char  ch;                              /* I/O character */

struct bodiop  iob1 = {&ch,1,0,2+MIN};    /* I/O parameter block */

do
   {
      pio (scuid,PIORE1,0L,&iob1,stabuf,WAIFIN);  /* read */
      ch = toupper (ch);                          /* cvt to UC */
      pio (scuid,PIOWRI,0L,&iob1,stabuf,WAIFIN);  /* write */
   }
while (ch != '\n');
```

## 13.6  CREATE UNIT

Most routine I/O is targeted to the System units, which are created during start-up. Nevertheless, a task can also create a new unit dynamically. This might be done for special application-dependent equipment, such as a communication device or analog-to-digital converter.

The C function to create a peripheral I/O unit is:

```
long int  unitid;              /* unit identifier */

unitid = crpun (u68584);
```

The argument, *u68584*, points to a structure containing the parameters for the unit:

```
struct ucd
   {
   long int  uky;       /* key */
   int       (*drv)();  /* addr of driver program */
   long int  uns;       /* key of unsolicited interrupt task (0=none) */
   int       *ddp;      /* addr of driver-dependent parameters */
```

```
    char      pid;      /* id of processor receiving interrupts {MP} */
    char      spr;      /* spare byte */
    char      ivn[4];   /* vector num for interrupts 0-3 (0 = none) */
};
```

If there is already a unit with the given key, then the function returns with **DUP-PUN**. This is not considered an error, so that the error signal, 26, is not sent. **BADPRM** is given if any of the verifiable components of the *ucd* are out of range. Components such as interrupt vector numbers are generally verifiable, while the driver address is not. If the internal facilities for creating units are exhausted, the response is **QUEFUL**. For success, the function returns the unit identifier.

Certain components of the *ucd* need further explanation. If a read request is being serviced when an input character arrives, the character is processed, which typically results in the storage of that character within the requester's input buffer. However, suppose the input is unsolicited, that is, there is no active input request. A driver can ignore the input, or it can start a task which will then issue a read to capture subsequent characters. For a Console, component *uns* specifies the key of the task that is to be started if the unsolicited input character is an ESCAPE. Similarly, the *uns* task might be called to handle an out-of-paper interrupt from a printer or a door-open interrupt from a floppy disk.

The argument *ddp* is the address of a structure containing further parameters. The nature of the structure is driver-dependent. Often the structure contains physical data, such as the BAUD rate for serial devices, or the total number of blocks for disks.

For single-processor installations, component *pid* is 0. Otherwise, it is the index of the processor to which the interrupt lines are attached (0–15).

MTOS-UX can accommodate an interface that generates up to four different interrupts. The interrupt numbers are contained in the *ivn* array. If there is only one interrupt, its number goes into *inv*[0], and *inv*[1] to *inv*[3] are set to 0.

The UCD is often in ROM. However, after the unit is created, the UCD is never referenced by the OS. Thus, if the UCD is in RAM, that area is available for reuse once *crpun* returns.

As a concrete example, the *ucd* to create the system console using the MK68564 SIO on a VME130 board is:

```
#define SYSC  0x53595343
#define dSYD  0x2E535944
```

```
int CONDRV ();          /* driver entry point */

struct
  {
    char *bas;          /* base addr of SIO */
    char  lvl;          /* interrupt level */
    char  chn;          /* channel: 0 = A, 1 = B */
    char  bau;          /* BAUD rate code: -1 = read switches */
    char  fil;          /* spare byte */
  } conPrm = {(char *)0xFFFB0040, 5, 0, (char)0xFF, 0};


struct ucd  u68564 =
             {SYSC, CONDRV, dSYD, (int *)&conPrm, 0, 0x5C, 0x5E, 0, 0};
```

## 13.7 PHYSICAL I/O AT THE TASK LEVEL

Some operating systems accomplish physical I/O primarily at the task level. Thus, a "driver" task is restarted every time the hardware generates an input-buffer-full, output-buffer-empty, or other I/O-related interrupt. The idea is to give the programmer complete freedom to write and debug drivers with the same facilities that are available to tasks.

While the goal is laudable, the cost in terms of unnecessary execution time usually makes this approach unattractive. A context switch to the driver task takes about as long as any simple service call. Thus, to output 80 bytes of ASCII text would be equivalent to about 80 service calls.

Under MTOS, the driver is part of the kernel. Interrupts are handled without a context switch (by saving and restoring a few work registers). A context switch is needed only for the last interrupt—the one that completes the service.

Although kernel-level drivers are not able to make standard (task-level) service calls, they can still obtain all the services that they are likely to need via an equivalent mechanism. Drivers can allocate memory, start a task, queue a message, pause, set an event flag, and more.

Kernel-level drivers also differ from task-level drivers in yet another significant way. A kernel driver inherently has a priority greater than that of any task. (Outstanding kernel-level work is always completed before resuming task work.) As a result, there is no danger that a kernel driver will lose an input character because it could not capture it before the next one arrives. Task drivers are subject to such data overruns.

Despite the advantages of working at the kernel level, the ease of debugging at the task level remains attractive, especially for complex drivers, such as those that do packet encoding and decoding. In such cases, it is common to divide the overall work between a kernel driver and supporting task. The task does the high-level protocol and packet work. The driver just blindly sends and receives fully formed packets as unstructured blocks of text.

## 13.8  SPECIAL INTERRUPTS

Normally, all external interrupts (other than the clock) are handled by a driver. Nevertheless, some special interrupts may not fit comfortably into the driver paradigm. The most common is a power-failure interrupt. For these, it may be necessary for the OS to service the interrupt and then start a given task. The code sequence:

```
int pfl_sub ();          /* define pfl_sub as a procedure */

long int  pfl_tid;       /* id of power failure task */
    ...

result = contsk (0L,pfl_tid,66L,pfl_sub);
```

connects the power failure task (whose identifier has been previously stored as *pfl_tid*) to the power failure interrupt (66 in this example) on processor 0. Prior to starting the selected task, the OS will call procedure *pfl_sub*. The procedure executes immediately, in the context of the OS. Thus, it cannot issue task-level service calls. The purpose of the interrupt handler procedure is to perform hardware-related manipulations that cannot wait for the task, or that require the privilege level of the OS. If the last argument of *contsk* is 0, no procedure is called.

The task starts executing at its default priority, which is likely to be the highest value for an emergency-recovery task. The argument presented to the task is four times the interrupt number. This permits one task to service several interrupts. Although the example focused on a power failure interrupt, the machinery is very general. Any task can be connected to any interrupt.

## 13.9  SUMMARY

Physical input/output is concerned with the transfer of information between a task and an external peripheral device. Physical I/O differs from logical I/O in that for the former the task must supply all details of the transfer, including assignment of blocks for a disk access. For logical I/O (which is covered in the next chapter), most of the physical details are hidden from the task.

Physical I/O is mediated by drivers and units. A driver is a kernel-level program that translates a task's input or output request into the sequence of individual steps that are needed to cause the interfacing hardware to perform the required transfer. Typical steps involve reading and writing the control and status registers of a peripheral controller chip, or its supporting interrupt controller. There is a separate driver for each type of device (console, printer, disk, etc.). Even within a given class, say, consoles, each arrangement of interfacing hardware requires a different set of steps, thus, a different driver.

Normally, a driver is a reentrant program that is able to service several similar peripheral devices simultaneously. A unit is the dynamic data needed to run a driver on behalf of a specific physical device. A unit is a dynamic object that can be created just as a task or memory pool can.

A request for physical input/output is made by issuing a *pio* service call. The parameters of the call select the unit (which also selects the driver), specify the function (such as read or write), supply any needed auxiliary information, and stipulate the priority and the coordination factors.

## EXERCISES

**13.1** Compose a utility function to output a given character to the requester's Standard Console and to the System Printer, if there is one. What would happen if the Standard Console were the System Printer? How can this problem be overcome?

**13.2** Suppose a task builds a message in a fixed buffer area. It expects to output the message via *pio* and then build another message in that same area. What coordination mode or modes can be used in the *pio* request? Suppose that the task allocates a new buffer area for each message. How should coordination now be accomplished?

**13.3** Implement the Portable C functions get string (*gets*) and put string (*puts*). These are described in Figure 14-6.

**13.4** For many of the peripheral chips that are used to interface to a console, it is possible to perform both input and output simultaneously and independently. Why is it still hard to design a console driver that could handle two requests at the same time—one for input and one for output? Is it any easier if the "console" is used only to send messages between computers (as an interprocessor link)?

# Chapter 14
## FILE SYSTEM

=============================================================

A file system (**FS**) enables a task to maintain information on a mass storage device, such as a disk, without being concerned with the details of how the data is physically placed on the device. Thus, file system I/O is a higher level of abstraction than the physical I/O that was described in the previous chapter.

A file system deals with a generic mass storage device called a *volume*. Characteristically, it has a (large) number of storage blocks that are both alterable and randomly accessible. A typical volume is an entire disk or a contiguous portion of one. It can be read/write memory (the so-called RAM disk). Each alterable block (a sector of a disk; a byte or word of memory) is addressed via an index number which runs from zero to the number of available blocks minus one. Thus, the volume is a contiguous, but unstructured physical medium on which information can be stored.

A file system is the mechanism by which information is placed on the volume so that later the information can be retrieved. To facilitate its access, the information is commonly organized into groups of logically related data. Each group is called a *file*. One file might contain the raw data picked up by a weather radar beam during the last 20 sweeps. Another file might contain the corresponding profiles of wind shear or other factors computed from the raw radar data. To be able to specify a particular file, each has a unique name with respect to the volume.

The logical organization and structure of the information within a file is understood only at the task level; to the FS a file is just an ordered sequence of bytes (a "byte stream"). At one extreme, a file may be empty (zero bytes); at the other, it may encompass all the available space on the volume.

There are many different industry standard and proprietary file systems that are used in real-time applications. They differ in how the information within a file is stored, the degree of freedom in assigning file names, and other details. Some popular standard file systems are MS-DOS, UNIX System V, and UNIX System 4.2 (Berkeley).

A file management system (**FMS**) is a program that lets a task use a file system. An FMS is an implementation of the storage rules and other conventions set by the FS. For a given FS there can be many equivalent file management systems.

Most file systems distinguish between two types of files: directories and data files. The difference is more in usage than in substance. A *directory* is a file built, maintained, and accessed only by the FMS. Its content describes other files and enables the FMS to access them. In contrast, a *data file* stores information supplied by the users. The content of a data file is immaterial to an FMS.

Some file systems further subdivide a file into subsequences of contiguous bytes called records. A *record* is a set of data that is grouped together as a single coherent unit because all the data pertain to the same time, event, person, and so on. For example, if we have a file of customers, each record might consist of the following data:

| bytes: | 00 - 25 | Name |
|---|---|---|
| | 26 - 60 | Address |
| | 61 - 99 | Products purchased (item, date and status) |

In this case, the size of each record is fixed at 100 bytes. Record size may also vary record by record.

When used, records are accessed by an index number that runs from zero to the number of records currently in the file minus one:

```
file:  byte 0, byte 1, ... , byte r-1,    byte r, byte r + 1, ...
       |                                  |
       record 0                           record 1
```

With MS-DOS and UNIX the record is fictitious; the record size is neither stored in the file nor in the directory for the file. A record can be as long as you want it to be for each read or write request. The unit of actual storage is a byte. With some other file systems (such as VERSA-dos), the record size is stored within the directory if all records have the same size, or are stored with each record if the size can vary from record to record.

So far, we have been discussing only the logical nature of files. Their actual physical storage (i.e., the blocks they occupy on the volume) depends upon the type of file and the type of FS. Often the logically contiguous stream of data within a file is physically scattered over the volume. Auxiliary information is also stored that permits the FMS to access the contents of a file. The auxiliary information is invisible to the user of the file system.

## 14.1  SELECTING A FILE SYSTEM IN REAL-TIME APPLICATIONS

In many real-time systems, the FS is used for storage and retrieval of data only while the application is in progress. There is neither a requirement to prepare files before the application begins nor to access the files after the application ends. In these cases, there is no need to be compatible with any industry standard. Furthermore, to achieve high processing rates, the FS can exploit proprietary storage and access techniques that were developed especially for embedded real-time environments.

In other cases, the FS is used to couple the real-time and nonreal-time aspects of an overall application. Database files may be prepared off-line and then read by real-time tasks; data developed and stored in files by real-time tasks may be analyzed later by off-line programs. When these requirements are added, there is some advantage to having the real-time FMS use a standard file system format. Nevertheless, you pay for this advantage. All the popular standard file systems were developed for protected, general, multiuser, nonreal-time environments. They require more processing than does a file system that has been optimized for dedicated, real-time applications. Thus, compatibility with MS-DOS or UNIX incurs a loss of efficiency, but avoids the bother of conversion between the real-time and standard formats.

MTOS-UX sidesteps the decision on file format by providing a few different file systems, the most popular of which is compatible with MS-DOS. Each FMS is written in C as a set of task-level subprograms. They employ ordinary OS services, such as *pio* for physical I/O and *waisem/rlssem* for mutual exclusion.

Each FMS has certain functions that take advantage of the special characteristics of the underlying file system. Once these functions are built into the application, it is locked into using that FMS. However, in most applications, all that is ever needed are such basic services as open a file, read a record, write a record, and close a file. For these, the OS provides portable access interfaces that are the same for all file systems. Two libraries of access procedures are available: the UNIX System Interface and the Standard (Portable C) Library, as specified in Chapters 7 and 8 of "The C Programming Language" by Kernighan and Ritchie (Ke78). We will begin by illustrating these independent modes of using a file system.

## 14.2 HIERARCHICAL FILE SYSTEM

Both UNIX and MS-DOS permit directories to contain still other directories in arbitrarily long sequences. This allows data files that are logically related to each other to be placed in a hierarchical organization that reflects that relation. The top of the hierarchy is a master directory called the *root*. The bottom layers contain the data files. The names of the directories in the chain that leads from the root to a given file is called the *pathname* for the file.

A typical hierarchy of files is illustrated in Figure 14-1. The root directory contains two files, a data file called STATIC-DATA and a directory called RT-DATA. RT-DATA, in turn, has a set of directories for individual days. The days are further subdivided into hours. Finally, each hour of each day has a data file called IMG.

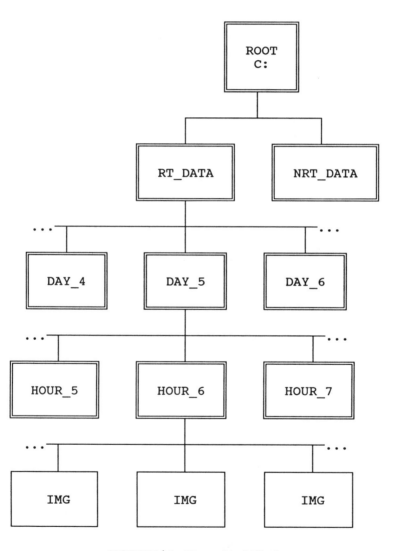

FIGURE 14-1: Hierarchical File System

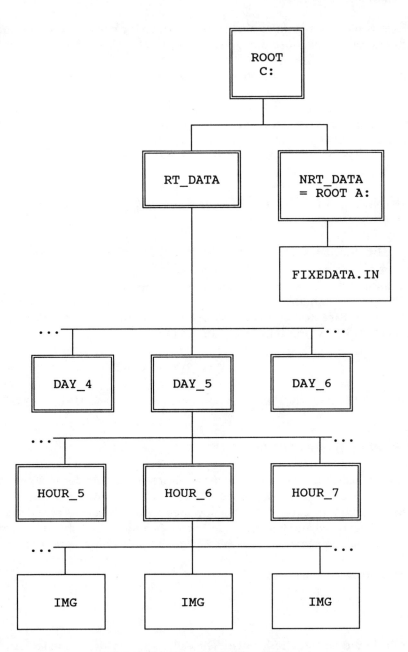

FIGURE 14-2:  Mounting a New Volume

## 14.3  VOLUME AND FILE NAMES

Various file systems differ slightly in the rules for naming volumes and files. To be concrete, we will use the conventions for MS-DOS. The main differences are in the maximum number of characters within a volume or file name, and in the separator between the directory name or names and the file name.

Under MS-DOS, each volume is designated by a colon preceded by a single letter. (The letter is assigned when the volume is entered in the FS installation data base.) This name is used by all requests that refer to the volume. A typical volume name is "A:" or "B:" for a floppy disk and "C:" for a hard disk.

File names are from one to eight characters long plus a zero to three character extension (i.e., FILENAME.EXT). The character set for forming names and extensions is:

ABCDEFGHIJKLMNOPQRSTUVWXYZ0123456789-_!@#$%^()"{}

Recall that the file systems support multilayered directories. Thus, a file is described by a pathname that starts with a volume name ("C:"), continues with one or more directories ("RT-DATA\DAY_5"), and ends with a file name ("HOUR_6.IMG"). A typical full pathname is then

"C:\RT-DATA\DAY_5\HOUR_6.IMG".

Notice that MS-DOS uses '\' as the name separator, whereas UNIX uses a '/'.


## 14.4  SUPPLEMENTAL I/O LIBRARY

As noted earlier, most real-time applications need only the services that are contained in either the UNIX compatible or Portable C libraries. Nevertheless, certain important functions were not specified within either library. These functions initialize the FS and permit the full name of a file to be abbreviated. We will describe these supplemental services (Figure 14-2) before proceeding to the standard libraries. As with all operating system facilities, the FS must be prepared prior to its first use:

fsinit ();

This call should be made only once. The call may be made by any task, even one that does not subsequently request FS services. It is also necessary to declare the physical unit on which the files are stored. Assuming that "C:" has been entered in the FS installation data as the name of a possible volume, the call:

    mount ("C:", "", 0L);

mounts (i.e., prepares) the volume for use by the FS. The second argument determines where the root directory of the new volume is placed in the overall directory organization of the file system. Note that for this first call, this argument is a null (empty) string. That places the root directory of the "C:" volume at the head of the entire file system. Figure 14-1 depicts the file structure after "C:" is mounted. The last argument is not used. It exists only for syntactic compatibility with a similar UNIX function.

    Subsequent calls mount additional volumes to expand the file structure:

    mount ("A:", "C:\NRT-DATA", 0L);

The second argument shows that the root directory of "A:" is to replace the existing directory "C:\NRT-DATA" (Figure 14-3). Because volume "A:" is logically under volume "C:", a file on "A:" has two equivalent names. The same file is accessed by either:

    "C:\NRT-DATA\FIXEDATA.IN"
or
    "A:\FIXEDATA.IN"

    The dismount function:

    umount ("A:");

closes all files under volume "A:" and releases the internal volume-related facilities for reuse by another volume.

    A task can always give the full pathname in any service that calls for a file. However, it is usually easier to set the directory portion and then use only the shorter file portion. The function:

    chdir ("C:\RT-DATA\DAY_5");

stores the given null-terminated string so it can be concatenated to subsequent file names. Up to 80 characters can be retained. The directory string can always be determined by a corresponding call:

int *chdir* (fn) — installs *fn* as the current directory. If *fn* begins with '\' or ':' then *name* completely replaces the current directory string. Otherwise, *fn* is assumed to be a subdirectory of the current directory and *fn* is concatenated with that current directory string. In either case, the function returns **NOERR** for success or **EOF** for failure.

int *clsfslib* () — deregisters the calling task as a legal user of the FS libraries. Whether the caller was previously registered or not, the function always returns **NOERR**.

int *fmtdev* (vol, fmt) — formats the volume specified by *vol*. Parameter *fmt* is available for auxiliary information. The function returns **NOERR** if successful, or **BADPRM** if not.

int *fsinit* () — prepares the FS and interface libraries. The function returns **NOERR** if successful, or **BADPRM** if not.

int *fumount* (vol) — forceably dismounts the volume specified by *vol* and makes it unavailable for further FS operations until remounted. The function is effective even if files are open when it is invoked. The requesting task must be in the root directory of the root volume. The function returns **NOERR** if successful, or **BADPRM** if not.

int *getdir* (bfr) — copies the full pathname of the current directory into *bfr* as a null-terminated string. The pathname can be up to 80 characters long.

int *mount* (vol, dir, x) — mounts the volume specified by *vol* replacing the directory specified by *dir*. Parameter *x* is not used. The requesting task must be in the root directory of the root volume. The function returns **NOERR** if successful, or **BADPRM** if not.

int *opnfslib* () — registers the calling task as a legal user of the FS libraries. The function returns **NOERR** if successful, or **BADPRM** if not.

int *search* (fn, rec, dr) — searches the current directory for a file named *fn*, starting at directory record *rec*. If found, the directory record is copied into user buffer *dr*. *fn* may contain '?' which matches any one character or '*' which matches 0 or more characters at the end of a name. The function returns **EOF** for failure or the record number at which the first match occurred for success.

int *umount* (vol) — dismounts the volume specified by *vol*. The requesting task must be in the root directory of the root volume. The function returns **NOERR** if successful, or **BADPRM** if not.

FIGURE 14-3: Supplemental File Functions

```
    char  curdrs[80];

    getdir (curdrs);
```

## 14.5  UNIX-LIKE I/O LIBRARY

A file must be opened before it can be accessed:

```
#include "STDIO.H"

long  fd1;                /* file descriptor for file 1 */

chdir ("C:\RT-DATA\DAY_5");

fd1 = open ("HOUR_6.IMG", 0L);   /* open file for read only */
```

The first argument points to the file; the second is the access mode.  Mode 0 is read only, mode 1 is write only, and mode 2 is read and write. The request *open* returns a file descriptor if the open succeeds or **BADPRM** (–1) if an error occurs.  A file descriptor is an internal file identifier, akin to the identifier for a task or other object.

Note that all parameters of library calls are assumed to have been passed as long integers or pointers.  Thus, the mode is given as 0L, not just 0.

With the default installation values, there can be up to five files open simultaneously for each task.  The five is a configuration parameter that is readily changed.

A file must already exist or it can't be opened via *open*.  The UNIX-like library requires a separate request for creation:

```
long  fd2;                /* file descriptor for file 2 */

fd2 = creat ("FILE_2", 0L);
```

Function *creat* either creates a new file or deletes the content of an old one. Either way it leaves the file open in read-write mode and returns a file descriptor. A value of **BADPRM** means that the function failed.

The first argument points to the file name.  Under UNIX, the second argument stipulates the protection modes for read, write, and execute, respectively. As a kernel intended primarily for embedded, real-time applications, MTOS-UX does not have protection. Thus, the second argument is not used and may as well be 0L.

By definition, UNIX files are byte streams; there is no sense of a multibyte record as a unit of access. The UNIX-like read and write reflect this stream attitude by transferring a given number of bytes into or out of a user area. The first argument of the read and write routines is a file descriptor, the second is the address of the text for send or buffer for receive, and the third is the number of bytes to be transferred. The following sequence employs the access routines to make a copy of a file:

```
#define BSIZE  256L              /* max number of bytes per access */

long  count;                     /* number actually transferred */
char buf[BSIZE];                 /* I/O buffer */

while ((count = read (fd1, buf, BSIZE)) > 0)

    write (fd2, buf, count);
```

For *read*, a return value of **BADPRM** indicates failure: Either *fd1* is incorrect or a read error occurred. Any other value is the number of bytes read. Thus, a value less than BSIZE shows that the read terminated by reaching the end of the file. For *write*, the return value is **BADPRM** or the number of bytes written. For a nonerrant write, if the third argument is not returned then the volume is full.

Under UNIX, file descriptors 0, 1, and 2 are reserved for the standard input, output, and error files, respectively. Under MTOS-UX, use the literals **stdin** (instead of 0) and **stdout** (instead of 1 or 2). Either name means the requester's Standard Console. Thus,

```
char ch;

read (stdin, &ch, 1L);
```

is equivalent to:

```
getchar ();
```

(For one character, *getchar* is faster than *read*.)

When a file is opened, an internal access pointer is initialized to the beginning of the file (value 0). Each read or write advances the pointer by the number of characters transferred.  The function *lseek* can be invoked to reset the pointer. For example, to "rewind" a file, invoke:

    lseek (fd1, 0L, 0L);

    The last two arguments (commonly known as the *offset* and *mode*) jointly determine the new value of the access pointer.  When the mode is 0, the pointer is set equal to the offset:

    lseek (fd1, 2000L, 0L);

sets the pointer to byte 2000.  For mode 1, the offset is added to the current value of the pointer; for mode 2, the offset is subtracted from the end of file.  Attempting to seek to a point before the beginning of the file is an error.  If the resultant pointer would be beyond the end of the file, it is set to just after the last character in the file.  The function returns **NOERR** if successful, or **BADPRM** if not.

    The function *tell* returns the current position:

    long  curpsn;

    curpsn = tell (fd1);

When access is no longer needed, the files are closed to destroy the pathway into the files:

    close (fd1);
    close (fd2);

When a closed file is no longer needed at all, its name may be removed from its parent's directory:

    unlink ("FILE_2");

The space occupied by the file is freed and the file ceases to exist.

    In a similar vein, MTOS has an implementation of all of the UNIX functions described in Chapter 8 of Kernigham and Ritchie.  Figure 14-4 is an alphabetic listing of the UNIX file functions.  They are available only if the optional file system is installed.

int *close* (fd)

closes the file whose descriptor is *fd*. Returns **NOERR** (= 0) if successful, or **EOF** (= −1) if not. *fd* may not be **stdin** or **stdout**.

int *creat* (fn, dummy)

creates and opens the file pointed to by *fn*. If there is already such a file, its contents are deleted. The function returns **EOF** if an error occurs. Otherwise, the return value is a file descriptor.

int *lseek* (fd, ofs, md)

sets the current access position pointer for file *fd*. For *md* = 0, the pointer is set to *ofs* bytes from beginning of file. For *md* = 1, *ofs* is added to current position. For *md* = 2, *ofs* is subtracted from end of file. *ofs* is a long integer. Attempting to seek to a point before the beginning of the file is an error. If the resultant pointer would be beyond the end of the file, it is set to just after the last character in the file. The function returns **NOERR** if successful, or **EOF** if not.

int *mkdir* (fn)

creates an (empty) directory with name *fn*. The function returns **NOERR** for success or **EOF** for failure.

int *open* (fn, md)

opens the file pointed to by *fn* in the given mode. Mode 0 is read only, mode 1 is write only, and mode 2 is read and write. In all cases, the file must already exist or it can't be opened. The function returns **EOF** if an error occurs, and a file descriptor if the open succeeds.

long *read* (fd, bfr, nr)

reads *nr* bytes starting at the current access position pointer for file *fd* into user buffer *bfr*. The access pointer is advanced after the read. The function returns the number of characters read if successful, 0 if at end of file, or **BADPRM** if an error is detected.

int *rename* (ofn, nfn)

changes the name of file *ofn* to *nfn*. The file may not be currently open in any mode. The function returns **NOERR** for success or **EOF** for failure.

int *seek* (fd, ofs, md)

is an earlier version of *lseek*. In *seek*, *ofs* is limited to 65,535 (although the argument is still a long word). Futhermore, *md* may be 3, 4, or 5, as well as 0, 1, or 2. For the larger values, *ofs* is internally multiplied by 512, and *md* is internally reduced by 3 after which the function behaves like *lseek*. The function returns the current access pointer if successful, or **EOF** if not.

long *tell* (fd)

returns the current access position pointer for file *fd* if successful, or **EOF** if not.

int *unlink* (fn)

deletes file *fn*. The file may not be currently open in any mode. The function returns **NOERR** for success or **EOF** for failure.

FIGURE 14-4: UNIX-Like File Functions

long *write* (fd, bfr, nr) transfers *nr* bytes from user buffer *bfr* into file *fd*, starting at the current access position pointer. The access
pointer is advanced after the write. The function returns
the number of characters actually transferred if successful or terminated for lack of room. **BADPRM** is returned
if an error is detected.

FIGURE 14-4: UNIX-Like File Functions (cont.)

## 14.6 PORTABLE C I/O LIBRARY

The C language specifies a library of I/O and file system functions that are
similar in intent, but different in detail from the UNIX interface. A full complement of Portable C routines is provided for those who wish to be compatible
with these standards.

C and UNIX share the same attitude towards files: A file is an unstructured
stream of bytes. They also use the same type of pathname for stipulating a file.
Recall that a slight difference between the UNIX and MTOS-UX library is that
UNIX uses a slash ('/') to separate the names of directories and files; MTOS, following MS-DOS, uses a backslash ('\'). In addition, for MTOS the root directory
of a volume is always given by a letter followed by a colon.

Both Portable C and UNIX require a specific open before file access is
permitted. One way in which Portable C and UNIX diverge is in the identifier
that is returned from an open and then submitted in subsequent requests. Portable C employs a file pointer (of type **FILE** *) while UNIX employs a file descriptor (a small positive integer). Despite the difference in type, however, a pointer
and a descriptor are logically equivalent; they each serve as a file specifier.

The open for Portable C is:

```
#include "STDIO.H"

FILE *fp1;          /* file pointer for file 1 */
FILE *fp2;          /* file pointer for file 2 */

fp1 = fopen ("HOUR_6.IMG", "r");
fp2 = fopen ("FILE_2", "w");
```

The first argument specifies the file name. In the MTOS-UX implementation, the
UNIX and Portable C library share a common current directory string for all file
I/O. Thus, if the last invocation of *chdir* had "C:\RT-DATA\DAY_5" as its argu-
ment, the file opened by the first *fopen* is "C:\RT-DATA\DAY_5\HOUR_6.IMG".
The second argument specifies the mode of access. The mode can be "r" to read,

"w" to write, and "a" to append to the end of the file.  For mode "r" the file must already exist or the function returns an error value of **NULL**.  For "a" the file is created if it does not exist.  For mode "w" if the file already exists, its contents are deleted; if the file does not exist, it is created.

Upon success, *fopen* returns a file pointer.  Type **FILE** is defined in the header **STDIO.H**.  Once a file is open, we can access its contents.  This is illustrated by a trivial file copy program:

```
char  ch;                /* file character */

while ((ch = getc (fp1)) != EOF)
    putc (ch,fp2);
```

Notice that the basic C file functions, *getc* and *putc*, work with one character per request.  The UNIX *read* and *write* are more efficient since they can deal with large blocks of characters.

When the files are no longer needed, they can be closed:

```
fclose (fp1);
fclose (fp2);
```

Figure 14-5 is an alphabetic listing of the entire Portable C file functions.  They require the file system to be installed.  Figure 14-6 is an alphabetic listing of the non-file Portable C I/O functions.  They need only *pio* and are always provided.  Note that the I/O functions use the requester's Standard Console for **stdin** (standard input) and **stdout** (standard output).

| | |
|---|---|
| int *fclose* (fp) | closes the file whose pointer is *fp*.  Returns **NOERR** if successful, or **EOF** if not.  *fp* may not be **stdin** or **stdout**. |
| int *fflush* (fp) | writes any changed data from the internal buffers to the storage device for file *fp*.  The function returns **NOERR** if successful, or **EOF** if not. |
| char *\*fgets* (str, max, fp) | reads from file *fp* into *str* until either *max* − 1 characters are stored or a *CR* is read and stored.  Any line feeds encountered are ignored, that is, not stored.  The function returns **NULL** if end-of-file is reached before storing any characters or an error is detected.  Otherwise, *str* is returned.  *fp* may be **stdin**. |
| FILE *\*fopen* (fn, mode) | opens the file pointed to by *fn* in the given mode.  Modes are "r" for read only, "w" for read or write, and "a" for read or append to end of file.  For mode "r", the file must |

already exist. For mode "w", if the file already exists, its contents are discarded. For modes "w" and "a", if the file does not already exist, it is created. The function returns a file pointer if successful, or **NULL** if not. After a successful open, the current access position pointer is set to the beginning of the file for modes "r" or "w" and to the end of the file for mode "a". Simultaneous opens are permitted if all use mode "r". For modes "w" or "a", an open will fail if the file is already open.

int *fputs* (str, fp)     writes the contents of string *str* to the file *fp*. The terminal null is not written. It does not append a carriage return or line feed after the last character. The function returns **NOERR** if successful, or **EOF** if not.

int *fseek* (fp, ofs, md)     sets the current access position pointer for file *fp*. For *md* = 0, the pointer is set to *ofs* bytes from beginning of file. For *md* = 1, *ofs* is added to current position. For *md* = 2, *ofs* is subtracted from end of file. Attempting to seek to a point before the beginning of the file is an error. If the resultant pointer would be beyond the end of the file, it is set to just after the last character in the file. The function returns **NOERR** if successful, or **BADPRM** if not.

long *ftell* (fp)     returns the current access position pointer for file *fp*. The function returns **EOF** upon error.

int *getc* (fp)     returns the next character from file *fp*. The function returns **EOF** upon error or end of file.

int *putc* (c, fp)     writes *c* to file *fp*. The function returns *c* if successful, or **EOF** if not.

int *ungetc* (c, fp)     puts the given character back into file *fp*. The character is not actually stored in the file, but is held in a one-character buffer until the next *getc* or *fgets*. If there is already a character waiting in the buffer, the function fails. Any call to *fseek*, *lseek*, or *seek* clears the buffer. The function returns *c* if successful, or **EOF** if not. *fp* may be **stdin**.

FIGURE 14-5:  Standard (Portable C) File Functions

## 14.7 SUMMARY

A file system is a set of rules for placing information on a mass storage device so that the information can subsequently be retrieved. Some popular standard file systems are MS-DOS and UNIX.

MTOS makes several file systems available by hiding the implementation details behind a trio of interfaces. One is the UNIX interface, as described in

Chapter 8 of Kernighan and Ritchie. It provides all the basic functions required to open a file, read, and write its contents, and then close the file. This is a sufficient set of services for most real-time applications. A second interface contains a logically equivalent, but linguistically different set of basic functions. These are the Portable C services from Chapter 7 of Kernighan and Ritchie.

Both the UNIX and Portable C methodologies share a common view on fundamental issues. Both distinguish two types of files: data files to house information supplied by the application and directories to hold information generated by the FS itself. Both treat a data file as an unstructured stream of bytes. And both permit one directory to contain information about other directories so that the tasks can build arbitrarily deep hierarchies of files. The third interface contains a few functions that were missed in the UNIX and Portable C sets. These cover initialization of the FS and manipulation of default path names.

Because the implementation details are hidden, tasks can read and write files that are physically compatible with MS-DOS, employing services that are logically compatible with UNIX.

| | |
|---|---|
| int *getchar* () | reads one character from the requester's Standard Console. The function returns **BADPRM** if an error occurs. Otherwise, the return value is the input character. |
| char *\*gets* (str) | reads characters from the requester's Standard Console and stores them in *str* until a **CR** is read. Any line feeds encountered are ignored, that is, not stored. The **CR** is not stored, but a null is. The function returns **NULL** ( = 0) if an error occurs or there are no characters (other than the null). Otherwise, the return value is *str*. |
| long *printf* (fmt[, args]) | writes any given arguments to the requester's Standard Console, as directed by the format string. The function returns number of characters written if successful, or **BADPRM** if not. |
| int *putchar* (c) | writes *c* to the requester's Standard Console. The function returns *c* if successful, or **BADPRM** if not. |
| int *puts* (str) | writes *str* to the requester's Standard Console. A CR and LF are substituted for the terminal null. The function returns **NOERR** if successful, or **BADPRM** if not. |

FIGURE 14-6:  Standard (Portable C) I/O Functions

## EXERCISES

**14.1** Write a program to count the number of words in a given file and display the result in decimal on the console. For these purposes a word is defined as an alphabetic string that is delimited by one or more nonalphabetic characters, including end-of-file.

**14.2** Write a program to list all the files in a given directory. (Use named parameters such as DIRLEN to represent the length of a directory record and NAMOFF to represent the offset from the beginning of the directory record to the file name.) Under what conditions (other than physical failure) will the listing be inaccurate?

**14.3** Write a program to compress an ASCII file by replacing multiple spaces by 0x80 + the number of spaces. (0x85 substitutes for five successive spaces.) The compressed file must have the same name as the original one.

# Chapter 15
## MULTIPROCESSING

==============================================================

Many real-time applications—even if they are coded with complete efficiency—cannot run with just a single processor. In some cases, the average or peak processing requirements exceed the capability of the processor that has been selected for the applications. Thus, the system must employ multiprocessing (MP), that is, must run with two or more processors working in unison, directly sharing the application load. Systems with four to six CPUs are common.

There may be other reasons for going to multiple processors. Suppose that an application requires a large number of serial, parallel, or other communication ports, or similar peripheral equipment. Often, the most practical option is to include several off-the-shelf communication boards. If those boards happen to have a CPU on them (as is usually the case), it may be advantageous to harness that processing power to increase the responsiveness or maximum capacity of the application.

Not every system with multiple CPUs is an MP configuration, however. Often complex peripherals (such as disk controllers, communication interfaces, and graphics terminals) have processors within them. But these CPUs do not execute application code; they just run the peripheral. To be an MP installation, more than one CPU must directly execute application code.

MTOS-UX can be run on either single-CPU or multiple-CPU hardware. However, for the remainder of this chapter, we will be concerned only with MP installations.

## 15.1 BASIC CONSIDERATIONS

A popular arrangement for real-time multiprocessing is to have several single board computers (SBCs) connected to a common backplane. VME and Multibus boards are often used, although in principle, any bus will do. Each SBC normally has a CPU, local read-write and read-only memory, one or more serial interfaces, and an on-board clock. In most cases, the system as a whole also includes some additional peripheral controller boards, plus one or more global memory boards. The global memory boards can be addressed by all SBCs. This physical arrangement produces "tightly coupled" multiprocessing (TCMP).

Figure 15-1 depicts a typical TCMP installation. In this example, there are three processors. To be concrete, we will continue to discuss a three-processor system. The number three has no special significance. Because there are three processors, at any instant three different tasks can be executing simultaneously. And we mean truly *simultaneously*: all three tasks executing at the same time. In a single-processor (SP) system, we could only simulate simultaneous execution by running the three tasks *concurrently*. In either case, progress can be made along three task threads of execution. With SP, that progress occurs serially by running one task for a while, then switching to the second, and finally switching to the third. With MP, that progress occurs simultaneously by running all three tasks in parallel.

Three single-board computers (CPU and local memory) plus one global memory board:

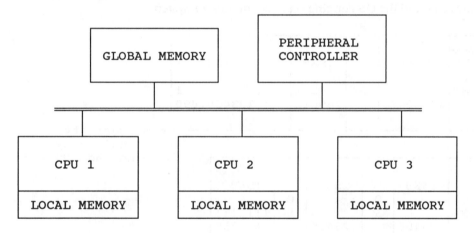

FIGURE 15-1: Typical Tightly Coupled Multiprocessor System

Very often, a task will start executing on one processor, be interrupted, and then continue on another processor. This is invisible to the task. The OS automatically takes care of CPU assignment in an effort to balance processor load and keep all CPUs busy all the time.

The benefit of MP can be a significant increase in overall system throughput. This can be seen in Figure 15-2, with even a two-processor configuration. Suppose that there are four tasks, but only one CPU. As explained above, the tasks run serially, sharing the CPU. If that CPU is never idle, the total elapsed time to complete the task work is the sum of the processing times of each separate task, plus any time spent by the OS for clock processing and other internal chores.

With a two-processor MP installation, as long as at least two tasks are ready to execute, they will do so. Ideally, the elapsed processing time could be cut in half.

Four tasks and the OS running on a one-processor system:

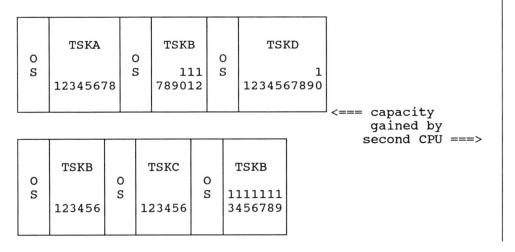

FIGURE 15-2: Increased Throughput with Multiprocessor System

In practice, the improvement in performance is never as great as the number of processors; having two CPUs gives less than twice the throughput. One reason is that there may be times when the number of tasks ready to execute is not as great as the number of processors. In that case, a CPU must idle until a task is ready. Another reason is that the OS must execute some extra code to coordinate the sharing of its internal data. However, this applies only to OS data, not to task-level information. Once you have multitasking, you must protect shared, alterable task data with a semaphore or equivalent machinery, even for an SP system. A third reason is that processors may have to wait their turn to access global memory through the backplane. Nevertheless, this problem can be reduced by proper system design, such as placing task and OS code in local memories to avoid passing through the backplane. We can now see that the actual improvement for MP depends upon many factors, including the distribution of code and data among local and global memories, the rates at which references are made to various types of memory, and the ratio of service-call to nonservice-call code in the application.

Even though execution is distributed over several processors, MTOS runs the entire set of CPUs as a single, integrated system. The CPUs are managed just as basic resources, in the same way that memory is managed: When a resource becomes available, it is allocated to the most important task that is waiting for it. A CPU goes idle only when there is no task at all that can run on it.

Furthermore, all task-level objects and facilities (such as mailboxes, semaphores, and peripheral units) are equally available to all tasks, as though there was only one CPU. For example, a task that is currently running on CPU 1 can form a message in global memory and then send that message via a mailbox to a task that will run on CPU 2. That task, in turn, can display the message on a console that is physically connected to CPU 3.

An MP system can be designed so that one CPU is the master and assigns work for the remaining CPUs to perform as slaves. MTOS-UX is not organized this way. All CPUs are equivalent; there are no masters and no slaves. As a result, simply by making all shared data global, the existence of the multiple processors can be hidden from the application tasks. Without changing a single line of task code, an application that runs on one processor will continue to run on several processors—only faster. This is particularly advantageous when the number of processors cannot be determined before the application is put into service or must be changed after the system is "completed."

The transparency of the MP can be critical when one or more processor boards fail in the field with the application already burned into ROMs. Most commonly, a board will fail when the system is being shut down or started up. If this is the case, the OS will ignore any boards that are unable to execute their initialization code. The same application code will continue to work, with execution degraded only with respect to capacity. (It is sometimes necessary to include some application code that evaluates the health of the hardware and makes adjustments to the start-up data base, but this is getting into details.)

When the failure occurs while the application is in progress, the recovery is more difficult. The subject of fault tolerance and dynamic failure recovery in MP installations is beyond the scope of this book.

## 15.2  SOFTWARE CONSIDERATIONS AND REQUIREMENTS

Each task may be designated as either local or global. A local task is bound to a specified processor; it can run on no other CPU. In contrast, a global task can run on any available CPU. Thus, a global task may start executing on CPU 0, be interrupted, and then continue on CPU 1. The switching of CPUs is invisible to the task.

The main advantage of global tasks is automatic load leveling. When a local task ('L') is ready to run, it must wait for its home CPU to be available. If there is any other task of higher priority that can use the CPU, task 'L' will not be able to proceed. This may be true even if there are idle CPUs. If 'L' were global, however, then it would never wait while a CPU idles.

The advantage of local tasks is reduced contention for the global memory. In many TCMP systems, the main bottleneck is memory access through the common backplane. For a global task, the stack (which is the residence of local variables for C and most other high-level languages) and all alterable data must be in global memory. Thus, every data reference must pass through the system bottleneck. For a local task, the stack and all data can be in local memory; the backplane need not be involved.[1]

To decide if a task should be local or global, the system designer must balance the time lost through idle CPUs against the time lost through possible increased memory access contention. If the processor boards have data caches, this balance may be difficult to determine analytically. It is usually easy to experiment with different task arrangements and thus to arrive at a good system empirically.

## 15.3  HARDWARE CONSIDERATIONS AND REQUIREMENTS

The OS makes minimal demands upon the hardware. Each processor must have the following items:

1. **CPU**: Generally all CPUs must have the same instruction set architecture; you cannot mix 68030s and 80386s in a single system. (One problem is that these processors do not use the same method of addressing memory

---

[1]One should not be too quick to generalize, especially in such an active field as hardware design. It is well known that some very popular busses, such as VME, do not perform well with even five or six active devices contending for global memory. Nevertheless, there are systems that do not have this limitation. At the 1987 Ada Expo in Boston, Westinghouse demonstrated a tightly coupled multiprocessor system based on its AMSP hardware. The application ran under MTOS-UX on 16 processors simultaneously without excessive loss of efficiency.

and thus could not share a common data base.) Nevertheless, because they are very similar, it is possible to mix 68000s, 68010s, 68020s, and 68030s.

2. **Interval timer**: This constitutes the real-time clock. At least one processor board must receive a periodic clock interrupt, with the period normally in the range 1 to 255 ms. Fractional values, such as 16 2/3 ms, can be easily accommodated.

3. **Local read-write memory** (RAM): This is needed for the OS stack and local (processor-dependent) data. The starting address of the local RAM is arbitrary; it need not be the same for every processor.

4. **OS code area**: Often, each processor board has its own copy of the OS code in a local memory. This reduces bus contention at the expense of duplicate memory. Alternately, a single copy of the OS can be placed in a global memory board for execution by all CPUs. In terms of system robustness, local copies are superior to one global copy. If the memory containing the global copy fails, you lose the entire system; if one of the local copies fails, all you lose is one processor.

The OS code is never (intentionally) altered by the OS itself. Thus, the code may be placed in read-only memory. However, in some installations, it may be desirable to download the code into read-write memory and execute from there. This is permitted.

5. **OS global RAM**: The OS requires RAM for its common data: static variables, tables, lists, and other structures. These must be placed in global RAM. Normally this is on a memory board that is separate from the processor boards. A given element of this global memory must have the same address when accessed from any processor board. "Dual-ported" memory on one of the processor boards may be used, but it must be accessed through its global address, even on its home processor board.

Since the OS can execute on more than one processor simultaneously, it protects its own data base via some internal semaphores. They are locked with special instructions, such as **TAS** (test and set) for the 680xx family and **XCHG** (exchange) for the 80x86 family. These instructions read a given location in memory, (possibly) modify it, and then write the result back, all as a single, indivisible operation. The bus must support the indivisibility of such instructions, that is, the bus must remain locked during the entire read-modify-write cycle. Local variables are never used as semaphores so that indivisibility is not required for the local bus.

6. **Priority Interrupt Controller**:  Some processors, such as the 80x86, expect each board to have a PIC.  The 680xx does not require a separate PIC since interrupt control is built into the CPU.

## 15.4  LOOSELY COUPLED MULTIPROCESSING

The ability to run multiple processors as smoothly as one arises from the tight coupling of the processor boards.  Every processor can directly and immediately access a (potentially large) portion of memory via the common backplane.  That common memory can contain shared task data as well as shared OS variables.  No processor "owns" the data; every processor is free to access it.  Of course, alterable shared data must be protected with a semaphore to prevent potentially harmful access by more than one task or more than one copy of the OS.  At the task level, this would be true even for a single processor because of spontaneous task switching.  At the OS level the need for protecting shared internal data introduces only a modest amount of overhead.

There is an alternate approach known as loosely coupled multiprocessing (LCMP).  With LCMP the individual processors are logically isolated so they must exchange information over communication links (e.g., RS-232 or Ethernet).  Each piece of data must be located on one processor ("network node") or another.  The node that houses the data becomes, in effect, the keeper of the data.  Sharing some data then involves a sequence of messages between the node that wishes to use the data and the node that keeps it.  In some systems, the current user initially gets a copy of the data from the keeper and then returns a (possibly altered) copy at the end.  In other systems, each access requires a separate read or write message.  The communication delays and message processing overhead needed to sustain a LCMP arrangement can be quite significant.

Loose coupling places important limitations on the mode by which tasks can communicate with each other and with the outside world.  With TCMP it is common to communicate information by reference, that is, by placing the information in global memory and then sending the *address* of the information via a message buffer.  This is possible since every processor can read the global memory.  With LCMP, communication must involve a mailbox, and the mailbox message that the OS copies into the receiver's buffer must contain all of the information.  Furthermore, the information must also be transmitted in its entirety over the communication link, unless both the sender and receiver happen to be executing on the same processor.  The same considerations apply to I/O unless the peripheral is local to the task that is using it.

Under certain conditions the designer of a multiprocessor system has no choice as to loose or tight coupling.  For example, if the component processors must be physically separated (for security or for convenience in working with other equipment), then loose coupling is mandatory. Similarly, TCMP is ruled out if the number of processors exceeds the practical capacity of the backplane. In some cases, the best arrangement is a loosely coupled arrangement of nodes, each node of which is a tightly coupled set of processors.

## 15.5 SUMMARY

A multiprocessor system is one in which more than one CPU directly executes application code. The advantage of MP is greater system processing power, even though you don't quite get $N$ times the throughput with $N$ CPUs.

MTOS-UX is inherently an MP system; the support for multiple processors was built in at design time. It employs tight coupling; that is, each processor can directly share memory with the other processors via a common backplane. Furthermore, the MP is fully symmetric: All CPUs are equivalent.

When each task is created, it is designated as either global or local. A global task can run on any processor, while a local task is bound to a given processor. A local task has a local stack and local variables. As a result, local tasking can reduce backplane contention and thus can lead to increased throughput. Nevertheless, global tasking can provide automatic load leveling. As long as there is any global task ready to run, a CPU will not be idle. In this way, global tasking also leads to increased throughput.

To save memory, all CPUs can share a single (global) copy of the OS. Alternately, each processor board can have its own (local) copy to reduce backplane traffic. The same dichotomy applies to each global task.

## EXERCISES

**15.1** Suppose that in a certain application, OS service calls require about 10% of the task time. In going from one processor to two, the application code runs 5% slower (because of increased bus contention) and the OS calls run 30% slower (because of extra protection, such as data locking). Estimate the overall advantage of running a two-processor system. What would be the change if the OS calls were 20% or 40% slower, all other factors being equal?

**15.2** One critical set of tasks runs about 45% of the time in an MP installation. Those tasks are global; both their code and data are in global memory. Assuming that a "typical" instruction runs 30% faster when executed out of local memory, how much faster will the overall application run if the code for just those tasks is moved from global to local memory? Assume that OS calls amount to 10% of the task time and that the OS services do not run any faster out of local memory.

**15.3** Some programming languages have constructs that let the user indicate which blocks of statements can be processed in parallel. For example, Dijkstra (Di65) suggests:

```
par_begin
   block1;
   block2;
   ...
   blockN;
par_end
next_statement;
```

Blocks 1 to *N* can proceed in parallel; they must all complete before *next_statement* begins.

How can such a construct be implemented using services described in previous chapters? Under what conditions is such a construct likely to increase the speed at which the entire set of statements is executed (compared with purely sequential processing)? Consider the nature of the blocks of statements, the overhead incurred in starting and synchronizing the parallelism, and the effect of multiple CPUs.

# Chapter 16
## DEBUGGING AND EXCEPTION RECOVERY

===============================================================

Real-time operations are subject to faults and exceptions that arise from several sources. As a minimum, the OS must be able to handle such abnormal events and survive all but the most severe cases. Ideally, the OS should help pinpoint the source of the problem and thus aid with debugging.

To set the stage for the discussion to follow, we can list some typical types of faults:

1. A task issues an unimplemented instruction or attempts to violate instruction privilege rules.

2. A task itself attempts to access memory incorrectly, such as trying to write to a nonalterable or nonexistent location.

3. A task causes the OS to make a bad memory access by supplying an incorrect buffer pointer or similar parameter.

4. A task issues an OS service request with inappropriate or inconsistent parameters, such as a request to send a mailbox message to an event flag group.

5. A task directly overwrites an OS code or data area.

6. A task causes the OS to overwrite one of its code or data areas by supplying a bad buffer address.

7. The stack length given when a task was created was too small so that the stack grows beyond its lower limit.

8. The hardware generates an unexpected physical interrupt.

9. Electrical noise destroys or alters an expected physical interrupt.

10. An interface chip, timer, or memory cell fails.

11. An unanticipated overload saturates the system so that internal memory is exhausted or some other shared facility is overwhelmed.

While hardware failures do contribute their share of troubles, most faults stem from task-level programming errors (common "bugs"). Let us explore these a little further.

Sometimes, a programming error makes the task violate the intent of the application function, but has no manifestations that the OS can detect. For example, when presented with a request for service, the OS can verify if the parameters are syntactically correct. Thus, it can flag an attempt to send a message to an event flag group. However, the OS cannot verify if the request is semantically meaningful. There is no way to detect that a request is silly, useless, or otherwise illogical with respect to the goals of the application.

Normally, the OS is concerned only with faults that are caught during the processing of a service request or that produce an interrupt that the OS must handle. However, the OS may also be called upon to support a Debugger by supplying it with internal information (such as the status and properties of a task) and by performing special services (such as installing a breakpoint).

## 16.1 SERVICE CALL VERIFICATION

The OS makes certain checks each time a task issues a service request. In any system, the level of verification is a compromise between service overhead and probability of error detection: Checking for errors takes time. In a dedicated real-time system, the need for high performance often leaves little time to validate parameters for every routine service call. Furthermore, once an application is debugged, the benefit of repetitive error checking is doubtful.

In this regard, MTOS-UX takes a middle ground between a tightly controlled OS that would run extensive or even exhaustive checks on every parameter and a loosely controlled OS that would not bother to check the parameters at all. For all service requests, MTOS-UX verifies that the identifier of any target object (such as a mailbox) currently exists and is of the required type. It also makes a separate range check on each supplemental parameter, such as a coordination mode and time units specifier. Whenever possible, it then verifies the internal consistency of the entire set of parameters.

The response to finding a bad parameter is to return the general **BADPRM** or a more specific indicator of the error as the value of the service function. In addition, signal 26 is sent to the requesting task. As with any signal, the task sets its own response to such an occurrence (see Section 7.1).[1]

A task can handle parameter errors either by examining the return value for each specific request, or through the general mechanism of signal 26. During debugging and early product development, the requesting task should check the value returned from every service call that can possibly fail:

[1]The description of the handling of bad parameters and most other program errors applies only to tasks written in assembler, C, FORTRAN, or Pascal. As will be explained in Chapter 17, Ada requires a different approach.

```
if ((service_request () & 0xFFFFFF00) = = 0xFFFFFF00)
  {
   ... ;              /* code to handle error found by OS */
  }
```

To avoid the confusion of having to handle the same error twice, the response to signal 26 during this phase of the code development can then be "ignore the signal":

```
setsig (SIG26,SIGIGN);
```

The cost in time and memory of all this task-level results checking might be too great for a final product. In this case, most or all of the in-line checking could be eliminated. Signal 26 would then be set to catch any residual faults detected by the OS:

```
setsig (SIG26,SIGBLK);    /* block errant task & then handle error via
                             debugger */
```

or:

```
int ParmErr ();           /* define parameter error recovery procedure */

setsig (SIG26,ParmErr);   /* handle error directly within errant task */
```

MTOS-UX also checks that the stack is not currently beyond its lower limit each time a service request is issued. If a stack error is found, the task is sent signal 30. Because of the severity of this error, a task is not permitted to ignore signal 30; because a procedure response requires additional stack usage, a task is not permitted to handle signal 30 via a recovery procedure. Only the Debugger can rescue a task after it overflows its stack segment. Unless the region of memory below the stack was not in use at the time of the overflow, the effects of such an error are likely to involve tasks other than the one that caused the problem.

Processors that permit the OS to define the stack memory region directly (80386) or via a Memory Management Unit (68030) will generate an interrupt upon an attempt to overflow the stack. In these cases, signal 30 is sent before any damage is done to the adjacent area.

## 16.2  RECOVERY FROM CODE FAULTS

Certain interrupts are the direct and immediate result of attempting to execute a particular instruction within task, kernel, or driver code. Examples of instructions that may cause such interrupts include unimplemented operation codes ("illegal instructions"), restricted instructions ("privilege violations"), and instructions that make an improper memory reference (write to read-only memory, access nonexistent memory, or violate address boundary rules).

Not every code-generated interrupt is an error, however. The basic method of calling for an OS service from a task or driver involves generating a software interrupt via a TRAP, software interrupt, or similar instruction. A Debugger often uses a software interrupt to produce a breakpoint. Furthermore, some high-level languages use special interrupt instructions to enter a floating point routine when there is no floating point hardware. Thus, the OS must be able to handle all code-related interrupts and recover from those that were generated because of a coding error.

When an interrupt occurs, the CPU saves some contextual information (such as the current program counter) and then vectors to a handler routine within the OS. (During the early phase of program development, some interrupts may be handled by an on-board monitor, but we may ignore this detail for now.) The OS uses the saved context and type of interrupt to decide if the interrupt is legitimate or not. The handling of proper interrupts need not concern the user; we will restrict our attention to errors.

For code error, MTOS-UX determines if the errant instruction was within a task or within the OS and its extended components (drivers). If a task is at fault, MTOS-UX sends a specific error signal to that task. (Signal 19 is sent for arithmetic exceptions, such as divide by 0; signal 28 is sent for memory access error; etc.) As always, the task elects to ignore the error, handle it via a procedure, or be halted and let an operator examine the problem with the Debugger.

The Debugger is defined as whatever task has key '.SYD'. A standard Debugger is supplied with the system, but it does not have to be installed. If there is no Debugger task in existence at the time it is needed to handle a signal, the signal is discarded and the errant task is terminated in hopes of containing the problem.

While an application is being developed, the normal practice is to install the Standard Debugger, or some customized variant of it. The kinds of errors that may arise at that early stage are just too numerous to code into error-recovery procedures. In contrast, the final embedded product may not have an operator, or even an I/O console. Thus, recovery procedures—possibly very complex ones—may have to be used once the product is in the field. Unfortunately, error-recovery logic is usually not given enough thought until well into field trials.

Code errors within the operating system itself are treated differently. If the error is just a bad memory access, MTOS-UX assumes that it has been given a faulty pointer: It outputs an error message (via the Error Logger task) and then continues at the next instruction. For any more serious errors (such as an illegal instruction), it must assume that its code or data has been damaged beyond repair. It outputs a "fatal error message" (via a stand-alone, ROM-able driver) and then shuts down. With a multiprocessor installation, all processors shut down together.

## 16.3  NONCODE FAULTS

The OS also starts the Error task as part of the handling of unexpected external interrupts and similar hardware faults. The Error task formats and displays a message indicating which fault was detected. The fault is assumed to be unrelated to the code being executed at the time the interrupt was generated. Thus, no note is taken of that code. Except for activating an Error task, the operating system takes no action in response to noncode faults; it is the programmer's responsibility to find the source of the problem, and correct it. Often the source is a defective peripheral board.

Since the operating system can completely recover from noncode faults, it is tempting to ignore them completely. For the rare, noise-induced spurious interrupt, there is no harm. Nevertheless, more frequent noncode faults often precede equipment failure and should be investigated.

## 16.4  DEBUGGER TASK

The Debugger is a task that is identified to the OS by virtue of having the key '.SYD'. There is no requirement that the same Debugger be deployed throughout the life cycle of an application. The powerful debugging facilities that are essential during program development may be too dangerous to make available to the ordinary operator in the final product. Thus, the final Debugger may have only limited facilities: inspect, but not change, for example. Alternately, there may be password protection in a final Debugger that would be a nuisance for the development version. The Standard Debugger refers to the version that comes with the OS.

Since the Debugger is an ordinary task, it can be invoked by any of the normal services, such as *start*. But this is usually not done. Instead, the Debugger is started by two special mechanisms: unsolicited console input and signal response.

Unsolicited console input is any keystroke that is entered without a corresponding read request having been issued. Someone just spontaneously types at the console. If an unsolicited control-D is entered while the Debugger is

Dormant, the OS starts the Debugger. The console at which the control-D was typed automatically becomes the Standard Console for the Debugger task. This permits any available console (ASCII I/O device) to serve as the Debugger's terminal.

Once the Debugger is started, it issues a prompt and then calls for input. Thus, the operator enters control-D in order to begin a Debugger "conversation," that is, a series of requests input by the operator with corresponding responses output by the Debugger. Unless the operator's request is to exit (terminate the conversation), the Debugger seeks a new request after responding to the current one.

The Debugger can also be started when a task makes a detectable error, reaches a breakpoint, or finishes an instruction in trace (single-step) mode. As explained, the actual mechanism is for the OS to send a signal in each case. When the task's response to the signal is to invoke the Debugger, the OS prepares a message containing the signal number and task context data, queues the message to a special Debugger message exchange, and then starts the Debugger if it is not already running. The Debugger always seeks such a message (without wait) before calling for input from the console. Any time it finds a message, it formats a corresponding "At Breakpoint" or other bulletin and displays it on its current Standard Console.

To avoid a potential deadly embrace, Debugger I/O must always be performed with the preemption bit set in the request parameters (see **PREEMP** in Section 13.3). The deadly embrace occurs when a task that has reserved the Debugger's console is halted because of an error, breakpoint, or trace: The halted task needs the Debugger to unblock it; the Debugger needs the console to proceed with the unblocking.

## 16.5  DEBUGGER REQUESTS

Within the general framework outlined in the previous section, the designer of a Debugger is free to implement any type of request deemed appropriate for the application under development. The Standard Debugger has two types of requests: those that do not depend upon the multitasking or real-time nature of the system and those that do. Inspect-and-Change-Memory is typical of the first class. It permits the operator to examine and possibly alter memory as defined by address, length, format (such as byte, word, or long word), and (for multiprocessor installations) processor number. The logical content of the memory is not an issue; the address could be within a task, a pool, a portion of the OS, or a region not even involved in the application. Because of the generality of Inspect-Memory, an operator could, say, determine the status of a given task, if he knows the address of that information within the OS's internal tables.

Change-Memory gives an operator the power to destroy any unprotected data area.

In a multitasking environment, the most useful Debugger requests are of the second type. They permit the operator to display the properties of the OS or the tasks that run under it, and provide a controlled and limited ability to alter certain properties. A typical request is to display a summary of the current status of all tasks. In response, the Debugger lists the task key, the state (Running, Ready, Blocked waiting for I/O, etc.), priority, program counter value, and similar dynamic data. A variant of this request invokes a considerably more detailed report on a single specified task.

Other requests permit the operator to set a breakpoint (BP) at a given address with respect to the code section of a given task, to halt or continue a task, and to inspect and change register values of a halted task.

The mechanism for setting a breakpoint and the corresponding limitations to the BP facility depend strongly upon the instruction set architecture. Some CPUs (such as the 80386) have internal BP registers. They are loaded with the desired BP addresses. When the CPU is about to execute an instruction at one of those addresses, it automatically generates an exception. In such cases, BPs can be set even if the code is in ROM. However, the number of active BPs is limited to the number of BP registers. Furthermore, the BP is limited to reaching a given address.

If the CPU does not have built-in BP support, but the code is in RAM, a BP is traditionally set by substituting a short breakpointing instruction, such as a TRAP or illegal instruction at the BP address. Upon executing the BP instruction, the Debugger is reentered. It replaces the original instruction and then reports the arrival at that location. There is no inherent limit to the number of BPs that the Debugger software could support. Breakpointing is still restricted to reaching a given address.

Finally, if there is no BP support within the CPU and the code is in ROM, breakpointing can nonetheless be achieved by tracing the code. The Debugger is automatically reentered after each instruction. The Debugger then compares the current program counter with its BP table. It either reports that it is at a BP or executes one more step to repeat the loop. Since the Debugger has access to both all of memory and the value of the task's registers, the BP can now involve these factors. Complex conditional BPs can be set up. Nevertheless, running in this mode can take 10 to 30 times as long as normal execution.

All Debugger requests that depend upon a knowledge of the tasking structure require the close cooperation of the OS. Within MTOS there is a special OS service, *debug*, through which a Debugger can request information about the status of the system and can alter certain aspects of it. For example, *debug* is the source of task status information; the Debugger does not have to know the structure of the OS internal tables. The OS must also cooperate by blocking a task when a breakpoint is reached and in permitting another task to execute through the breakpoint if it happens to be within a procedure that they share.

It should be apparent that Debugger support must be built in as an integral part of the OS. The Debugger influences the scheduling of tasks, as well as the handling of signals and interrupts.

## 16.6  GENERAL MONITOR

A Debugger task is only one of several kinds of tools available to develop a real-time application. The others are monitors, emulators, and bus state analyzers. All four tools are different; all may play a role in the development process.

A general monitor is a ROM-resident program that is designed to be the first piece of code to execute when power is applied to a processor board. It initializes the hardware on the board (prepares interrupt vector and other tables required by the CPU, initializes serial communication chips, writes to local memory if write-before-read is needed to set parity, etc.). After the monitor is finished with its initialization, the board is ready to execute code under the monitor as master. (Master in the sense that unless the interrupt vectors are changed, all interrupts will be handled by the monitor.)

The monitor then displays an identifying header on its console and calls for input from the operator. Services normally available include load a program from a local disk or from a host computer over a serial link; save a program on a local disk or at a host computer; inspect-and-change memory (often with the ability to disassemble code as an inspect option and assemble code as a change option); inspect-and-change hardware registers; set, display, and remove breakpoints; trace (single-step) through code; and execute code. There is often a HELP display to indicate the available features.

Generally, the tracing capability is limited to executing the next single instruction (or possibly a given number of next instructions) and then displaying the current state of the CPU. Monitors traditionally do not have the supporting hardware needed to store the history of the last several states and then display this upon demand.

In addition, the operator is normally quite restricted in his or her ability to select a breakpoint condition. Most monitors have the ability to BP when the CPU is about to execute the instruction at one or more absolute addresses. If this is implemented by substituting a TRAP or interrupt instruction at the selected address, the instructions must be in alterable memory. If the CPU itself supports breakpointing, the code can be in ROM. In some cases, a BP can be generated when a particular memory address is accessed, but this requires auxiliary hardware on the board, or direct support within the CPU. Since a monitor does not know the value of the registers while a program is executing, register values are excluded from the BP facility.

Almost always, the general monitor is supplied by the company that makes the processor board. The same monitor is provided to all board users, real-time as well as nonreal-time. As a result, the general monitor has no knowledge of the application or of the operating system that will run the application. Debugging with a general monitor therefore must be at the lowest level; high-level requests, such as display task status, cannot be implemented. This is one essential difference between debugging under a general monitor and under a Debugger task.

Another essential difference is the state of the system between operator requests. A Debugger is just a task. While it waits for a request to be input, other tasks may continue to execute. In contrast, most monitors "freeze" the system while waiting for a request. As far as the monitor is concerned, there is only one user program (the application is not distinguished from the OS). That single program is run only when the operator types TRACE or GO (or their equivalents); the program stops completely when a trace, BP, error, or other monitor interrupt occurs. This can be an advantage. While the system is frozen, the operator can perform an extensive examination of memory without fear that conditions will be changed by program execution. Of course, in a multiple processor configuration, global memory is still subject to change since other processors may continue to run.

A third difference is that a monitor can handle any code: application as well as operating system. Many of the most powerful features of a Debugger task, such as trace and BP, cannot be applied to the OS itself. Similarly, the monitor needs very little in the way of support; unless certain critical interrupt vectors are destroyed or diverted away from the monitor, the monitor can run. Even if the vectors are gone, a Reset (or simulated power up) will always restore the monitor to service, often leaving application memory intact. However, a Debugger task requires that the OS be operational enough to run tasks. If the OS can't be started or requires a cold restart, critical evidence about the failure may be lost.

The primary place for a monitor is in the early stages of program development. Initially, it may be needed to debug the hardware dependencies of the OS itself. For example, for an embedded system to run under the OS alone (without the monitor), the OS must be able to initialize any special hardware that is in the system, to set up and service the real-time clock, and so forth. Such board-dependent code has to be debugged. Here, a monitor is a good tool. After that, the monitor may be asked to download the application into alterable memory and to "patch it" (correct code and data tables) prior to execution. This role may continue until the system is ready to be burned into read-only memory. The final ROM-based, embedded product may not need a monitor at all.

During application development, the Debugger task gradually assumes greater responsibility for supporting debugging, taking over from a monitor (or equivalent tools to be described shortly). In the intermediate stages, both monitor and Debugger may be needed. But this leads to conflict. For example, there is usually only one Trace vector; who shall service it? The resolution for MTOS-UX is that the OS always receives the interrupt. It determines from context whether the traced instruction is in the OS or in a task. If in a task, it continues to process the trace. However, if OS code is being traced, the handler returns the CPU to the exact state it had just after the Trace interrupt and then jumps into the monitor at its Trace entry point.

### 16.7  OS-SENSITIVE MONITOR

The general monitor supplied by the manufacturer of a processor board is designed to work with any software that happens to be loaded onto the board. Thus, the monitor is insensitive to the OS (if any) that underlies the board's application program. Nevertheless, there is no inherent reason that monitor-level debugging cannot be performed with full knowledge of the operating system. In fact, this approach was taken with an alternate MTOS debugger that runs as a monitor, rather than as a task.

An OS-sensitive monitor can have all the benefits of a general monitor. It (1) can provide a uniform debugging environment for task and OS code, (2) can freeze the system until the operator gives a GO or TRACE command, and (3) can perform even if the OS is not yet completely installed or is damaged by a task error. Equally important, a monitor that is familiar with the resident OS can display OS-specific data, such as the status of the tasks, message exchanges, and other dynamic objects.

Traditionally, a monitor is a self-contained program that needs only a console for input of operator commands and output of debugger reports and messages. In such a stand-alone mode, the monitor has no mechanism to reference the source code or to consult tables of auxiliary information, such as the absolute address that corresponds to a given program label. As a result, the operator must independently determine the address of a program label or variable to set a breakpoint or perform inspect-and-change.

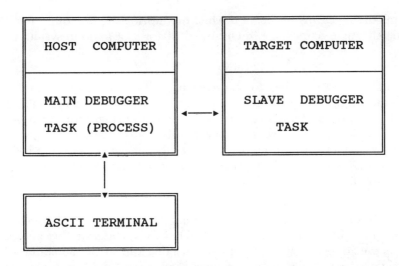

**FIGURE 16-1: Running a Debugger/Monitor in Conjunction with a Host Computer**

Most of the foregoing limitations and operator inconveniences vanish when the monitor-debugger runs with the aid of a host computer. Such an arrangement is depicted in Figure 16-1. The monitor is split into two programs. The main program executes on a host computer under UNIX, VMS, or MS-DOS. The main program is responsible for all console operations; it performs the potentially lengthy chores of command line interpretation and formatted display.

The main program is linked to a slave program that resides on the target hardware. The slave performs very simple, highly specific commands generated by the main program. Typical commands are read or write a given address and trace one instruction within a given task. The slave also reports back to the main program when a breakpoint is reached.

Since the main program runs under the OS of the host computer, it can access any source code and auxiliary link data that is stored within the host's file system. Thus, the monitor can automatically translate a program label or variable name into an absolute address. Now debugging can proceed at the symbolic source level, with breakpoints set by line number or program label, and variables examined or altered by program name.

## 16.8 EMULATOR AND BUS STATE ANALYZER

An emulator is yet another debugging tool that potentially provides great flexibility and convenience for certain functions, primarily tracing and breakpointing. The emulator consists of a hardware and software combination that performs the functions of the CPU while monitoring the execution for BPs and errors. Alternate names are in-circuit emulator (ICE) and in-system emulator (ISE).

In many cases, the operator can specify a BP as a complex chain of events, such as the storage of any odd value at a given address after a particular register attains a given limit. Emulators also provide the normal monitor functions of program download and save, memory/register inspect-and-change, and execution control. Thus, an emulator is similar to a monitor, but one with an unparalleled ability to BP when an operator-selected combination of hardware and software conditions occurs.

The last class of debugging tool, a bus state analyzer (BSA), is also a combination of hardware and software. It attaches to a processor chip and passively monitors the address, data, and control lines that appear on the chip leads. The BSA simultaneously records the sequence of addresses and data (in its own high-speed memory) and analyzes them for the occurrence of a breakpoint. Since the BSA has access to memory read and write signals, the BP can involve these factors. (Break when a certain range of values is stored within a given address is one possibility.) However, since the bus state analyzer does not have direct access to register values, these cannot be included. When a BP is reached, the BSA can be asked to display a selected portion of the saved history of bus accesses or record and display a given number of subsequent accesses. Often, the display can be presented as a sequence of assembly instructions. For complex chips, this is no trivial matter since prefetch, pipelining, and an on-chip cache distort the relation between actual instructions executed and the signals that appear on the chip leads.

A BSA will halt the CPU while the operator examines the trace display after a BP is reached. However, a BSA is purely a monitoring device. It cannot display what it has not already seen and recorded. Thus, it cannot perform general memory/register inspect-and-change. In this respect, an emulator is stronger than a BSA.

Some BSAs have a profiling capability. They sample the program counter periodically and then display the percentage of the time the program is executing within specified address regions. The results are often depicted as histograms. Such profiling information enables the programmer to discover sections of code that may be worth optimizing because they occupy so much of the CPU's time. Idle time, OS overhead, and similar operational information can also be estimated.

## 16.9  SUMMARY

Debugging is a skill that can be aided by various classes of tools.  The major classes are:

**1. A debugger task** that runs on the target processor under the target OS:  Such a task can perform general functions, such as inspect-and-change-memory, and OS-specific functions, such as display-task-status.  However, since it runs under the target OS, a debugger task is unable to debug board-specific modules of that OS.  Furthermore, if a task error renders the OS inoperative, a debugger task becomes inoperative as well.

**2. A general monitor** that runs on the target processor, but has no relation to any co-resident OS:  The monitor performs even in the absence of an OS.  A general monitor can help debug kernel and driver code, as well as application modules.  But it cannot directly report OS information, except as the content of independently-determined physical addresses.

**3. An OS-sensitive monitor** that runs on the target processor:  Although it does not require the target OS to operate, it is aware of the nature and internal organization of that OS.  Such a monitor combines the advantages of convenient access to OS and task-level information with the ability to debug the OS itself and to run even if the OS is inoperative.  Furthermore, when an OS-sensitive monitor is operated in conjunction with a host computer, debugging can be at the symbolic source level.

**4. An emulator** or a **bus state analyzer**:  These are very useful when the capture and display of program data must be triggered by a complex condition, such as the storage of a given value at a given address.  (With the other tools, data display is most commonly evoked by operator command while the program is stopped at a breakpoint.  Breakpoints, in turn, are limited to reaching a preselected program address.)

## EXERCISES

**16.1**  Suppose memory access errors must be handled by a task itself rather than through the Debugger.  How can this be done without any modification to MTOS-UX?

**16.2**  The Debugger is a C task that can be retained or not in the field version of an embedded application.  Which Debugger functions might "safely" be included in a version to be released in an uncontrolled environment?  Assume that if a command can be entered it will be entered, even if the user doesn't know what the result will be.  How would this change if all code were in ROM and an MMU were present to isolate OS code and data from all tasks?

**16.3**  During field trials of a certain embedded system, it is noticed that a message destined to be output over an interprocessor link is cleared out before it can be transmitted.  This occurs rarely and randomly.  Which debugging tools are best suited to investigate this problem?

It is also noticed that under "mild" conditions (i.e., not peak load) all the internal queuing blocks eventually become unavailable.  Evaluate the relative merits of various debugging tools in this case.

**16.4**  What special problems are introduced when there is more than one processor in the system?  Emulators and BSAs often have the ability to output an external signal when a BP is reached and to use an external signal as a BP event.  How might these be used?  What might be the equivalent for a monitor?

# Chapter 17
## ADA AS THE TASKING LANGUAGE

So far, all the illustrative code has been in C. The justification is the current popularity of C for real-time applications. Nevertheless, the Department of Defense (DoD) has mandated Ada for its embedded real-time programs, and this practice may spread to other government and industrial segments. What about Ada? Can Ada just be substituted for C as the tasking language, or is there more involved?

Ada is significantly different from C. The main difference is not in the syntax since:

    var1 = var2 + var3;        /* add 2 numbers in C */

is not essentially different from:

    var1: = var2 + var3;        -- add 2 numbers in Ada

Nor is the difference in the strong typing within Ada. (C is fairly permissive about adding and equating various types of integers; Ada requires that all variables be of the same type unless we specifically redefine + and = for the mixed types.)

### 17.1 ADA REAL-TIME MODEL

For our purposes, the critical difference is that Ada attempts to define and control the real-time behavior of a program, whereas that is not a *language* question within C. Ada has several programming units, one of which is a task. This is exactly the same type of object that we have been discussing throughout this guide—an independent thread of execution that can be run in parallel with other tasks. In C, we had to impose this extralinguistic notion of a task by calling upon the operating system to create the task. In Ada, the task is an inherent feature of the language. The Ada declaration "**task** *INITSK*;" is sufficient to make *INITSK* a task.

The basic concept of a task as a unit of execution is the same under MTOS-UX and Ada's implicit real-time kernel. Nevertheless, the detailed behavior of the task is not the same. One difference is that an Ada task need not have an ex-

ecution priority, and when it does, there is no service to change it.[1]   Under
MTOS, every task has a priority that is dynamically alterable.

Another difference is that Ada does not distinguish creation and starting as
separate functions requiring separate requests. When an Ada task is "elaborated"
(created in the same sense that a local variable is created), it automatically begins
execution.  When it terminates, it is deleted never to run again (unless
recreated.)

In addition, Ada takes a highly protective attitude toward its tasks (as well as
all of its objects). This leads to a complex set of semantic rules concerning the
termination of a task and the interaction of one task with another. For example,
a "parent" task **P** may begin by creating two "children" tasks **C1** and **C2**. The children inherit access to the local variables within the parent.  Since these variables
disappear when **P** terminates, the termination of **P** is forestalled until **C1** and **C2**
have themselves terminated or reached a special position from which termination is the only alternative.

```
task C;              -- specification for calling task

task body C is       -- body for calling task
   RESULT:  INTEGER;      -- result returned by SERVICE_1

   ...

begin
   S.SERVICE_1(10,RESULT);        -- call for SERVICE_1
   S.SERVICE_2(0,-1);             -- call for SERVICE_2

   ...

end C;
```

FIGURE 17-1: The Ada Rendezvous: Calling Task

Ada's built-in real-time features are not limited to tasking.  The language also
supplies pauses (via the **delay** statement), error recovery (via the exception
handler), time-of-day support (via **package** CALENDAR), physical I/O (via **package** TEXT_IO), and communication/coordination (via the rendezvous).  Here
again, MTOS-UX and Ada diverge on fundamental issues.  For example, MTOS-
UX provides a very rich set of primitives for communication and coordination,
including event flags, semaphores, controlled shared variables, mailboxes, message buffers, and signals.  With Ada, there is only one mechanism: the rendez-

---

[1]The priority of a task may be changed when it is the server within a rendezvous, but the priority
immediately reverts to the original value when the rendezvous is over.

vous. All other forms of intertask interaction must be fabricated at the task level via the rendezvous.

```
        task S is                -- specification of task with two entries

          entry SERVICE_1(  ARG_1:  in  INTEGER;
                            ARG_2:  out INTEGER);

          entry SERVICE_2(  ARG_3:  in  INTEGER;
                            ARG_4:  in  INTEGER);

        end S;


        task body S is          -- body for service task

        begin
          loop
            select
              accept SERVICE_1(ARG_1:     in  INTEGER;
                               ARG_2:     out INTEGER)
                do ...          -- code for service
              end SERVICE_1;

            or

              accept SERVICE_2(ARG_3:     in  INTEGER;
                               ARG_4:     in INTEGER)
                do ...          -- code for service
              end SERVICE_2;
            end select;
          end loop;
        end S;
```

This is only one of several forms for the rendezvous. The variants are in the alternatives used within the **select** statement.

FIGURE 17-2: The Ada Rendezvous: Serving Task

The Ada rendezvous is basically a procedure call that is issued by one task and executed by another task (see Figures 17-1 and 17-2). The caller, C, indicates its desire to have the procedure run by naming a specific procedure (or set of alternate procedures). The procedure is given as a particular entry point within a particular task. Thus, the caller always targets a specific task (or set of tasks). Correspondingly, the server, S, indicates its willingness to execute one of its procedures by issuing an **accept** statement. Although the **accept** also mentions a specific procedure (or set of procedures), the server has no control over which task it serves. In fact, unless the identity of the caller is included as one of the procedure arguments (by an agreement outside of the scope of the language), S does not know the identity of C.

The rendezvous automatically provides coordination between C and S. If the **accept** is issued first, S waits for the call; if the call is made first, C waits for the **accept**. In either case, the rendezvous begins with a match of call and **accept**: C is blocked, any input arguments to the procedure are transferred to S, and S begins to execute the procedure code. When the procedure has completed, any output arguments are transferred from S to C, the rendezvous is dissolved, and both tasks continue independently. Although there are options to limit the wait, C does not have the ability to continue without coordination or to defer coordination via an event flag or signal.

```
task SF_1 is              -- specifications (common to any implementation)
   entry Get;
   entry Release;
end SF;


task body SF_1 is         -- first implementation
   begin
      loop
         accept Get;       -- wait for caller to issue Get
         accept Release;   -- wait for caller to issue Release
      end loop;
end SF;
```

FIGURE 17-3: Simple Binary Semaphore Implemented via Ada Rendezvous

Figures 17-3 and 17-4 show how to implement a simple, binary semaphore with a rendezvous. At first glance this appears to be equivalent to its MTOS-UX counterpart (or at least the subset that specifies **WAIFIN** as the coordination mode). But there is an oddity in the Ada semantics that makes a rendezvous-based service behave very differently: The calls must be processed in the order of arrival (first-come, first-served) (LRM83, Section 9.5.15). This is a critical issue. Most writers of real-time programs expect that if two or more tasks are waiting for a semaphore, the one of highest priority will always get it first. With Ada, that expectation will not necessarily be met.

```
task body SF_1 is                    -- second implementation

   AVAILABLE: BOOLEAN: = TRUE;
   begin
     loop
       select
         when AVAILABLE = >
           accept Get;          -- wait for caller to issue Get
           do AVAILABLE: = FALSE;  end Get;
       or
         when not AVAILABLE = >
           accept Release;      -- wait for caller to issue Release
           do AVAILABLE: = TRUE;  end Release;
       end select;
     end loop;
   end SF_1;
```

Note: When a semaphore is coded as shown here, each SF would need a separate task program. More general techniques are available.

FIGURE 17-4: Alternate Simple Binary Semaphore Implemented via Ada Rendezvous

Another, more subtle, difference is that the Ada equivalent of the semaphore, message exchange, and similar coordination/communication facilities are primarily executed at the task level. The Ada kernel only maintains the caller/server queues and performs the context switches. Thus, when task **R** gets a semaphore by rendezvous with server task **SF_1**, two task-to-task context switches are required: **R** to **SF_1** and **SF_1** to **R**. With MTOS-UX there is only one context switch since the OS performs the semaphore code directly. The extra overhead makes a rendezvous-based service slower than the corresponding OS-based service.

The concept of deferred coordination is available in Ada. But as with all secondary coordination mechanisms, the programmer must construct it from the rendezvous. For example, Habermann and Perry (Ha82, p. 385) show how to issue a "receipt" at the start of an I/O request and later how to perform a semaphore wait until the I/O is finished. Nevertheless, with this scheme a new

SF task is created for each receipt. Creating and disposing of tasks are slow operations compared with their OS counterparts.

## 17.2  USING ADA: TASKING ISSUES

Given all these differences in real-time behavior, can Ada replace C as the task language in an application controlled by a full-service OS, such as MTOS-UX? Yes, with only a few adjustments to the MTOS specifications and semantics. The areas of change are tasking and exception handling.

An Ada program must have an underlying kernel or its equivalent to support the language's task model and other real-time features. MTOS-UX has been served as that kernel (for the TeleSoft TeleGen2 compiler). The result was an Ada compiler that runs standard ("plain vanilla") Ada programs. These execute without any reference to MTOS. In fact, the compiler was not even altered; only a few of the code generator support packages that link with the compiled code had to be replaced.

However, for the compiler to pass the stringent Ada validation test suite, the normal MTOS semantics had to be augmented with additional rules from the Ada Language Reference Manual (LRM83). As a result, the MTOS task create and terminate requests became superfluous; they were discarded in favor of the Ada equivalents. Thus, a task becomes known to the compiler via a task specification and a corresponding task body. A typical specification (for a task that is not to be the server in a rendezvous) is:

**task type** INPTSK **is**         -- specification: declares INPTSK as a task object

    **pragma** PRIORITY (200);   -- optional declaration of task priority

**end** INPTSK;

**for** INPTSK'STORAGE SIZE **use** 3000;   -- optional declaration of stack length

The specifications let the compiler know that **INPTSK** is a task. The compiler translates these into the code both to create the task and to start it running. The optional **pragma** PRIORITY statement sets task priority to the given value. Without such a specification, MTOS assigns the lowest possible value, 0.[2] The optional STORAGE_SIZE statement sets the stack length to the given value. Without a specification, stack length is fixed at a (compiler-dependent) default value.

---

[2]A **pragma** is a suggestion that the programmer makes to the compiler. The compiler is free to ignore it. The suggestion can involve coding or execution decisions, compiler implementation options, and the like. Since **pragmas** must be recognized by the compiler, they require a change to the compiler.

The task body contains both declarations for any local task variables and the code to be executed by the task:

```
task body INPTSK is        -- body: defines local variables
                           --  and code to execute
    ...                    -- specifications of local task variables
begin                      -- entry point for task
    ...                    -- code for task
end INPTSK;                -- end of task
```

Except for priority and stack size, there are no predefined agreements in Ada on other task characteristics that an OS might need (such as MTOS key). We forfeited the ability to bring such TCD information directly into the creation when we had to discard the create-task service call because it conflicted with Ada's implicit creation of task objects. We might have introduced a special **pragma** to transmit TCD values. However, this alternative was discarded since it would have necessitated a change to the compiler.

As mentioned before, Ada tasks can run perfectly well without a key or other special OS attributes. (All tasks are assigned a default key, '.Ada'.) Nevertheless, it is beneficial to be able to specify values, rather than accept defaults. Thus, we simply retrofit the TCD information after the task starts:

```
task body INPTSK is                   -- alternate body with optional
                                      -- retrofit of TCD attributes
with MTOSUX_H;  use MTOSUX_H;  -- basic definitions (MTOS_KEY, etc)
with MTOS_TSK;  use MTOS_TSK;  -- task services
    ...
    INPT:        constant MTOS_KEY:= 16#494E5054#;  -- 'INPT'
    INPT_TCD:    constant MTOS_TCD:= (INPT,0,250,0,0,0,0);
    DUMMY:       MTOS_RESULT:= Set_TCD (INPT_TCD);
    ...
begin             -- entry point for task
    ...           -- code for task
end INPTSK;       -- end of task
```

How these statements combine to set TCD values takes a few paragraphs to explain.

An Ada **with** statement is equivalent to a C #include. A **use** statement permits an element in an included package to be referenced without prefixing the element with the name of the enclosing package.  (After **use** MTOS_TSK we can write *set_TCD*; before the **use** we would have needed the full name MTOS_TSK.*set_TCD*.)

Code to allocate space for any local variables and to assign them initial values is executed before the main body code (the part that follows the **begin**). We take advantage of that ordering to introduce TCD information via the statements:

| | |
|---|---|
| INPT: | **constant** MTOS_KEY:= 16#494E5054#;  -- 'INPT' |
| INPT_TCD: | **constant** MTOS_TCD:= (INPT,0,250,0,0,0,0); |
| DUMMY: | MTOS_RESULT:= Set_TCD (INPT_TCD); |

The general form of an Ada variable declaration is:

<name>:  <type>   [:= <initial value>];

where the part in square brackets is optional.  The initial value, in turn, can be constant or can be computed dynamically, as by a function call.  In this specific case, the initialization of *DUMMY* forces a new service call, *Set_TCD*, to be called during the elaboration (creation) of the local task variables. The two nonzero components of the TCD are, respectively, the key and the inherent priority.  The zero components cover certain additional characteristics that need not concern us here. After this call, the *INPTSK* task runs at priority 250. (Until then it was running at the priority supplied by the **pragma** or at some default value if the **pragma** was not given.)

As with their C cousins, Ada tasks can have a variety of overall organizations, depending upon the way they normally start executing.  Three typical organizations accommodate tasks that run periodically, tasks that run when a message arrives and tasks that run when started by a *Start-Task* request.  This is just a sample of some of the forms an Ada task can take when running under MTOS.


## 17.2.1  Structure of a Periodic Task

A periodic task is one that runs after a fixed interval without having to be started by another task. In C, this behavior was achieved by calling *trmrst* at the end of the cycle to have the OS restart the task after the specified interval.  The C task always restarted at its entry point.

In Ada, the periodic task is organized as a (possibly empty) initial section, followed by an "endless" loop:

```
task body INPTSK is       -- typical body of a periodic task
  with MTOSUX_H;  use MTOSUX_H;

    ...

  with MTOS_TSK;   use MTOS_TSK;
    INPT:          constant MTOS_KEY: = 16#494E5054#;  -- 'INPT'
    INPT_TCD:      constant MTOS_TCD: = (INPT,0,250,0,0,0,0);
    DUMMY:         MTOS_RESULT: = Set_TCD (INPT_TCD);

    SVC_RESULT:  MTOS_RESULT;      -- value returned by SVC
    WORK_AREA:   MTOS_ADDRESS;     -- base of work area
      ...
  begin                -- entry point
    RESULT: =
            Allocate_From_CMP (−1,2000,WORK_AREA'ADDRESS,WAIFIN);
                -- allocate 2000 bytes from global TPA for work area
                -- can write 'ALLOC' instead of 'Allocate_From_CMP'
        ...                 -- other initialization (nonrepeated) code
    loop
        ...                 -- cyclic code
      RESULT: =
            Terminate_Task_With_Restart_After_Given_Interval (25 + MS);
                -- pause for balance of cycle time
                -- short form PAURST (25 + MS)
                -- end of task in MTOS sense
    end loop;
  end INPTSK;        -- end of task in Ada sense
```

The task first executes any calls required to create and initialize its local variables and then begins the task code proper at the **begin**. (There may be an invisible break in execution while the OS starts other tasks; in this guide we are not dealing with that level of detail.) The task performs its one-time initialization work, such as allocating a work area. The task then proceeds into the first cycle of the loop.

Within the loop, the task can request any OS services, including those that send messages and that start other tasks.

At the end of the loop, the task calls another new service, *Terminate_Task_With_Restart_After_Given_Interval*. An alternate name is *PAURST*. (Each service has a "long" and a "short" Ada name). In the example, this causes the task to pause until 25 ms after the last start time. *PAURST* takes the place of *trmrst* in the C world. Upon return, the **end loop** takes the task to be top of the loop.

While the task operates as a loop, it never ends in the Ada sense. Each call of *Terminate_Task_With_Restart_After_Given_Interval* ends the task in the MTOS sense. Of course, if the task executes an Ada **exit** to leave the loop, the task would reach its Ada end, and then terminate and disappear. (In Ada "exit" means from the nearest loop, not from the task as a whole.)

We can compare the task code with what might be done without any special OS services:

```
task body INPTSK is          -- "pure Ada" form of a periodic task

   with CALENDAR;  use CALENDAR;  -- defines TIME, SECONDS, etc

   NOW:          TIME;          -- current time
   START_TIME:   DURATION;      -- in seconds
   LOOP_TIME:    DURATION;      -- in seconds
   ...

   begin          -- entry point
      ...                          -- initialization (non-repeated) code

      NOW:= CLOCK;                 -- capture start time
      START_TIME:= SECONDS (NOW);  -- extract seconds

      loop
         ...                          -- cyclic code

         NOW:= CLOCK;                 -- capture end time
         LOOP_TIME:= SECONDS (NOW) - START_TIME;
         if LOOP_TIME < 0.0 then
            LOOP_TIME:= LOOP_TIME + 86400.0:   -- spanned end of day
         end if;

         delay 0.025 - LOOP_TIME;      -- pause for balance of cycle time

         if START_TIME < (86400.0 - 0.025) then
            START_TIME:=
               START_TIME + 0.025;        -- compute scheduled start time
         else
            START_TIME:=
               START_TIME + (0.025 - 86400.0);        -- spanned end of day

         end if;

      end loop;
   end INPTSK;
```

This version does all of the time calculations at the task level. Function *CLOCK* was described in Section 6.7; function *SECONDS* extracts the number of seconds within the day (0 .. 86400.0) from a given time.

## 17.2.2 Structure of a Message-Activated, On-Demand Task

Many real-time applications have tasks that run on demand when a message arrives at a message buffer or mailbox. **CVT1** is such a "worker"; its organization as an Ada task is:

```
task body CVT1 is          -- typical body of a message-activated task

   with MTOSUX_H;  use MTOSUX_H;
      ...
   with MTOS_TSK;  use MTOS_TSK;

   CVT1:        constant MTOS_KEY:= 16#43565431#;  -- 'CVT1'
   CVT1_TCD:    constant MTOS_TCD:= (CVT1,0,200,0,0,0,0);
   DUMMY:       MTOS_RESULT:= Set_TCD (CVT1_TCD);

   SVC_RESULT:  MTOS_RESULT;            -- value returned by SVC

   MSB1:        constant MTOS_KEY:= 16#4D534231#;  -- 'MSB1'
   MSB1_ATTR:   constant MTOS_MSB_ATTR:= MSBGBL+100;
                     -- global buffer with room for up to 100 messages

   MSB1id:      MTOS_BID;               -- id of message buffer

   type DATSET is          -- transaction block
     record                          -- equivalent to C struct
       DATVAL:   array(1..62) of  SGN_WORD;   -- data values
       MSTIME:   array(1..6)  of  CHARACTER; -- ms counter
       DATVAL:   array(1..10) of  SGN_LWRD;   -- other parameters
          ...
     end record;

   type pDATSET is access DATSET;       -- pointer to transaction block
   NEWDS:       pDATSET;                -- addr of new data set block
      ...

   begin          -- entry point

      MSB1id:= Create_MSB (MSB1,MSB1_ATTR);
                     -- creates global message buffer
                     -- short form 'CRMSB'
                     -- just returns id if buffer already exists

         ...          -- other initialization code
```

```
loop
    RESULT: =
    Get_Message_From_MSB_With_Wait (MSB1id,NEWDS'ADDRESS);
                    -- waits for message to arrive
                    -- short form GETMSN
                    -- start and end of task in MTOS sense
        ...         -- code for operations on message
end loop;
end CVT1;        -- end of task in Ada sense
```

As before, the task first creates and initializes its local variables and then begins the task code proper at the **begin**. **CVT1** performs its one-time initialization
work, in this case creating the input message buffer. (Recall that this service just
returns the identifier if the buffer already exists.) The task then enters its main
loop.

In this example, the loop begins with a wait until the next message arrives.
The task processes the message, perhaps sending it on to the next buffer. The
statement **end loop** sends the task back to wait for another message.

Unless something exceptional occurs, the task never leaves the main loop
and hence never gets to the **end** CVT1 code. Thus, the task never terminates in
the Ada sense. Of course, we can use a conditional **exit** statement to force the
task out of the loop. Strictly speaking, the task also never terminates in the
MTOS sense of going Dormant. But we can consider the arrival at the
*Get_Message_From_MSB_With_Wait* as the logical end of each cycle of execution.

A task with the organization of CVT1 is activated by posting a message to the
beginning or end of the message buffer exactly as in C. The analogous organization and activation method would apply if a mailbox was substituted in place of a
message buffer.


### 17.2.3  Structure of a Start-Activated, On-Demand Task

As noted in Chapter 11, communication via messages is most beneficial
when the sender (1) does not need to select a specific receiver task, (2) does not
need to coordinate with that receiver (especially with the completion of the work
done by the receiver), and (3) does not need to set the priority with which the
receiver starts to run. In other cases, it may be more efficient to communicate
via the run-time argument of a *Start_Task*.

The Ada organization of a task that runs on demand in response to a *Start_Task* (or *START*) request is similar to that of a message-activated task:

```
task body WORK is                       -- typical body of a start-activated task
    with MTOSUX_H;   use MTOSUX_H;
    ...
    with MTOS_TSK;   use MTOS_TSK;
    with UNCHECKED_CONVERSION;
    WORK:           constant MTOS_KEY: = 16#574F5248#;  -- 'WORK'
    WORK_TCD:       constant MTOS_TCD: = (WORK,0,150,0,0,0,0);
    DUMMY:          MTOS_RESULT: = Set_TCD (WORK_TCD);

    SVC_RESULT:     MTOS_RESULT;  -- value returned by SVC

    type DATSET is          -- commonly, these definitions
     record                 -- would be in a package "withed"
        ...                 -- by all tasks that use them
     end record;
    type pDATSET is access DATSET;

    NEWDS:          pDATSET;       -- addr of new data set block

    function CONV is new
        UNCHECKED_CONVERSION (SOURCE = > MTOS_ADDRESS,
                                      TARGET = > pDATSET);
        -- "converts" the address returned by Wait_For_Start as a run-time
        -- argument to the address of a data set block
    ...
begin               -- entry point

    ...             -- initialization (nonrepeated) code

    loop

        NEWDS: = CONV (Wait_For_Start);  -- waits for Start_Task to be issued
                        -- short form is WAISTR;  returns address
                        -- of new data block (run-time argument)
                        -- start of task in MTOS sense

        ...             -- code for operations on data block

        RESULT: = Terminate_Current_Start (NOERR);
                        -- terminates current start
                        -- short form is TRMSTR
                        -- end of task in MTOS sense
    end loop;

end WORK;           -- end of task in Ada sense
```

As always, once the task is created, it immediately begins executing its initial section and then proceeds into the loop.

Now the task issues yet another new service, *Wait_For_Start* (*WAISTR* for short). This blocks the task until a *Start_Task* request is issued. (Recall that in Section 11.4 we interpreted task status Dormant as "wait-for-start"; *WAISTR* makes this notion concrete.) Upon receipt of a *Start_Task* targeted to **WORK**, MTOS releases that task. **WORK** continues at the priority specified in the *Start_Task*. *Wait_For_Start* also returns the value of the run-time argument as specified in the *Start_Task*. (The **UNCHECKED_CONVERSION** function *CONV* tells the compiler that it is legitimate to treat the run-time argument as the address of a data block, even though they are of different types. The strong type checking of Ada makes such formalities necessary.)

At the end of the cycle, the task is expected to issue *Terminate_Current_Start* or *TRMSTR*. This is the mate to *Wait_For_Start*. The argument is the equivalent of the return argument *rtnarg* of the C function *exit* (see Section 5.7). *TRMSTR* ends the run in the MTOS sense and so performs any final processing required by the coordination mode specified in the *Start_Task*.

Once the starting task has been released via *TRMSTR*, the worker task is free either to branch back to wait for the next *Start_Task* (by executing the **end loop**) or to perform other processing first. **WORK** may also go to the final **end** statement and thus terminate in the Ada sense. Thus, by separating the one C call *exit* into the two Ada calls *Wait_For_Start* and *Terminate_Current_Start*, we have achieved greater flexibility.

### 17.2.4 Overall Structure of an Application: Main Program

In terms of project development, maintenance, and control, it is often desirable to place each task or closely related set of tasks in a separate program module. It is also common practice with Ada to separate the specifications for tasks and procedures from the corresponding bodies (since often only the specifications need be visible to other people on the project).

Eventually all the separately compiled units must be linked together to form an overall application program. For this we need a main program, which is usually a parameterless procedure that "acts as if called by some environment task" (i.e., the OS) (LRM83, Section 10.1.8). As an example, we may define a procedure called APPLICATION to enclose the three tasks just described:

```
with TEXT_IO;  use TEXT_IO;      -- contains functions similar to "printf"

procedure APPLICATION is         -- nominal main program
```

```
        task INPTSK;                        -- minimum specification
        task body INPTSK is separate;  -- of separately-compiled task

        task CVT1;
        task body CVT1 is separate;

        task WORK;
        task body WORK is separate;

            ...                  -- specifications for common data
            ...                  -- and shared procedures

        begin                    -- entry point of main program:
                                 -- tasks defined above are created and started

    PUT_LINE (CR&VT&"Main program for application has started");
                                 -- PUT_LINE is specified in TEXT_IO
        end APPLICATION;         -- main program waits for all Ada tasks
                                 -- to be terminated
```

As with a task, the code needed to elaborate the variables, procedures, and tasks declared in the main program is executed before arriving at the entry point for the body of that program. Thus, by the time we reach the first statement of the main program (PUT_LINE), tasks **INPTSK, CVT1,** and **WORK** have already been created.

The main program executes under an "invisible" task (with key 'INIT') that is created by MTOS-UX itself for the purpose of housing the Ada programs. **INIT** is thus the ultimate parent of all other Ada tasks. The priority of **INIT** is arbitrarily set at 200. Thus, with a single-CPU system, at the entry point of the main program task **INPTSK** (priority 250) has already started executing, but tasks **CVT1** (priority 190) and **WORK** (priority 150) have not. With four or more CPUs, all four tasks start simultaneously.

By the Ada tasking rules, were the main program to reach **end** APPLICA-TION, it would wait for the termination of its children, **INPTSK, CVT1,** and **WORK.** This will not happen in the routine operations just shown since each child is in an endless loop. Each child might end, however, if the response to a shutdown signal included an Ada **abort** statement. Under these conditions, the parent **INIT** would also terminate, to end the application.

## 17.3  EXCEPTION PROCESSING: SIGNALS VERSUS HANDLERS

MTOS and Ada each provide a method to treat a task exception, be it an arithmetic fault, a bad parameter in a service request, or a lack of sufficient memory to perform a requested service. Here 'MTOS' is shorthand for "MTOS-UX supporting a task written in assembler, C, or any language other than Ada," in other words, the semantic rules of MTOS-UX as described in the previous chapters.

With MTOS-UX, a *signal* is sent to the errant task. The response to the signal is (1) to ignore the signal (continue as if the fault had not been detected), (2) to start the Debugger after halting the task, (3) to execute a preselected, task-level procedure, or (4) to terminate (abort) the task (Figure 17-5). There is a fixed number of signals (32). A task can also send a signal to itself or to any other task.

| Number | Default[3] | Use |
|--------|-----------|-----|
| 0-15 | SIGADA | available for end-of-service coordination and for communication |
| 16-30 | SIGADA | available for communication |
| 31 | SIGTRM | abort task |

FIGURE 17-5: Signal Usage for MTOS-Supported Ada

The response to a given signal may be changed at any time via a service request. Once set, the response remains in effect no matter where the program counter happens to be when the signal is received.

With Ada, an *exception* is raised in the errant task. The response to the exception is always to execute a predetermined, task-level piece of code (a "handler"), which may, in turn, terminate the task. There are a fixed number of predefined exceptions (five), plus any number that the programmer introduces via the **exception** statement. A task can also raise an exception in itself and, if it is the server in a rendezvous, can propagate an exception back to the caller.

An Ada exception handler is a set of instructions whose boundaries are marked with language delimiters:

> **exception**      -- beginning of handlers, such as:
>   **when** NUMERIC_ERROR = >
>     ...          -- handler for arithmetic failures
>   **when** PROGRAM_ERROR | STORAGE_ERROR = >
>     ...          -- handler for code errors or memory access errors

[3]Possible responses are **SIGIGN** (ignore), **SIGBLK** (become blocked if Debugger is present; raise **MTOS_SIGNAL** exception if not), **SIGTRM** (Ada abort), **SIGADA** (raise **MTOS_SIGNAL** exception), and perform given procedure.

```
       when others  = >
             ...                  -- handler for any exceptions other than those
             ...                  -- mentioned above
       end; -- end of handlers
```

A set of handlers need not cover every possible source of exception. There need not be a **when others** handler. Furthermore, there can be a set of handlers for a task as a whole, for each procedure, and even for a block of one or more instructions. Thus, we can have:

```
   begin              -- start a block
      VAR: = VAR + 1;
   exception
      when NUMERIC_ERROR = >
         VAR: = 0;  -- overflow, reset to 0
   end; -- end of block (above handler no longer applies)
```

When an exception is raised, the Ada run-time support code automatically "searches" for the handler that applies to that exception at that point in the program. Because of this nesting of handlers, the response to a given Ada exception is statically determined when the task is written and depends upon the location of the program counter at the time the exception is raised.

Much of the difference in exception processing between MTOS and Ada is superficial. We may logically equate "sending a signal" to "raising an exception" and a signal procedure to an exception handler. Furthermore, in many practical applications, we can map the code regions in which a particular signal response applies. (*Set_Signal_Response*, *setsig*, is issued as we leave one region and enter another.)

Nevertheless, there is a critical difference that is not so easily waved away: A signal procedure is *called*, while a handler is *jumped to*. Thus, after a signal is processed, execution (normally) continues at the next instruction after the errant one. In contrast, exception processing continues with the first instruction after the handler. This might be at the end of the task (which forces termination of the task).

The inherent semantic differences between signals and exceptions are too strong to arrive at a composite that would retain the flavor of signals and still pass the Ada validation suite. But we can find a proper place for each notion separately. Signals are intended for "asynchronous" events, that is, events for which the sending of the signal bears no direct relation to the current value of the PC. Signals sent by the task service *Send_Signal*, *SNDSIG*, are a good example. So are the signals utilized in the deferred coordination mode **CSIGn**. Signals were applied to error processing in the C/assembler version of MTOS only because these languages did not provide any good alternatives. With Ada, the need for signals in fault processing has been superseded.

Exception handling is intended for "synchronous" events, that is, events for which the raising of the exception can be directly correlated with the current value of the PC. Thus, in an MTOS-supported Ada compiler, a code-induced error raises an Ada exception: An arithmetic error raises **NUMERIC_ERROR**, a memory access failure raises **STORAGE_ERROR**, an illegal instruction raises **PROGRAM_ERROR**, and so on. Similarly, the OS raises **STORAGE_ERROR** if it detects a stack overflow at the start of a service request. Finally, if the OS encounters any other problem in a service before that service function returns, it raises a general exception **MTOS_BAD_SVC**. Problems are detected before the function returns in the following three cases:

**1.** The coordination mode is **WAIFIN**.

**2.** A wait limit of 0 is imposed by adding **IMONLY** to any coordination mode.

**3.** The nature of the error makes it immediately apparent, such as attempting to send a mailbox message to a memory pool.

By the same logic, no exception is raised when a failure occurs after the PC has moved away from the request, as would be the case for a time out with no coordination (**CTUNOC**) or deferred coordination (**CLEFn** or **CSIGn**).

Since there may be more than one service request within the domain of a handler for **MTOS_BAD_SVC**, there is a new service (*Get_Bad_SVC*) to supply auxiliary fault information. Specifically, it delivers the fault code that would have been returned by the service and the PC value to which the service would have returned. It is expected to be called within a handler:

```
BAD_RESULT:      MTOS_RESULT;      -- fault code, such as BADPRM
BAD_ADRESSS:     System.Address;   -- return address of bad service
BAD_SVC:         STRING (1..37): =
                      "Task NAME had bad SVC at 16#12345678#";

exception
   when MTOS_BAD_SVC = >
      BAD_RESULT: =
           Get_Bad_SVC (BAD_ADRESSS'ADDRESS);      -- get parameters
      MTOS_DBG.CVTHEX (BAD_ADDRESS,BAD_SVC,29);
                                   -- convert address to hex
      PUT_LINE (BAD_SVC);          -- print message
```

```
              ...                -- code to recover from bad service call
        end;
```

It is good practice to provide a handler for every exception that might arise in a task. As a minimum, every task should end with a **when others** handler that prints a message for any otherwise unhandled exceptions. This final handler could call another special service, *Get_Exception*, which returns both the address of the fault and the name of the exception as a null-terminated string.

```
        task body SERV is
            BAD_ADRESSS:  System.Address;    -- address of exception
            EXC_STG:      STRING (1..74):=
                              "Task SERV had exception at 16#12345678#: ";

            ...

        exception
            when MTOS_BAD_SVC = >
                BAD_ADDRESS:= Get_Exception (EXC_STG (42)'ADDRESS); -- get data
                MTOS_DBG.CVTHEX( BAD_ADDRESS,EXC_STG,31);
                                                -- convert address to hex
                PUT_LINE (EXC_STG);             -- print message
        end SERV;
```

The argument of *Get_Exception* is the address at which the exception string is to be stored. The return value is the fault address. The latter is made visible via a convert_to_hexadecimal procedure that the Debugger provides.


## 17.4  MTOS DEBUGGER

The MTOS Debugger task is available in either C or Ada. Both versions are essentially identical in the services they provide and the interface they present to the user. The only differences are minor. For example, the Ada version displays the Ada status as well as the MTOS status for the Display_Task request. Thus, the Ada Debugger might indicate that a task is a server in a rendezvous (as far as Ada is concerned) and is running (as far as MTOS is concerned). Similarly, the Ada version shows the task's Static Link and Global Frame, whereas these have no meaning for the C version.

In C, the Debugger is normally created by including its TCB in the automatic task creation section of the USEr/OS Interface (module USEOSI). For Ada, the Debugger is created by instantiating an object of **type** DEBUGGER:

```
with MTOS_DBG;   use MTOS_DBG;
    ...
procedure APPLICATION is
    task MAIN_TSK;
    task body MAIN_TSK is
        DBGR:  DEBUGGER;      -- Debugger task
        ...
    end MAIN_TSK;
    ...
end APPLICATION;
```

The Debugger task will be created, initialize itself, output a message, and then wait to be restarted by an unsolicited control_D entered from any console.


## 17.5  OVERLAPPING SERVICES

Some services can be invoked by an Ada construct or by a direct call to MTOS.  For example, a pause of 1 second can be obtained by either:

```
    delay 1.0;                      -- pause in Ada
```
or:
```
    RESULT: = Pause (1 + SEC);    -- pause in MTOS
```

In either case, the requesting task is blocked for 1 second, or until the pause is canceled by another task.  There is only a subtle difference.  With the **delay** there is no way to determine if the pause ended early by a cancel request; with *pause* the value of *RESULT* returns that information.

Sometimes Ada and MTOS services complement each other.  Ada has **package** CALENDAR that supplies clock/calendar information in a convenient format.  But there is no predefined Ada service to set the clock or calendar.  MTOS has the needed *Set_TOD*.


## 17.6  ADA OR C FOR REAL-TIME APPLICATIONS

The DoD has mandated Ada for new real-time applications (with few, if any, exceptions).  Thus, for this class of programs there is no longer a choice of language.  In the commercial field, however, we can choose between C (as a synonym for any language that has no tasking facilities) and Ada. Having seen examples of C and Ada, we know some of the technical differences. What other factors should be considered?

Ada is a more difficult language to learn and use than C. It takes more experience to cope with some of the subtle features and rules of the Ada semantics. However, a good Ada compiler, especially one embedded in a language-sensitive editor, can help greatly by pinpointing language problems, and even suggesting solutions. Also, most routine programming is accomplished with only a small subset of any language. It may not be necessary for everyone on an Ada project to be an expert in all features.

C lets you do almost anything you want; it is a convenient language in which to write good programs quickly. By the same token, C can make it easy to write bad programs, that is, programs with coding errors or with coding obscurities that hinder maintenance. Submitting a C program to the style checker program *Lint* often helps uncover some of these problems.

In contrast, Ada greatly restricts what you can do in a program. It automatically checks that arithmetic operations are being performed consistently (no adding addresses to time units) and that the arguments submitted when a procedure is called exactly match those declared when the procedure was specified. This tight type checking can make it difficult to write programs quickly. By the same token, it makes it difficult to introduce many kinds of errors. There are also provisions to turn off some of the checking (**pragma** suppress) and to defeat it (UNCHECKED_CONVERSION).

The speed with which programmers write code is only one (often minor) reason for selecting a language. The major reason is the effect of language on the overall product development, support, and maintenance cycle.

Ada is the first prominent language specifically designed with the software engineering aspects of application code in mind. As stated in the introduction to the Language Reference Manual (LRM83, Section 1.3), the three overriding concerns in designing the language were "program reliability and maintenance, programming as a human activity, and efficiency." As a result, Ada provides considerable computer-supported software development aids. For example, the language requires that changes to the specifications of a task, procedure, package, or other unit automatically invalidate any other units that depend upon those specifications. However, there is no reason a corresponding set of utilities could not support C. Computer-aided software engineering is an active field, and it is not restricted to Ada.

In the efficiency of the compiler-generated code, there is no clear advantage of one language over another: There are good and bad compilers for both languages.  The quality of the generated code is constantly being improved by optimizers that work on both the "intermediate form" that goes into the code generator and the assembler or machine code that comes out.  Because of the greater complexity of Ada, this optimization can take more time than with C.  Because of the greater knowledge generally retained in the Ada environment, the optimization can be deeper with Ada than with C.  In either case, the more optimization that is applied to the code, the harder it is to debug, at least at the resultant assembler code or machine code level.

The sluggishness of certain Ada run-time facilities is notorious.  For example, some companies have refused to let their programmers use the Ada rendezvous because it is considered too slow.  Whether speed problems are inherent in these facilities or just the result of some early implementation difficulties is still an open question.

Some of the communication and coordination services provided by MTOS could have been approximated by the rendezvous paradigm.  Nevertheless, these OS services were retained to have an efficient alternative to the rendezvous.

An Ada program should be more portable than a C program.  One reason is that the strict validation procedures for Ada compilers should reduce the dependence of program behavior upon the compiler.  Another is that Ada encourages you to specify the precision with which each variable is carried.  Even so, there are many behavioral characteristics of the Ada semantics that are "implementation-dependent."  An example is the treatment of tasks that do not specify any priority.  [The Ada Run-Time Environment Working Group (ARTEWG) of ACM/SigAda has developed an extensive list of such dependencies in hopes of eventually improving portability.]  The LRM simply states that any program whose proper execution depends upon such compiler or run-time properties is "erroneous."  That doesn't seem very satisfactory.

Finally, current Ada compilers are larger, slower, and generally more costly than are C compilers.  Partly this results from the greater complexity of the Ada language, partly from the yearly validation requirements that must be satisfied to be a registered Ada supplier.  While the differences might decrease over the next few years, it is likely that Ada will remain at a disadvantage in this respect.  Luckily for champions of Ada, the potential savings in the cost of program development, maintenance, and upgrading through improved software engineering can far outweigh any disadvantages stemming from the cost of the compiler.

## 17.7 SUMMARY

Ada attempts to define and control the real-time behavior of a program by including a tasking model and other real-time facilities directly within the language. In this respect, Ada is significantly different from C, FORTRAN, Pascal, and similar tasking languages.

The rendezvous is the only facility for coordination and communication that is built into Ada. All other forms of intertask interaction must be fabricated at the task level from this single mechanism. Furthermore, the rendezvous has some unfortunate semantics, such as a requirement that waiting tasks be serviced first-come, first-served. This makes coordination based on the rendezvous unsuitable for some real-time applications.

Because of the real-time features, an Ada implementation requires an underlying real-time kernel, or its equivalent. A commercially-available operating system, such as MTOS-UX, can serve as that kernel. Were the role of the OS limited to supporting the Ada tasking model, the nature of the kernel would not be apparent at the task level.

The rich set of MTOS services can be accessed by Ada tasks. The specifications for the services are contained in a set of interface packages. This enables the Ada programmer to enjoy all the facilities that are provided to the C programmer.

Generally, the Ada tasking model is similar to that employed with C. Nevertheless, there are some semantic differences, especially in the rules for creating and deleting a task. As a result, an Ada task needs a special organization when it is to duplicate the behavior of a C task.

At this time, there does not appear to be a simple answer to the question: Which language is best suited to writing real-time applications? Many factors are involved. We will have to see how the language definitions, compilers, and program development support facilities evolve for C and Ada. For now, we are left with an unanswered question.

## EXERCISES

**17.1** The Ada call/accept of a simple rendezvous (one target procedure as opposed to a list of alternates) is very close in function to the MTOS-UX start/terminate. In what ways are they different?

**17.2** Sketch an Ada implementation of a message buffer. Hint: Examine the semaphore shown in Figure 17-3.

**17.3**  In Ada, there is generally no execution overhead to support exception handling until an exception occurs. (Handler tables are static.) However, when an exception occurs, considerable processing is often needed to find the handler that applies to the current value of the program counter. What does this imply about the use of exception generation as a means of reporting status from a procedure or propagating status outward from the inner layers of nested code? How should status be reported and propagated in Ada?

**17.4**  Ada favors synchronous operations: The rendezvous always blocks the caller until the procedure is finished. What problems can arise when we introduce no coordination or deferred coordination?

**17.5**  The analog of the kill signal is Ada's **abort** statement, which can be targeted to any task. (It is one of the few examples of asynchronous actions imposed by one task on another.) What problems does the **abort** impose on a task writer? What does this imply as the proper use for **abort**?

# BIBLIOGRAPHY

**(Be82)** Ben-Ari, M. *Principles of Concurrent Programming*. Englewood Cliffs, N.J.: Prentice Hall, 1982.

**(Br73)** Brinch Hansen, P. *Operating System Principles*. Englewood Cliffs, N.J.: Prentice Hall, 1973.

**(Br87)** Brooks, F. "No Silver Bullets," Information Processing '86, H. J. Kugler, ed., Elsevier Science Publishers B. V. (North-Holland), 1986. Reprinted in *UNIX REVIEW*, Vol. 5, no. 11, Nov. 1987.

**(Co87)** Cornhill, D. Task Session Summary. In *Proceedings of ACM International Workshop on Real-Time Ada Issues* VII, 6, pages 29-32. Ada Letters, 1987.

**(De78)** DeMarco, T. *Structured Analysis and System Specification*. New York: Yourdon Press, 1978.

**(De84)** Deitel, H. M. *An Introduction to Operating Systems*. Reading, Mass: Addison-Wesley, 1984.

**(Di65)** Dijkstra, E. W. "Cooperating Sequential Processes," Technological University, Eindhoven, Netherlands, 1965. Reprinted in F. Genuys ed., *Programming Languages*. New York: Academic Press, 1968.

**(Fa88)** Falk, H. "CASE Tools Emerge to Handle Real-time Systems," *Computer Design*, Vol. 27, no. 1, Jan. 1, 1988.

**(Gl87)** Gleick, J. *Chaos*, New York: Penguin Books. 1987.

**(Go84)** Gomma, H., "A Software Design Method for Real-Time Systems," *CACM*, Vol. 27, no. 9, Sept. 1984.

**(Ha82)** Habermann, A. N., and Perry, D. E. *Ada for Experienced Programmers*. Reading, Mass.: Addison-Wesley, 1982.

**(Ho83)** Holt, R. C. *Concurrent Euclid, The UNIX*\**System, and TUNIS*. Reading, Mass.: Addison-Wesley, 1983.

**(In84)** *MTOS-UX User's Guide*, Jericho, N.Y.: Industrial Programming, 1984.

**(Ke78)** Kernighan B., and Ritchie, D. *The C Programming Language*. Englewood Cliffs, N.J.: Prentice Hall, 1978.

**(Li73)** Liu, C. L., and Layland, J. W. "Scheduling Algorithms for Multiprogramming in a Hard Real-Time Environment," *JACM*, Vol. 20, no. 1, Jan. 1973.

**(Lo88)** Locke, D., Sha, L., et al. "Priority Inversion and Its Control: An Experimental Investigation," Second International Workshop on Real-Time Ada Issues, June 1988. Reprinted in Sha, L., ed., "An Overview of Real-Time Scheduling Algorithms," Software Engineering Institute, Dept. of Computer Science, Carnegie-Mellon University, Pittsburgh, June 8, 1988.

**(LRM83)** *Reference Manual for the Ada Programming Language*, ANSI/MIL-STD-1815A-1983.

**(Mo87)** Motorola Computer Group Technical Report, "VMEexec," M68NRTBVMEX/DD, 1987.

**(MOSI87)** Technical Committee on Microprocessors and Microcomputers of the IEEE Computer Society (New York), sponsor, "Draft Standard for Microprocessor Operating System Interfaces," P855/Draft 7, Nov. 1, 1987.

**(Pa88)** Page-Jones, M. *The Practical Guide to Structured Systems Design*, 2nd ed. New York: Yourdon Press, 1988.

**(Pa72)** Parnas, D. L. "On the Criteria to Be Used in Decomposing Systems into Modules," *CACM*, Vol. 5, no. 12, Dec. 1972.

**(Pl85)** Plum T., and Brodie, J. *Efficient C*. Cardiff, N.J.: Plumb Hall, 1985.

**(POS88)** Technical Committee on Operating Systems of the IEEE Computer Society (New York), sponsor, "Realtime Extension for Portable Operating Systems," P1003.4/Draft 2, Feb. 1, 1988.

**(Ri79)** Ripps, D. L. "Help a Real-Time Multitasking OS by Carefully Defining Each Task," *Electronic Design*, Vol. 27, no. 13, June 21, 1979.

**(Ri83)** Ripps, D. L. "Multitasking OS Manages a Team of Processors," *Electronic Design*, Vol. 31, no. 15, July 21, 1983.

**(Ry89)** Rynearson, J. (Mizar, Inc.) "In Search of a Real-Time Kernel Standard," presented at Sessions 103 and 503 of BUSCON/89-West, Santa Clara, Feb. 7 and 9, 1989.

**(Sa87)** Sakamura, K. "The TRON Project," *IEEE Micro*, p. 8 - 14, Apr. 1987.

**(Sa89)** Sakamura, K. Chair, TRON Products session, IEEE Computer Society Internation Conference, Comp Con 89, San Francisco, Feb. 27, 1989.

**(Sh87)** Sha, L., ed. "An Overview of Real-Time Scheduling Algorithms," Software Engineering Institue, Dept. of Computer Science, Carnegie-Mellon University, Pittsburgh, June 8, 1988.

**(Wa85)** Ward, P. T., and Mellor, S. J. *Structured Development for Real-Time Systems*, Englewood Cliffs, N.J.: Prentice Hall, 1985.

**(Yo79)** Yourdon, E., and Constantine, L. *Structured Design*, Englewood Cliffs, N.J.: Prentice Hall, 1979.

# INDEX

====================================================================

## A

ABS, 60
accept (Ada statement), 227
Active, 45
Ada, 11, 83, 149, 225, 244
ADDVAL, 26, 71
alarm clock, 94
*alloc*, 167
allocate block from fixed block
    pool, 163
*allocate from_cmp*, 233
allocate from common memory
    pool, 167
*alofbp*, 163
ALOLIB.C, 169
altering coordination attributes, 151
arithmetic exception, 214
ARTEWG, 246
assembly language, 11
asynchronous communication,
    115, 132
asynchronous events, 241
asynchronous procedure, 139
asynchronous storage, 69
at end of file (mailbox), 112
automatic task priority change, 73

## B

backplane, 202, 204, 206
bad parameter, 140, 212
BADPRM, 26, 61, 68, 69, 70, 212
BELL, 179
bidirectional exchange of
    information, 148

binary semaphore, 122
block (disk), 185
Blocked, 5
block-oriented devices, 177
block (pool), 161
block size (pool), 166
*bodiop*, 177
BP, *See* breakpoint
breakpoint, 214, 216, 218, 222
broadcast, 145
BSA, *See* bus state analyzer
bus, 202
bus state analyzer, 218, 221
busy/free flag, 145
buy vs. build, 10
byte-oriented devices, 177
byte stream, 185, 194

## C

C, 11, 58, 60, 187, 197, 225, 244
calendar, 83
CALENDAR (Ada package), 83,
    226, 244
*calloc*, 169
cancel pause, 82, 142, 143
*canpau*, 79, 82, 143
CARRIAGE RETURN, 178
chaotic behavior, 12
*chdir*, 191, 192, 197
children (Ada), 226
CLEFn, 97, 133
clock, 78, 79, 84, 234
clock/calendar, *See* time of day
*close*, 195, 196
close file, 195, 198
close mailbox, 113

252

# H

halt task, 217
handler, *See* exception handler
hardware interrupts, *See* interrupt
    (hardware)
hierarchical file system, 187
high-level languages, 11
HMS, 79
HRS, 79

# I

ICE, *See* in-circuit emulator
idle time, 27
illegal instruction, 214
immediate only, 91
IMONLY, 91
implementation-dependent, 27
implementation model, graphical,
    44, 52, 64, 65
in-circuit emulator, 222
indivisible instruction, 207
inherent priority, 60, 61, 232
INHPTY, 61
*inient*, 59
INIT, 60, 239
Initialization task, 51, 59, 60, 62
input/output, *See* physical input/
    output and logical input/output
inspect and change memory, 216
inspect and change registers, 217
in-system emulator, 222
internally-latched coordination, 145
internal name, 60
interrupt (clock), 79, 207
interrupt (hardware), 4, 12, 183
interrupt (power failure), 183
interrupt (software), 132, 214

in-use (semaphore), 121
invoking task services, 23
I/O objects, 16
ISE, *See* in-system emulator

# J

jitter, 77

# K

key, 59
kill signal, 133

# L

last-in, first-out, 102, 105
latched coordination, 145
LCMP, *See* loosely coupled
    multiprocessing
LIFO, *See* last-in, first-out
LINE FEED, 179
*Lint*, 245
Loader, 60
load program, 218
load sharing, 100, 151, 203
local event flags, 95, 148
local pool, 161
local task, 60, 206
local TPA, 104
logical input/output, 173
loosely coupled multiprocess-
    ing, 208
*lseek*, 195, 196